A READING OF
THE TALE OF GENJI

ROYALL TYLER

BLUE-TONGUE BOOKS

Charley's Forest NSW Australia

First published in 2009 by ANU E Press
under the title
The Disaster of the Third Princess: Essays on The Tale of Genji
ISBN 978-1921536663

Revised edition published in 2014 by CreateSpace
under the title
A Reading of The Tale of Genji
ISBN 978-1494852580

Republished in 2016 by Blue-Tongue Books

ISBN 13: 978-9945715-3-3
ISBN 10: 0994571534

A Reading of *The Tale of Genji*

CONTENTS

Preface   7

Introduction   9

Genji and Murasaki: Between Love and Pride   25

Genji and Suzaku: The Disaster of the Third Princess   81

Genji and Suzaku: The Possibility of Ukifune   119

Genji and The Luck of the Sea   157

Pity Poor Kaoru   187

Two Post-*Genji* Tales on *The Tale of Genji*   221

Feminine Veils over Visions of the Male   249

Abbreviations for Works Frequently Cited   273

Works Cited   275

PREFACE

Four of these seven essays were published under different titles and in earlier forms between 1999 and 2006, and a fifth appeared in Japanese translation in 2008.[1] The most recently written ("Genji and the Luck of the Sea") dates from 2007. Its initial version, like that of all the others, has been extensively revised and re-titled.

Sympathy for Murasaki in her struggle to hold her own in her relationship with Genji inspired the first essay and led, through analysis of Genji's marriage to the Third Princess, to further work on that theme and others. The standpoint throughout the collection is that of a translator intensely concerned with the text both in detail and as a whole. This gives the collection no special authority, a translator's views on a work being as debatable as anyone else's. It simply explains the essays' character. No suppression of the first-person pronoun can conceal their personal engagement.

The collection perhaps resembles a preliminary sketch for a consecutively organized study. The essays have been edited to fit together as well as possible, but they are not wholly integrated, and they sometimes overlap. Although they cover some important and worthwhile topics, they neglect many others. However, passing time and changed circumstances now discourage any thought of developing the sketch further. If this book sometimes contests others' views, such is the nature of reading and understanding. Diversity of opinion on this extraordinary work has a long history and is inevitable.

---

[1] In order, "'I Am I': Genji and Murasaki," *Monumenta Nipponica* 54:4 (Winter1999); "The Possession of Ukifune," *Asiatica Venetiana* 5 (2000, published May 2002); "Rivalry, Triumph, Folly, Revenge: A Plot Line through *The Tale of Genji*," *Journal of Japanese Studies* 29:2 (Summer 2003); "*Sagoromo* and *Hamamatsu* on *Genji*: Eleventh-Century Tales as Commentary on *Genji monogatari*," *Nichibunken Japan Review* 18 (2006); "Dansei no imēji o ou josei no bēru" ("Feminine Veils over Visions of the Male"), in Haruo Shirane, ed., *Kaigai ni okeru Genji monogatari* (Kōza Genji monogatari kenkyū 11), Benseisha, 2008.

INTRODUCTION

Rather than introduce *The Tale of Genji* in a general way, these seven essays offer a few fundamental perspectives on a work that has stood for a thousand years as a rich and varied masterpiece. They remain generally silent about the pleasures the tale offers (elegance, sensibility, wit, poignancy, and so on) and about many of the issues that it raises. No interested reader should find them unapproachable, but they admittedly assume a degree of familiarity with the work. Essential to each will be the widely recognized tripartite division of the tale into Part One (chapters 1-33), Part Two (34-41), and Part Three (42-54).[1]

This introduction will review each essay briefly and then summarize the principal reading developed in the earlier ones, concerning Genji and his brother Suzaku. Next, it will discuss the provisional character of any approach to the tale, the inevitable emergence of incommensurable views, and the position of Hikaru Genji in the work as a whole. Finally, it will turn to an issue raised in several of the essays: the difference in character between Part Three of the tale and the rest.

An overview of the essays

The first essay ("Genji and Murasaki: Between Love and Pride") follows Genji's long relationship with Murasaki, the woman most important to him during the greater part of his life, while the second ("Genji and Suzaku: The Disaster of the Third Princess") emphasizes his even longer relationship with his elder brother, Suzaku. Both relationships intersect when Genji marries Suzaku's favorite daughter, the Third Princess, at the beginning of Part Two. These two essays therefore view this turning point and its aftermath from different

---

[1] On this division, see Shirane, *The Bridge of Dreams*, xx.

angles. "The Disaster of the Third Princess" also discusses the supernatural influences that encourage Genji's triumph over the faction centered on his brother.

Taken together, these two essays propose an underlying dramatic structure for what easily appears to be a fragmented, episodic work centered on love relations. However, they do not question the importance of these relations, which naturally and properly remain the principal focus of reader interest. Rather, they propose a background unity that leaves the tale's main appeal intact and, at the same time, extends the range of the author's achievement. The third essay ("Genji and Suzaku: The Possibility of Ukifune") discusses the nature and experience of the tale's last heroine, her psychological condition, her likely future fate, and the significance of the exorcism scene in the penultimate chapter. It speculatively identifies the possessing power as the angry spirit of the late Suzaku, thus suggesting a possible thematic link between the first two parts of the tale and the third.

The fourth essay ("Genji and the Luck of the Sea") approaches the relationship between Genji and Suzaku in Part One from the perspective of myth. Genji's exile and triumphal return hark back to the *Nihon shoki* story best known in English as "The Luck of the Sea and the Luck of the Mountains" and referred to below in this collection as the myth of Hikohohodemi. The essay develops this parallel and links the myth to the history of the Sumiyoshi deity, who plays so vital a role in this phase of Genji's life.

The fifth essay ("Pity Poor Kaoru") discusses the main hero of Part Three. While many readers accord Kaoru psychological depth, "Pity Poor Kaoru" argues instead that the narrator's chief interest in him lies in manipulating his experience so as to elicit the greatest possible sympathy for him. It also contrasts the portrayal of Kaoru with that of Genji and discusses in this connection the distinctiveness of Part Three.

The sixth and seventh essays ("Two Post-*Genji* Tales on *The Tale of Genji*" and "Veils of the Feminine over Visions of the Male") treat more restricted topics. The former analyzes passages from the mid-11th c. *Sagoromo monogatari* and *Hamamatsu Chūnagon monogatari* in order to shed light on how their authors read *The Tale of Genji*. It particularly discusses ancient and modern views of Ukifune's failure to drown herself. The latter essay presents a motif that has stirred the curiosity of many readers: that of a man or men wishing that a beautiful man were a woman.

Genji's rise and the collapse of his world

The essays that consider Genji's life and career differ with the view expressed by Norma Field in her book on the tale: "Now for Genji to qualify as a fictional hero, he must be free of the taint of political desire, and there is no more powerful antidote for this than erotic desire."[2] They contend that "political desire" is fundamental to Genji as a fictional hero; that erotic desire is not for any man an antidote to political desire but belongs instead to an entirely different realm of life, even though the two may certainly become entangled; and that both are essential to Genji as a character and as a hero.

Field conceded:

> It should be admitted that political ambition, even though unbecoming to heroes, can provide a fictional interest different from that of erotic anguish. And Genji is ambitious, as we shall see, but his political manipulations are usually masked, at times transparently, by erotic tension.[3]

Attentive readers certainly recognize that the tale's love relationships play themselves out against a backdrop of political maneuvering and ambition. "Genji and Murasaki" and "The Disaster of the Third Princess," supplemented by aspects of some of the succeeding essays, offer a reading of this background narrative. They suggest that tension between Genji and the faction represented by Suzaku (Part One), and then increasingly between Genji and Suzaku personally (Part Two), gives the work a veiled thematic continuity that Part Three may conceivably prolong, and that the Hikohohodemi myth may have first suggested. The most visible aspect of this continuity has to do with Genji's rise, followed by the collapse of his private world.

---

[2] Field. *The Splendor of Longing in the Tale of Genji*, 27.
[3] Field. *The Splendor of Longing*, 29.

In agreement with the consensus on the importance of love in *The Tale of Genji*, Sumie Terada described the work's "central theme" as that of "frustrated love" *(les amours contrariées)* and observed that this theme appears at the very start, with the story of Genji's mother ("Kiritsubo").[4] The major love-related elements in the introductory "Kiritsubo" chapter (the Kiritsubo Emperor's loss of Genji's mother, Genji's early longings for Fujitsubo) indeed foreshadow future developments. Genji's yearning for Fujitsubo, prolonged by his relationship with Murasaki, remains alive for him until the end of his life. However, "Kiritsubo" also evokes the political pressure that forces Genji's father, against his wishes, to appoint Suzaku rather than Genji heir apparent. Later chapters follow through on this political struggle, which reappears, even after Genji's death, in the opening pages of "Hashihime" (the first of Part Three).

It is also in "Kiritsubo" that Genji marries Aoi, the daughter of the minister of the left. Suzaku, by now the heir apparent, expresses interest in her. However, her father gives her to Genji instead, and the emperor, the brothers' father, upholds his choice. Just as Suzaku's appointment as heir apparent marks for the faction focused on him a victory over the threat represented by Genji, this marriage constitutes Suzaku's first loss of a woman to Genji—a loss that Suzaku's mother, a major force on his side, resents bitterly. (Genji is of course too young at this point to have any initiative in the matter.) It will not be the last. In the realm of personal feeling, Suzaku's later loves (Oborozukiyo, Akikonomu), and his loss of them to Genji or Genji's interests, are a likely source of unspoken tension between him and his brother.

These essays therefore distinguish between two aspects of the relationship between Genji and Suzaku.[5] The first is political: the struggle between the factions of the right (Suzaku's side) and left

---

[4] Terada, "Présentation," 7. Terada's remarks introduce a volume of French essays on the tale.

[5] The *Genji* author has long been celebrated for her psychological insight. To dismiss from the relationship between Genji and Suzaku any psychological content beyond sweetly fraternal affection is therefore to hold that in their case the author set psychology aside and portrayed Suzaku, especially, less as a man than as a cipher genuinely free of any feelings not publicly attributable to an emperor.

(Genji's). A major aspect of this struggle, and one certainly familiar to the author and her intended audience, has to do with the imperial succession. The second, more personal aspect of the relationship between the brothers influences developments in the background of the tale just as Genji's loves provide the great foreground theme. The relationship need not involve personal antagonism. Nothing in the narrative suggests that Genji dislikes Suzaku, and there is no need to imagine him doing so. There is no need, either, to imagine Suzaku consciously resenting Genji's successes, still less plotting against him. However, the brothers are dissimilar not only in age, but also in ability and recognized standing. The younger, extravagantly gifted Genji is a commoner despite his father's personal wishes, while the elder Suzaku, whose lack of talent his own father clearly recognized, is heir apparent, emperor, and retired emperor. Birth and circumstance have placed the two in a relationship that invites difficulty between them and guarantees open tension between their allies. Under these circumstances, Genji's efforts first to redress the balance tipped against him at the start, and later on (after he accepts the Third Princess) to retain the relationship he still treasures with Murasaki, are certain to involve decisions and actions that neither honor Suzaku nor satisfy Suzaku's fondest wishes.

The proposed background story therefore goes as follows. Having been forced by external circumstance to favor his lackluster first son (Suzaku) publicly, the Kiritsubo Emperor does all he can to favor his brilliant second son (Genji) privately. Meanwhile Genji, feeling cheated of the honor to which his gifts and his father's favor properly destine him, maneuvers (with supernatural assistance) to overcome those who forced him into this position. After many vicissitudes he succeeds well enough to dominate the court, including Suzaku, completely. Part One and the parallel with the Hikohohodemi myth end at this point.

As many scholars have noted, and as any reader (especially of the original) may observe, Part Two represents a new departure for the author, who seems to have re-launched her tale at this point in a different mood and in a style not seen before. Part Two appears from the perspective of these essays to extend the story told by the Hikohohodemi myth in order to follow the brothers' fortunes after the victory of the younger, and with the same emphasis on the younger as before. Suzaku's efforts to find the Third Princess a husband immediately tempt his victorious brother, and Genji, whose success has clouded his judgment, accepts a prize that he neither needs nor examines. The marriage almost destroys his relationship with Murasaki and leads ultimately to her death. Meanwhile, Genji's continuing attachment to Murasaki gives Kashiwagi an opening to violate the Third Princess. Kaoru is born, and Suzaku and Genji confront each other first from a distance over the despairing Third Princess, then at last in person when, over Genji's protests, Suzaku makes the Third Princess a nun. By this time Suzaku has reason to resent profoundly the ruin that Genji has brought on the daughter he cherished above all else in the world. The narrative does not explicitly attribute any such sentiments to him, but it does not need to. No man in Suzaku's position could fail to have them. The example of Rokujō, described as unaware while awake of any hostility toward Aoi, even though her spirit attacks Aoi savagely while she sleeps, shows how accurately the *Genji* author recognized the possibility of a gap between conscious and unconscious feelings.

"The Possibility of Ukifune" argues on these grounds that Suzaku may be seen as becoming, after death, the angry spirit that eventually possesses Ukifune. Extravagant at first glance, the idea has been retained in this book for two reasons. First, the secondary literature on Ukifune's possession conveys such conflicting ideas about the spirit, and indeed often betrays (at least in Japanese) such reluctance to deal with the subject at all, that there is room for further speculation. Second, the work of collecting evidence to test the plausibility of the idea nourished this reading of the relationship between Genji and Suzaku, and of the intense drama played out in Part Two. This reading of Ukifune's possession therefore turned out to be stimulating and fruitful. Whether it is "true" or not, no one will ever know.

Reader orientations and incommensurable views

Most interpretations of the tale are impossible to prove to the satisfaction of all readers because, as Richard Okada noted of the

"Wakamurasaki" chapter alone, the narrative requires the reader to make, unaided, so many connections between this and that in the abundance of material that it offers.[6] The narrator seldom signals a connection, still less spells out its intended content (if there is one), and she therefore leaves making sense of it all largely up to the reader. Striving to grasp the tale as a whole is therefore like attempting to fix in one painting a landscape that changes with every hour, season, and play of light, and also with every shift in the viewer's mood and interests. The narrative offers more possible connections and inferences than anyone could gather into a single, coherent reading. Moreover, little external evidence confirms or denies what might have been the intentions (should these be felt to count) of author, patrons, and original audience. As a result, no reading of the work, in whole or in part, can reveal a hitherto unseen *fact* about it. It can only develop a perspective and seek to persuade the reader that this perspective, however limited, is at least legitimate and even, perhaps, congenial.

For this reason differing convictions, interests, and experience may yield strong, conscientiously supported, but also mutually incompatible views. The tale has been condemned as immoral and praised as a record of "the beautiful ways of antiquity,"[7] damned for depicting lèse-majesté and read as documenting the contradictions in the ruling class. Such perspectives may convince those suitably committed, but the narrative does not demonstrably confirm any of them. It does not confirm either the current conviction of some read-ers, academics among them, that Genji's marriage to Murasaki ("Aoi") is farcical and insulting to her, and that his first intercourse with her is an unforgivable crime. This, too, is a matter of perspective.

Some readings, although persuasive in their own terms, are therefore incommensurable because founded on perspectives too different to allow usefully reasoned comparison or refutation. An example is the gulf between the view of possessing spirits adopted

---

6 Okada wrote, "The situation [in 'Wakamurasaki'] not only calls into question notions of 'unity' and 'narrative development' but places on the reader-listener the burden of making the links between those moments and pretexts" (Okada, *Figures of Resistance*, 265). By "pretexts" he meant such works as *Ise monogatari*.

7 Kumazawa, *Genji gaiden*, 442.

here and that developed at length in English by Doris Bargen.[8] Several of the essays acknowledge Bargen's view and debate it to a degree, but the gulf just mentioned explains why they do not address it more fully. Like Mitani Kuniaki, writing somewhat earlier in Japanese,[9] Bargen gathered from a poem in Murasaki Shikibu's personal collection *(Murasaki Shikibu shū* 44) that Murasaki Shikibu took a sophisticatedly psychological view of possessing spirits and therefore wrote this view consistently into her fiction. Although the (fictional) narrator of a fictional work cannot be assumed to be identical with the author,[10] Bargen founded on faith in this identity, hence in authorial intention, her thesis that a possessed women in the tale is actually wielding, of her own unconscious volition, a "weapon" to recapture Genji's wandering attention and in this way proclaim her power, even as her "weapon" sickens or kills her.[11] It is not necessary to engage Bargen's thesis in detail if one accepts neither its foundation nor her concomitant treatment of fictional material as authentic anthropological data. Her identification of the spirit in "Tenarai" with Ukifune's father is likewise as impossible to prove objectively as the identification of the same spirit, here, with Suzaku. These readings simply represent different perspectives on the work.

---

[8] Bargen, *A Woman's Weapon*, especially pp. 23-27.

[9] Mitani's work is cited and discussed in "The Possibility of Ukifune."

[10] There is no reason, even without the poem, to assume that Murasaki Shikibu took the lore regarding possessing spirits wholly at face value. Many cultivated people in her time, especially those familiar with Chinese writings, probably had personal doubts on the subject. At the collective, public level, however, spirits and spirit possession seem to have been accepted as genuine. Murasaki Shikibu is unlikely to have exploited, through a fictional narrator and throughout a complex work of fiction, so dramatically effective a device in accordance with personal view so at variance with collectively accepted belief and practice.

[11] Bargen insisted *(A Woman's Weapon*, 93-94) that the spirit of Rokujō does not kill Aoi. However, her evidence for this reading proves nothing to anyone not already disposed for other reasons to accept it.

Genji's position in the tale

One important matter of perspective involves the position of Genji himself in the tale. Most readers over the centuries have apparently seen him as an attractive and impressive hero, and some modern authorities have described him as "ideal." By taking his quality and centrality as self-evident, however, such a view may also seem to slight the experience and importance of the women whose absorbingly difficult relationships with him give the work its most accessible appeal. Objections to his behavior with them date back at least to the late twelfth century,[12] and in recent decades some have even come to condemn or belittle him. Many have rejected his centrality in the work in favor of that of the women characters. This view is prominent in academic writing in English. Norma Field gave it influential expression when she wrote:

> The eponymous hero, far from being the controlling center of the work, is as much constituted by his heroines as they are by him. Yet, for reasons to be seen, he is curiously absent by comparison to his ladies."[13]

Genji and the tale's female characters of course stand in a reciprocal relationship to each other, as do living men and women. From the perspective of these essays, however, Genji functions as the "controlling center," or perhaps reference point, of the narrative. It is he who initiates every love relationship in which he engages, and to whose interests the narrative always returns. Moreover, his decision to accept the Third Princess makes him not a passive victim of erotic nostalgia, but the active agent in the unfolding of his fate. Seen this way he is not "curiously absent by comparison to his ladies." This does not make him better or more deserving than they, nor does it require the reader to admire him. The point is elsewhere. He is a charismatic figure whose actions change his own life as well as the lives of others. He is the hero of the tale.

---

[12] Higuchi and Kuboki, *Mumyōzōshi*, 198.
[13] Field, *The Splendor of Longing*, 17.

Reflections on Part Three

A recurring issue in these essays is the literary difference between Parts One and Two, taken together, and Part Three. It is great enough to seem perhaps to cast doubt on Murasaki Shikibu's sole authorship of the tale. However, these essays do not suggest multiple authorship. Murasaki Shikibu is the only identifiable author. Her diary associates her intimately with the work, and centuries of fame both for the tale itself and for the art motif of her writing its first chapters have put that association beyond challenge. What the essays implicitly question is instead the necessity of reading Part Three *through* faith in her sole authorship.

This authorship is indeed a matter of faith. The mentions of the tale in Murasaki Shikibu's diary probably do not refer to all fifty-four chapters. She may not have written every word of all of them. Some modern authorities have therefore questioned the authorship of one or more of the "three 'Niou Miya' chapters" (42-44), although others have then sought to refute their doubts.[14] In pre-modern times two commentators reported, without endorsing it, a rumor that the Uji chapters were by Murasaki Shikibu's daughter, Daini no Sanmi; and Yosano Akiko (1878-1942) more recently attributed both Parts Two and Part Three to her.[15] No Japanese specialist actually questions the authorship of the Uji chapters, but many share a "perception of disharmony" *(iwakan)* between them and the rest.[16]

In his discussion of the way the tale may have been composed, and of the diversity of its constituent elements, Haruo Shirane described it as "a highly diversified and far-ranging body of texts." He concluded:

> The reader of the Ukifune sequence, for example, can appreciate these five chapters both independently and as an integral part of the previous narrative. The reader approaches

---

[14] Takeda Munetoshi rejected "Takekawa" in 1949, Ikeda Kikan rejected all three chapters in 1951, Ishikawa Tōru rejected "Kōbai" in 1961, and Ishida Jōji rejected all three in 1971 (Kubo, "Zokuhen sakusha ibun," 208). Many others have contributed to the same debate, which continues.

[15] Rowley, *Yosano Akiko and The Tale of Genji*, 147-148.

[16] Kubo, "Zokuhen sakusha ibun," 207-208.

the new sequence with a memory of Murasaki Shikibu's earlier accomplishments and recognizes its individuality in light of her previous literary achievements.[17]

In this spirit many scholars have pointed out parallels of theme, motif, and so on between the Uji chapters and the rest, thus affirming an underlying continuity of intention and style that integrates these chapters with what precedes them. In the spirit of these essays, however, the balance tips the other way. Shirane's "recognizes its individuality in light of her previous accomplishments" becomes, so to speak, "wonders in light of what precedes the Uji chapters how the same person could conceivably have written them at any time in her life." This doubt is reasonable, even if it is not inevitable, once the weight of Murasaki Shikibu's immense prestige is set aside. It is meaningful because bypassing her name widens the range of possible readings of the Uji chapters and affects some existing ones.

In the decades immediately following World War II, the Uji chapters came to be seen as the culmination of the entire tale. "Pity Poor Kaoru" briefly summarizes Konishi Jin'ichi's view to this effect. That of Takeda Munetoshi, originally a student of Western literary theory, was perhaps even more influential. Takeda wrote in 1954:

> Part One was written from an idealistic perspective, although one cannot call the ideals in question very high. Part Two conveyed actual suffering from an objective perspective and so at last approached reality. Part Three, one may say, conveyed the times through individual experience, reflected human universality transcending time, and thus achieved symbolic truth in the most profound sense. With Part Three, *The Tale of Genji* comes at last to deserve being called a masterpiece.[18]

However, times have changed. Current appraisals of the Uji chapters avoid value judgments, and some scholars come close to inviting doubts about sole authorship. In a 1982 essay echoed by later writers, Mitani Kuniaki found in them a new approach to characterization that,

---

17 Shirane, *The Bridge of Dreams*, xxi.
18 Quoted by Akiyama Ken, "Kanketsuteki na seishin hatten ron," 138. The passage is from Takeda's *Genji monogatari no kenkyū*, Iwanami, 1954.

in keeping with their "hollowed-out" world, undermines the "myth of unity" of character. [19] ("Pity Poor Kaoru" discusses this topic.) Takahashi Tōru wrote similarly of "multidimensional fragmentation of the subject" in the Uji chapters, and of the inability of the Uji characters even to communicate among themselves; [20] and Kanda Tatsumi saw an "epistemological disjunction" *(ninshikiteki setsudan)* between the Uji chapters and the rest.[21] Opinions like these suggest the need to define what it means to say that the Uji chapters, brilliant as they are in themselves, are integral to the rest.

Mitani responded to this need by providing a definition that he rested on the opening words of "Niou Miya": "His light was gone, and none among his many descendants could compare to what he had been.[22] Genji's world, vividly present a moment ago, has gone dark. The Uji chapters have indeed been called a tale of "darkness."[23] As one literary critic wrote in 1949, "With [them], the atmosphere of *The Tale of Genji* turns dark and cold, as though one had stepped down into a cellar."[24] The opening words of Part Three are therefore fundamental to Mitani's view of these chapters as a "hollowed-out tale of absence,"[25] that is to say, the story of a world now without a center. The effect of this "darkness" is to give Genji's life a new, retrospective radiance. Kobayashi Masaaki similarly called these chapters an "anti-monogatari" that succeeds Genji's story in a Hegelian dialectic of light

---

[19] Mitani Kuniaki, "Genji monogatari daisanbu no hōhō," 94.

[20] Takahashi, "Aishū no tsumi: Ukifune no genzoku to bukkyō," 153-154.

[21] Kanda Tatsumi, *Monogatari bungaku, sono kaitai: Genji monogatari 'Uji jūjō' ikō*, Yūseidō, 1992: cited by Kobayashi, "Uji jūjō no genzai ni kaete," 352.

[22] *Hikari kakure-tamainishi nochi, sono mi-kage ni tachitsugi-tamaubeki hito, sokora no on-suezue ni arigatakarikeri.* TTG, 785; GM 5:17. For what it is worth, Chateaubriand (1768-1848) wrote almost exactly the same thing, in his own style, when looking back on the swiftly eclipsed empire of Napoleon *(Mémoires d'outre-tombe* 2:3-4; author's translation): "To fall back from Bonaparte and the Empire into what followed is to fall from reality into the void, from a mountaintop into the abyss...Of whom, of what is one to speak after such a man?...I blush to think that I must now drone on about a horde of infinitesimal beings, myself among them—dubious, nocturnal creatures that we were in a world the great sun of which was gone."

[23] Ōasa, "Monogatari no kōzō," 298.

[24] Odagiri, "Uji jūjō: chūsei bungaku e," 393.

[25] Mitani Kuniaki, "Genji monogatari daisanbu no hōhō," 76.

and darkness.[26] In short, Mitani attributed the value of Part Three above all to the way it renews the reader's pleasure, by contrast, in Parts One and Two.[27] However, whether the same author or another planned this effect remains imponderable.

The many parallels noted between Part Three and the rest likewise leave the issue moot. A simple example is the proposition that Kaoru's discovery of the Uji sisters ("Hashihime") "echoes" Genji's discovery of Murasaki ("Wakamurasaki"). [28] Perhaps it does. However, it also echoes the first episode of *Ise monogatari*, which is understood to underlie the "Wakamurasaki" scene as well, and which is in fact the closer of the two to *Ise monogatari* since it involves *two* sisters, both of marriageable age. Moreover, the real issue has to do with the flavor of the two scenes. The one in "Wakamurasaki" is casual, fresh, almost naïve, the one in "Hashihime" comparatively elaborate and theatrical. The reader may prefer either, but, granted the presence in both of the *kaimami* ("peeping through a crack") motif, they are at any rate extremely different. The value of the echo, or even its meaningful existence, is therefore unclear.

Other such parallels likewise stand or fall according to the reader's perspective. Ishida Jōji wrote that, "No understanding of Part Three is possible without an understanding of Part Two" [29] and cited as evidence the roles played by two "sisters" *(shimai)* in Part Two (Murasaki and the Third Princess, actually cousins whose lives are unrelated until the latter's marriage) and three sisters in Part Three (Ōigimi, Nakanokimi, Ukifune); the adultery between Kashiwagi and the Third Princess in Part Two, and Niou and Ukifune in Part Three; and Yūgiri's failed attempt to make love to Princess Ochiba in Part Two, and Kaoru's failures with Ōigimi in Part Three. However, these pairs illustrate Kanda's "epistemological disjunction" equally well. Viewed from the standpoint of contextual circumstance and literary character they are utterly dissimilar and shed no light on each other.

---

[26] Kobayashi, "Uji jūjō no genzai ni kaete," 349.
[27] Mitani Kuniaki, "Genji monogatari daisanbu no hōhō," 86.
[28] Shirane, *The Bridge of Dreams*, 140.
[29] Ishida, "Seihen kara zokuhen e," 22.

"Pity Poor Kaoru" suggests several times that a particular scene parodies one from much earlier in the tale. Parody, which is a recurring theme in the reception of the Uji chapters, has also been extended to cover them as a whole. Mitani's reading suggests parody with a particular effect in mind, and the eminent thinker Yamaguchi Masao put the matter as plainly as possible when he wrote, "The theme of *The Tale of Genji* is summed up and brought to completion by the parody of the Uji chapters."[30] Both seem to have had in mind *self-*parody, which the Uji chapters may indeed be; and yet they convey so pervasively different a view of people and life that the "*self-*" is not wholly convincing. A motif that seems familiar at first glance need not have in these chapters anything like its earlier value.[31] This, too, is a meaningful perspective from which to read them.

It is easy to explain why Murasaki Shikibu might not have written every word. In the main she undoubtedly followed through chapter by chapter, as Shirane suggested, on an evolving and expanding conception of her work. However, she may also have responded to outside stimulus (suggestions, requests, even orders) as her work grew in reputation. The populous, fastidious court society around her must have made widespread participation in any attractive pastime almost inevitable. (The "Eawase" and "Hotaru" chapters of *Genji* provide examples.) Her stories might have inspired others (individuals or rival coteries) to join in or even to compete. For diplomatic reasons she might have been unable to reject every suggestion or contribution and so ended up editing others' work into the whole as well as her own, roughly as Watsuji Tetsurō suggested long ago.[32] Or perhaps inter-salon rivalry even brought under the shelter of her name extended material over which she had relatively little control.

Perhaps such speculation is no more compelling than Maruya Saiichi's fancy, in his novel *Kagayaku Hi no Miya* (2003), that Murasaki Shikibu simply wrote up in *The Tale of Genji* the escapades that Fujiwara no Michinaga related to her while the two lay together in bed.

---

[30] Yamaguchi, *Tennōsei no bunka jinruigaku*, 161.

[31] An example is Mitani Kuniaki's reading of the exorcism scene in "Tenarai," discussed in "The Possibility of Ukifune."

[32] Watsuji, "Genji monogatari ni tsuite."

Still, nothing about her immortal achievement should be taken for granted.

GENJI AND MURASAKI:
BETWEEN LOVE AND PRIDE

The spark that brings Murasaki fully to life in *The Tale of Genji* flashes in the "Miotsukushi" chapter, when Genji offends her with his talk of the lady at Akashi and the daughter conceived there during his exile. "There I was, [she] thought, completely miserable, and he, simple pastime or not, was sharing his heart with another! Well, I am I!"[1] Her *ware wa ware* ("I'm me!") sharply affirms the distinctness of her existence.

Akiyama Ken wrote that studying Murasaki, more than any other character, reveals the essence of the tale.[2] She is Genji's private discovery and his personal treasure. Her fate in life depends so entirely on him that she might be a sort of shadow to him, without a will of her own, and yet at this moment, and later ones like it, she resists him. The pattern of give and take between the two is as vital to the unfolding of their relationship as it is to the development of the tale itself. Murasaki's precise social standing vis-à-vis Genji and the court society they inhabit is essential, too. These interrelated issues in turn bear on the great crisis of Murasaki's life: the disaster that strikes both her and Genji when Genji agrees to marry the Third Princess ("Wakana One"). The next essay will consider this crisis from the standpoint of Genji's relationship with Suzaku, his brother, while this one emphasizes Genji and Murasaki as a couple. Their relationship has its crises, and the marriage to the Third Princess strains it nearly to the breaking point, but it lasts until the loss of Murasaki leaves Genji a mere shell of the man he once was.

Three critical scenes punctuate the relationship. Shimizu Yoshiko called them Murasaki's "perils."[3] They are Murasaki's hurt when she

---

[1] TTG, 286; GM 2:292.

[2] Akiyama, *Genji monogatari no sekai*, 75.

[3] Shimizu, *Genji no onnagimi*, 44.

learns about the lady from Akashi ("Akashi" and "Miotsukushi"); her fear when Genji courts Princess Asagao ("Asagao"); and her shock when Genji marries the Third Princess ("Wakana One," "Wakana Two"). These scenes have usually been given roughly equal weight when previously treated as a set and discussed in isolation one from the other. However they follow a clear trajectory. Each time Genji talks to Murasaki about another woman who is or has been important to him she resents it; her anger upsets him; and his effort to calm her miscarries because it is at least in part blind and self-serving.[4] Each time there is more at stake for Genji, and the impact on Murasaki is more serious. It is therefore reasonable to see dramatic progression from one of these scenes to the next.

Many have wondered why Genji seeks with Akashi, Asagao, and the Third Princess the tie that so disturbs Murasaki, when he already has in her a wife who meets his personal ideal and for whom he cares deeply. The answer may be that Genji's desire for all three involves less erotic acquisitiveness than thirst for heightened prestige.

First, Genji's tie with Akashi, and the consequent birth of their daughter, opens for him the way towards that highest advantage accessible to a commoner: to be the maternal grandfather of an emperor. Reaching this peak—an aspect of his destiny fostered by her father's devotion to the Sumiyoshi deity and announced by prophetic dreams—does not depend entirely on his will, but it requires from him a cooperation that he gives gladly. What Murasaki sees, however, is attachment to a rival who, to make things worse, gives him a child when she herself cannot.

Second, Asagao and then the Third Princess promise to round out Genji's success—one that might be called less political than representational. By the time he courts Asagao seriously, let alone by the time he accepts the Third Princess, his supremacy is secure. He

---

[4] Doris Bargen, who included all three scenes in her discussion of Murasaki, pointed likewise to Genji's incomprehension and self-centeredness (Bargen, *A Woman's Weapon*, 109-149; see for example 137). The treatment of Murasaki here parallels hers in some ways, although it shares neither the foundations of her argument nor her conclusions.

does not need them politically, but he still wants one and then the other in order to seal his increasingly exalted station.

Thus Genji is a flawed man like others, despite his gifts, and for him public ambition comes into conflict with private affection. Murasaki's quality makes her his personal but not his social equal, and her value to him, as well as her valuation of herself despite his slights, makes this conflict a theme that runs through the tale.

The following discussion will cover the reception of Murasaki as a character and the penchant for "jealousy" *(shitto)* that distinguishes her. It will then turn to her childhood and her marriage to Genji. The main part of the essay covers in chronological order the three "perils" that culminate in Genji's marriage to the Third Princess.

Perceptions of Murasaki

Murasaki means so much to Genji, for so long, that she seems obviously to be the "heroine" *(onna shujinkō)* of Parts One and Two of the tale. However, Matsuo Satoshi argued in 1949 that she is no more prominent in Part One than any other female character and does not play a central role until "Wakana One."[5] In fact, Matsuo saw no connection between the Murasaki of Parts One and Two. Although his thesis became widely accepted, later writers proposed a qualified continuity after all. In 1993, after exhaustively discussing whether or not Murasaki is the heroine of both parts, Nagai Kazuko concluded that she is.[6] For some, however, doubt remains.

In any case, many do not respond to Murasaki. Tanabe Seiko wrote that in her youth she found her tiresomely perfect; Enchi Fumiko called her too "sheltered" to be a romantic heroine; Ōba Minako omitted her from her list of "female characters who have a brilliance, a strange beauty, and a romantic quality befitting the heroine of a monogatari"; and Norma Field wrote of her studied "banality."[7] Modest and untouched by scandal, she can seem colorless and perhaps even

---

[5] Matsuo Satoshi, "Murasaki no Ue: hitotsu no yaya kikyō naru shiron," 151-166.

[6] Nagai, "Murasaki no Ue: 'onna shujinkō' no teigiron," 157-74.

[7] Tanabe, *Genji monogatari kami fūsen*, 106-107; Enchi, *Genji monogatari shiken*, 79; Ōba, "Special Address," 19-40; Field, *The Splendor of Longing*, p. 175.

tediously privileged. Nonetheless, the text describes her repeatedly as a woman of extraordinary beauty, kindness, intelligence, and warmth. Shigematsu Nobuhiro evoked her this way with particular success.[8]

Only one writer found Murasaki worse than dull. Matsuo Satoshi described her in Part One as coarse, ignorant, vain, petty, cold, and incapable of self-reflection; while in Part Two, he wrote, she "coldly" asks Genji several times to let her become a nun, knowing perfectly well that such requests wound him, then "betrays all his hopes" by "coldly" dying.[9] Matsuo's mirror image is the feminist critic Komashaku Kimi, with her passionate attack on Genji and her correspondingly militant defense of Murasaki.[10]

Jealousy and self-affirmation

Murasaki's silent "I am I!" conveys a pang of the jealousy that is a major theme in Japanese writing about her.[11] The word is not quite fair to her, however, since it takes Genji's part. Jealousy is what he sees, while hurt, fear, and anger are what she feels. She protests an injury done her by the person for whom she cares more than anyone else in the world and on whom her wellbeing depends.[12] A symptom of her predicament in life is that in principle it is beneath her dignity to express such feelings at all.

Ware ("I"), even alone, occurs in many expressions that might not flatter a woman like Murasaki, since it easily suggests self-affirmation in a manner that the tale does not normally associate with feelings proper to a lady. The opening paragraph of "Kiritsubo" says of the

---

[8] Shigematsu, "Murasaki no Ue no ningenzō," 5-22.

[9] Matsuo Satoshi, Murasaki no Ue: hitotsu no yaya kikyō naru shiron," 157-58, 165.

[10] Komashaku, *Murasaki Shikibu no messêji*.

[11] Articles devoted to Murasaki's *shitto* include Iijima, "Murasaki no Ue no shitto"; Morita, "Murasaki no Ue no miryoku"; Saitō, "Murasaki no Ue no shitto: tai Akashi no baai"; and Saitō, "Murasaki no Ue no shitto: Akashi oyobi Asagao no Saiin." On her sense of self: Baba, "Jiga no ishiki o motsu Murasaki no Ue."

[12] Most writers accept without question Genji's view as the narrator presents it. For example, Fukasawa Michio saw in Murasaki's *shitto* the sole, precipitating cause of Genji's passage from glory to anguish (Fukasawa, "Murasaki no Ue: higekiteki risōzō no keisei," 20).

women who were jealous of Genji's mother, "Those others who had always assumed that pride of place was properly theirs ["who thought pridefully, Me!"] despised her as a dreadful woman."[13] *Ware wa* ("Me!") conveys not only the emotions of "those others" but their vulgarity in comparison with Genji's mother.

Waka poetry associates the expression *ware wa ware* with a sharp awareness of self in the vicissitudes of a private love affair. In three of four occurrences earlier than the tale a male speaker laments that because of love's longing he has lost his "self,"[14] while in the fourth a woman stolen from one lover by another feels estranged from any "self" she may properly possess.[15] However, two of three poems roughly contemporary with *The Tale of Genji* use the words as Murasaki does in "Miotsukushi." The full expression in both is *kimi wa kimi ware wa ware* ("you are you, I am I"). Izumi Shikibu evokes the distinction between "you" and "me" only to deny it ("Since nothing comes between us [to make us] 'you are you, I am I', how could our hearts be separate from each other?").[16] Ben no Menoto affirms it sharply: "You are you, I am I: that is the way for us, although we pledged ourselves to each other for life."[17] Murasaki's "I am I," which evokes especially "my" dignity in a private relationship, conveys the same mood.[18]

---

13 TTG, 3; GM 1:17.

14 *Gosenshū* (951) 518; *Shitagō shū* (Minamoto no Shitagō, 911-983) 187; *Asamitsu shū* (Fujiwara no Asamitsu, 951-995) 72.

15 *Gosenshū* 711, the last poem addressed to Heichū (d. 923) by his mistress, in the story about how Heichū's mistress was stolen from him by Fujiwara no Tokihira (871-909).

16 *Izumi Shikibu shū* 410.

17 *Ben no Menoto shū* 85.

18 In "Matsukaze" Genji makes the same words mean something quite different. Far from accepting Murasaki's reproach, he insists that she agree to *his* definition of her standing. On returning from a visit to the Akashi Lady he admonishes Murasaki, "In rank, there is simply no comparison between the two of you. You are you, after all: remember that." (TTG, 343; GM 2:422) More literally, he says, "Think, 'I am I!'" The fourteenth-century commentary *Kakaishō* observes, "He means that Murasaki should take pride in being who she is and reflect that no one comes higher than she" (Tamagami, *Shimeishō, Kakaishō*, 356).

For many Japanese readers, Murasaki's jealousy is her salient trait. Genji seems to enjoy it, despite his complaints, at least until the "Wakana" chapters. It gives her a piquancy that he savors. Tanabe Seiko remarked that it is what animates her and makes her human.[19] Shigematsu Nobuhiro contended that no woman as intelligent as Murasaki could fail to be jealous in her situation,[20] and Komashaku Kimi noted with pleasure that Genji's treachery and oppression had not after all "killed" Murasaki's sense of self.[21]

Murasaki certainly remains herself throughout her life, but her strongest feelings little become a lady, no matter how discreetly she conveys them. No avowed expression of jealousy is ever associated with Aoi, Genji's original wife, and Rokujō's jealousy toward Aoi is so far beneath her dignity that in her waking life she is not even conscious of it. Mitoma Kōsuke, who wrote of jealousy in Heian literature that ladylike behavior forbade it, observed that Toshikage's daughter, the ideal heroine in *Utsuho monogatari*, never shows any such feelings, and that jealousy never appears in *Ise monogatari*. He suggested that Murasaki gets away with it only because she is so beautiful.[22]

Since Murasaki's jealousy compromises her, some writers sympathetic to her feel obliged to explain it. They observe that her expressions of jealousy are fair and loyally meant. After all, the famous "rainy night conversation" *(amayo no shinasadame)* in "Hahakigi" enjoins a woman to let her straying husband know tactfully that she knows and cares, and so to win back his affection. However, the rainy night conversation explicitly does not discuss women of the "highest class" *(kami no shina)*, to which Aoi and Rokujō belong. Is Murasaki then not of this class? Feeling the difficulty, Akiyama Ken assigned her, at least as a girl, to the "middle class" *(naka no shina)* instead.[23]

On the other hand, the temper that helps to make Murasaki's standing ambiguous also makes her accessible. As Tō no Chūjō

---

[19] Tanabe, *Genji monogatari kami fūsen*, 127.
[20] Shigematsu, "Murasaki no Ue no ningenzō," 13.
[21] Komashaku, *Murasaki Shikibu no messēji*, 152.
[22] Mitoma, *Genji monogatari no denshō to sōzō*, 76.
[23] Akiyama, *Genji monogatari no sekai*, 77. See also Ko, "Murasaki no Ue no ron."

remarks in the "rainy night conversation," "Those of middle birth are the ones among whom you can see what a girl really has to offer and find ways to distinguish one from another."[24] Murasaki's tendency to resist Genji over certain of his affairs gives her a similarly distinct individuality, which is why some recent Japanese readers have admired her as a woman of independent spirit. Baba Taeko, for example, wrote that her sense of self gives her a remarkably contemporary appeal.[25] At the same time, Murasaki is of sufficiently distinguished birth that "middle class" will not really do. Surely her jealousy is a manifestation less of intrinsic personality than of contingent social predicament.

The child Murasaki

Many writers fail to see the mature Murasaki in the child. Tanabe Seiko wrote that what Genji glimpses through the fence, when he first discovers Murasaki, "has graven a little girl's appeal in the hearts of the Japanese," but she noted nothing individual in the scene. In fact, she held that until Genji's exile Murasaki remains a "doll bride." Akiyama Ken similarly called the young Murasaki a "living doll" without individual traits,[26] although for Ōasa Yūji and Shigematsu Nobuhiro, Murasaki is recognizably herself from the beginning.[27]

Genji discovers Murasaki when he visits a healer in the hills north of Kyoto. As soon as he sees her he wants her. That she is a little girl does not matter, because he sees the grownup already and is willing to wait. Her resemblance to his great and inaccessible love, his father's empress Fujitsubo, captivates him above all.

In a way, Murasaki satisfies the adolescent longing that Genji felt at the end of "Kiritsubo," when he "kept wishing with many sighs that he

---

24 TTG, 23; GM 1:58.
25 Baba, "Jiga no ishiki o motsu Murasaki no Ue," 249.
26 Tanabe, *Genji monogatari kami fūsen*, 109, 126; Akiyama, *Genji monogatari no sekai*, 82.
27 Ōasa, *Genji monogatari seihen no kenkyū*, 350-51; Shigematsu, "Murasaki no Ue no ningenzō," 10.

had a true love to come and live with him"[28] at his mother's home, now rebuilt after her death. Five years later, the "rainy night conversation" that broadens his knowledge of women includes this advice from the Chief Equerry (Sama no Kami):

> "It is probably not a bad idea to take a wholly childlike, tractable wife and form her yourself as well as you can. She may not have your full confidence, but you will know your training has made a difference."[29]

The idea of living apart from the world with a true love, and of forming her to his own ideal, is therefore present in Genji's mind by the time he first spies Murasaki:

> In among them came running a girl of perhaps ten or so, wearing a softly rumpled kerria rose layering over a white gown and, unlike the other children, an obvious future beauty. Her hair cascaded like a spread fan behind her as she stood there, her face all red from crying.
>
> "What is the matter?" the nun [her grandmother and guardian] asked, glancing up at her. "Have you quarreled with one of the girls?"
>
> "Inuki let my baby sparrow go! And I had him in his cage and everything!" declared the indignant little girl…
>
> "Oh come, you are such a baby!" the nun protested. "You understand nothing, do you! Here I am, wondering whether I will last out this day or the next, but that means nothing to you, does it! All you do is chase sparrows. Oh dear, and I keep telling it is a sin! Come here!"
>
> The little girl sat down…
>
> "You hate even to have it combed," said the nun, stroking the girl's hair, "but what beautiful hair it is! Your childishness really worries me, you know. Not everyone is like this at your age, I assure you."

---

[28] TTG, 18; GM 1:50. Genji is in only his twelfth year. While *omou yō naran hito* ("a true love") has been taken to refer to Fujitsubo, the expression is probably more speculative. He is dreaming of someone *just like* Fujitsubo.
[29] TTG, 25; GM 1:64.

Child though she was, the girl observed the nun gravely,
then looked down and hung her head. Her hair spilled forward
as she did so, glinting with the loveliest sheen.[30]

Genji soon discovers that her father is Fujitsubo's elder brother and
her mother a wellborn lady (now dead) with whom this gentleman
had an affair. Her qualities therefore suggest that she will fulfill the
promise of her looks. She is of good birth, she has a pleasing vividness
of presence, and she does not talk back. He has seen her accept a
scolding with downcast gaze and gathered that she would accept his
own guidance meekly. He therefore dreams of making her his. "How he
would love to have her with him," the narrator says, "and bring her up
as he pleased!"[31]

Murasaki is certainly not cheeky, but she is not passive, either. She
has a temper, she is possessive about her pet sparrow, and the way her
grandmother's plight fails to quell her high spirits suggests character
and a mind of her own. That so lively a girl should accept her
grandmother's rebuke suggests more depth than simple docility: the
capacity to honor her elders and to recognize that she is wrong. If she
can do that, she can also see that someone else is wrong and respect
herself for being right. She is not vain, but she has the intelligence to
be justly proud. Genji senses that quality in her, too.

It is unusual that Genji should be able to observe Murasaki so
directly and then imagine taking her home. She is well born, she is
pretty, she is delightful, and she knows right from wrong, but what
really encourages him to dream on is that she is so poorly protected.
She has no *ushiromi*, no one to uphold her interests in a ruthless world,
because her mother is dead and because her father dares not provoke
his ill-tempered wife (her stepmother) by recognizing her. Her
grandmother resists Genji's interest in Murasaki because she fears
how he might treat her; but when she, too, dies, Murasaki is left with
next to no prospects. Her father then makes up his mind at last to
bring her home, but Genji makes off with her first. Her father has no
idea where she has gone. While people gather that Genji now has

---

[30] TTG, 86-87; GM 1:208.
[31] TTG, 89; GM 1:213.

someone living with him, nobody knows who she is or realizes that she is a child.

Genji could not have abducted Murasaki if she had been her father's recognized daughter, nor might he then have been so keen to have her, since success would have made him responsible to a second father-in-law. As it is, she passes from having a doubtful future to having whatever future Genji will give her. She is his in a way the screened and guarded Aoi could never be, and this suggests that she is more or less disreputable.

It is a shame that a prince's daughter just ten years old should not be seen to act with Murasaki's charming spontaneity, and no one could really criticize her for what she does or the narrator for what she tells. Still, once Genji has taken her home, and she has accepted him, her innocent affection leads her to behave in ways unlike those expected of a young lady. As Shimizu Yoshiko noted, Murasaki behaves like a wanton when she sulks over Genji's plan to go out one night and falls asleep on his lap. Aoi's women pass on such rumors disapprovingly to their mistress. Shimizu also suggested that Aoi, whose gentlewomen do not know that Murasaki is a child, look down on Genji for his playfulness, his susceptibility, and his insistence on demanding from her the same kind of intimacy.[32] In this way Murasaki's situation in her early years tarnishes her a little, just as her jealousy may raise an eyebrow later on.

Murasaki's marriage

An inadequately protected girl in the world of tale, and still more those to whom her future matters, may fear that a suitor means only to toy with her. Genji's approaches appall Murasaki's grandmother because she cannot believe that he is serious and clearly suspects him of strange desires. No one would believe him today, either, but he has no intention of treating Murasaki lightly or of misbehaving. Wakashiro Kiiko, among others, acknowledged the honorable character of his conduct when she wrote, "If Genji were insensitive he could never

---

[32] Shimizu, *Genji no onnagimi*, 66-69.

have waited so patiently for the little girl to grow up."[33] His abduction of Murasaki is certainly startling (Enchi Fumiko found it "uniquely manly and quite wild"),[34] but in the long run it is no offense against her. While some condemn him for depriving her of her autonomy, she really has none to lose, and no hope otherwise of anything like such a marriage. Her stepmother would certainly see to that, lest Murasaki overshadow her own daughters.

Having treated Murasaki from the start with affection and respect, Genji at last consummates his marriage with her in the same spirit. It is understandable, however, that the radical feminist Komashaku Kimi should have viewed this consummation, from Murasaki's perspective, as rape, as did Setouchi Jakuchō; while Norma Field wrote of "a betrayal both horrifying and humiliating." [35] Genji's action has irreparably tarnished his character for some contemporary scholars and students, especially in the United States. In an effort to salvage his reputation Margaret Childs argued that he "seduces" rather than rapes Murasaki,[36] but the narrative really leaves no escape. Genji's first intercourse with Murasaki is a complete surprise to her, and the issue of consent does not arise.

Unequivocal condemnation of Genji over this issue involves an appraisal of Genji, and a reading of the tale as a whole, that upholds contemporary moral, legal, and social standards over an incident that the tale's author and her intended audience, whose world differed from ours, presumably enjoyed. Even in modern Japan, few writers on the tale criticize Genji over the issue, or even raise it. Tanabe Seiko called the marriage consummation scene wonderfully sexy, while Wakashiro Kiiko, who acknowledged Murasaki's dismay, observed only that the author had perfectly captured "a girl's feelings" *(onna-*

---

[33] Wakashiro, *Genji monogatari no onna*, 226.
[34] Enchi, *Genji monogatari shiken*, 77.
[35] Komashaku, *Murasaki Shikibu no messēji*, 136-38; Setouchi, *Genji monogatari no joseitachi*, 42; Field, *The Splendor of Longing*, 174.
[36] Childs "The Value of Vulnerability," 1071-1072.

gokoro).[37] There is right on both sides, and the disagreement can be resolved no further.

Genji actually tried to prepare Murasaki for this moment, but in vain. She did not even notice his attempts to stir her interest, once he believed her ready. "It was a pleasure to see that his young lady had turned out to be all he could wish," the narrator says, "and since he judged that the time had now more or less come, he began to drop suggestive hints; but she gave no sign of understanding."[38] The true character of her situation is beyond her, and Genji has long refrained from pressing her. His decision to act ends her innocence, but nothing in the narrative suggests long-term resentment on her part, nor does it upset anyone else at the time. Her women, who had assumed that the moment had passed long ago, are only surprised. Once the marriage cakes are eaten her nurse weeps with happiness, since under the circumstances nothing obliged Genji to go through a marriage ceremony at all.[39]

As Murasaki enters womanhood she is therefore all she should be. Her purity, untainted by any breath of desire, proves her quality, just as Genji's patience towards her proves his. To respond to his advances and consent to first intercourse she would have to divine what intercourse is and feel drawn to it, but if she did, she would not be a perfect young lady.[40] That she is still perfect after years of sleeping

---

[37] Tanabe, *Genji monogatari kami fūsen*, 122; Wakashiro, *Genji monogatari no onna*, 228.

[38] TTG, 186; SNSKBZ 2:70.

[39] The Introduction mentions a contention that the marriage is farcical and insulting to Murasaki. If it were, it would make a fool and a dupe of Murasaki's nurse. Mocking humor of this kind occurs in the Uji chapters, but not earlier.

[40] The example of Tamakazura confirms that a lady could not decently agree in advance, on her own initiative, to first intercourse. In "Wakana Two" Genji reflects as follows on her marriage night with Higekuro: "When [Tō no Chūjō] prevailed on an unthinking gentlewoman to help [Higekuro] make his way in to her, [Tamakazura] made sure everyone understood clearly that she had had nothing to do with it, that what was happening had full authorisation, and that for her part she was completely blameless. Looking back on it now, I can appreciate how very shrewd she was. It was their destiny to be together, and never mind how it began, as long as it lasts; but people would think a little less of her if they retained the impression that she had willingly acquiesced. She really did it very, very well." (TTG, 662; GM 4:261.) On the

beside him, and he therefore a perfect gentleman towards her, has something of the fairy tale about it, but what matters is that each should be worthy of the other. Since they are, it is up to Genji to act. That is why he who loves her is only charmed by her outrage, and why the issue never comes up again.

Unhappily, marriage does not make Murasaki secure, despite Genji's good will. She will always lack influential backing; being childless will always leave her a little vulnerable; and the flaw in her background will become a more and more pressing issue as Genji rises in rank.

The crisis over Akashi

In his twenty-sixth year Genji goes into exile at Suma, leaving Murasaki at home in charge of his affairs. Their three-year separation is painful (she is only nineteen when he returns), but it never occurs to her that he might not be faithful. Meanwhile, he misses her desperately and hesitates to take the opportunity that the Akashi lady's father is so eager to press on him. Still, he yields in the end to the Akashi Novice's urging, to the exotic enchantment of the place, and to the lady's personal distinction, so unexpected in a provincial governor's daughter. He returns from Akashi understandably full of his experience and, especially, of thoughts of the lady and the child she is soon to bear.

Genji feels "deeply content" once reunited with Murasaki, and he sees "that she would always be his this way." At the same time, however, "his heart went out with a pang to [Akashi], whom he had so unwillingly left."

> He began talking about her, and the memories so heightened his looks that [Murasaki] must have been troubled, for with "I care not for myself" she dropped a light hint that delighted and charmed him. When merely to see her was to love her, he

---

same theme Jennifer Robertson wrote: "Before and even after the Meiji period, published writers and critics—the vast majority of whom were male—relegated sexual desire in females to courtesans and prostitutes" (Robertson, *Takarazuka*, 62).

wondered in amazement how he had managed to spend all these months and years without her, and bitterness against the world rose in him anew.[41]

Despite the wonder of rediscovering Murasaki, anticipation of the birth and then the thought of his new daughter prolong the enchantment. A prophetic dream has already let him know that the little girl is a future empress and that in her his own fortunes are at stake.

However, Murasaki does not yet know about the birth, and Genji does not want her to hear of it from someone else. To mask all it means to him he behaves like a guilty husband, first claiming indifference and a commendable resolve to do his tedious duty, then passing to diversionary reproaches.

"So that seems to be that," he remarked." "What a strange and awkward business it is! All my concern is for someone else, whom I would gladly see similarly favored, and the whole thing is a sad surprise, and a bore, too, since I hear the child is a girl. I really suppose I should ignore her, but I cannot very well do that. I shall send for her and let you see her. You must not resent her."

She reddened. "Don't, please!" she said, offended. "You are always making up feelings like that for me, when I detest them myself. And when do you suppose that I learned to have them?"

"Ah yes," said Genji with a bright smile, "who can have taught you? I have never seen you like this! Here you are, angry with me over fantasies of yours that have never occurred to me. It is too hard!" By now he was nearly in tears.[42]

Fearing Murasaki's rebuke, Genji takes the offensive and obliges her to defend herself instead. Still, it is true that she does not quite understand. The child means more to him than the mother, and in time he will have Murasaki adopt her for that reason. Meanwhile, Murasaki remembers "their endless love for one another down the years, ...and the matter passed from her mind."

---

[41] TTG, 276; GM 2:262. Murasaki alludes to *Shūishū* 870: "I care not for myself, who am forgotten, but grieve for the life of him who made me those vows."
[42] TTG, 285; GM 2:291.

In the ensuing silence Genji goes on, half to indulge his feelings and half to pursue loyal confidences. In so doing he manages to hurt Murasaki after all.

> "If I am this concerned about her," Genji said, "it is because I have my reasons.[43] You would only go imagining things again if I were I to tell you what they are." He was silent a moment. "It must have been the place itself that made her appeal to me so. She was something new, I suppose." He went on to describe the smoke that sad evening, the words they had spoken, a hint of what he had seen in her face that night, the magic of her koto; and all this poured forth with such obvious feeling that his lady took it ill.
>
> There I was, she thought, completely miserable, and he, simple pastime or not, was sharing his heart with another! Well, I am I! She turned away and sighed, as though to herself, "And we were once so happy together!"[44]

The pattern of this conversation recurs in the two other crisis passages yet to be discussed. There, too, once the danger seems to have passed Genji indulges in reminiscing about his women, especially Fujitsubo in the second and Rokujō in the third. In each case someone then becomes angry: Murasaki here, then the spirit of Fujitsubo, and finally the spirit of Rokujō. The role played by the three women in these scenes suggests their critical importance to Genji himself.

The injury Murasaki feels is of course painful, and her response springs from a fine quickness of spirit, but the scene is still touched by the lyrically beautiful anguish of those exile years. She is hurt but not yet in danger. No provincial governor's daughter, not even one as unusual as Akashi, can actually threaten her.

---

43 He foresees his daughter's becoming empress.
44 TTG, 285-286; GM 2:292.

Asagao: the question of Genji's motive

Three years after the birth of Genji's daughter, Murasaki finds that her distress then was nothing to what she feels now as Genji courts Princess Asagao. She is acutely aware that, as Richard Okada put it, "she is forever vulnerable to threats posed by other women,"[45] but in the meantime things have gone well. The lady from Akashi has come no closer, Genji has pursued no new affairs, and she has had the joy of adopting the little girl. Genji, now palace minister, has not yet built his Rokujō estate, but he is already the key figure at court.

Genji has known the highly respected Asagao for years. She first appears in "Hahakigi," when he overhears women "discussing a poem that he had sent with some bluebells to the daughter of His Highness of Ceremonial, although they had it slightly wrong."[46] He seems to have attempted a liaison with her already in his youth, but although he remained in touch with her, she refused all new approaches. Once she had become Kamo Priestess ("Sakaki") he pressed her nearly to the point of scandal, considering that a Kamo Priestess properly remained untainted by any suspicion of such concerns. When her father's death obliges her to resign ("Asagao"), she retires to his house and begins there the life of Buddhist devotion that her role at the Kamo Shrine forbade. She clearly does not mean to marry. Social constraints discouraged the daughter or granddaughter of an emperor from marrying, and besides, she long ago noted that Genji only toyed with Rokujō and decided that she would not let that happen to her.

She has hardly retired from Kamo when, without a word to Murasaki, Genji lays siege to her. No doubt he has always liked her. In "Aoi," for example, the narrator observes that Genji "was struck by how truly in her case 'distance is the secret of lasting charm.' Distant she might be, but she never failed to respond just as she should."[47] However, this does not sound like passion. What does he want with

---

[45] Okada, *Figures of Resistance*, 358, n. 51.

[46] TTG, 37; GM 1:95. Asagao is translated "bluebell," rather than "morning glory," because the word is more likely to have referred in Heian times to the modern *kikyō*, a bluebell-like flower.

[47] TTG, 182; GM 2:58.

her? There are two lines of thought on the question. One, the simpler, is associated with Saitō Akiko. The second, dominant and more complex, was proposed by Shimizu Yoshiko and developed by other scholars, including Akiyama Ken and Suzuki Hideo.

Saitō suggested that Genji had always been drawn to Asagao by the difficulty of success and had courted her even at Kamo for the same reason he made love to Oborozukiyo (with whom he began a perilous affair in "Hana no En"): because of the risk.[48] The "Asagao" chapter begins: "The Kamo Priestess had resigned because of her mourning. Genji, whose peculiarity *[kuse]* it was, as always, never to break off a courtship he had once started, sent her frequent notes." [49] Saitō gathered from this that Genji's initial approaches to her are only "lukewarm"[50] and that her rejection is what challenges him to conquer her resistance at all costs. Norma Field agreed that Genji pursues Asagao because "her very resistance poses a challenge he cannot overlook."[51] While Saitō's reading recognizes the urgency of Genji's interest in Asagao and the need to explain it, it gives Genji, shrewd and powerful courtier though he is, no intelligible motive but a blind refusal to give up.

Several years earlier, Shimizu Yoshiko suggested that Genji courts Asagao out of nostalgia for Fujitsubo.[52] Fujitsubo died in the previous chapter ("Usugumo"), in the third month of Genji's thirty-second year, and "Asagao" begins in the ninth month of the same year. Genji must feel her loss deeply. The first time he visits Asagao, he finds at her house the Dame of Staff (Gen no Naishi) over whom he and Tō no Chūjō quarreled comically fourteen years before ("Momiji no Ga"). According to Shimizu, this reminder of a past now lost—the world of his father's court—wakens memories of Fujitsubo, and he courts Asagao as his sole surviving link to those days. He desires her because she is now to him a token of Fujitsubo.

---

[48] Saitō, "Murasaki no Ue no shitto: Akashi oyobi Asagao no Saiin," 32-42.

[49] TTG, 366; GM 2:469.

[50] Saitō, "Murasaki no Ue no shitto: Akashi oyobi Asagao no Saiin," 37.

[51] Field, *The Splendor of Longing*, 177.

[52] In "Fujitsubo chinkonka": Shimizu, *Genji no onnagimi*, 43-49.

In the chapter's closing scene, which Shimizu discussed at length, Genji and Murasaki sit with blinds raised before their moonlit garden, deep in snow. Murasaki has expressed her fears about Asagao, and Genji has sought to allay them. He then sends the girls of the household down into the garden to roll a snowball and begins to talk about Fujitsubo, who once did the same. He contrasts her favorably with Murasaki (her niece). Next he muses about some of his other women. When he has finished, Murasaki speaks a poem, and Genji sees her with new eyes:

> Leaning forward a little that way to look out, she was lovelier than any woman in the world. The sweep of her hair, her face, suddenly brought back to him most wonderfully the figure of the lady he had loved [Fujitsubo], and his heart, which had been somewhat divided, turned again to her alone.[53]

That night, Fujitsubo reproaches him bitterly in a dream.

For Shimizu, Genji's memories of Fujitsubo spill forth willy-nilly before the snowball scene, and he only goes on talking about the others (Asagao, Oborozukiyo, Akashi) to cover his indiscretion. As he talks, he realizes that Murasaki looks exactly like Fujitsubo, and his longing for Asagao vanishes. However Fujitsubo, who loved him, has heard him from the afterworld. She feels not only insulted that he should speak of her to another woman, but also jealous that, to him, the other woman should have now become, as it were, she; hence she reproaches him in his dream. Shimizu did not wonder why Genji pursues Asagao so stubbornly, nor did she seem to believe that Murasaki's fears, which she hardly discussed, ever had substance.

A few years later, Imai Gen'e analyzed Murasaki's poem in order to illuminate her mood in the chapter:[54]

> *Frozen into ice,*
> *water caught among the rocks*
> *can no longer flow,*
> *and it is the brilliant moon*
> *that runs freely through the sky.*

---

[53] TTG, 374; GM 2:494.
[54] Imai, "Murasaki no Ue: Asagao no maki ni okeru."

Having shown that the poem had always been read simply as an evocation of a beautiful winter scene, Imai argued that in reality it conveys deep distress: it is Murasaki who is "frozen into ice" and Genji who "runs freely through the sky" (spends night after night away, courting Asagao). Imai demonstrated that Genji misrepresents his interest in Asagao to Murasaki and that she recognizes his duplicity. He also stressed that Murasaki is upset about Asagao and that while Genji has not actually done anything yet, so that he has nothing definite to tell her, her anxiety is understandable. For Imai, Genji's silence, which is meant only to spare her feelings, alarms her more than would the truth.

While Shimizu gave Genji a motive, and Imai understood the depth of Murasaki's distress, both therefore considered her fears unwarranted. Their Genji may do as he pleases and is not accountable to Murasaki, and she has nothing to worry about as long as he has not actually succeeded in commit-ting Asagao to himself.

Akiyama Ken's interpretation of "Asagao,"[55] published soon after Shimizu's essay appeared, shared Shimizu's belief that the snow scene resolves key tensions and Saitō's that Genji's pursuit of Asagao is helplessly compulsive. However, he particularly stressed the operations of the author, finding Asagao's sudden appearance in the foreground of the narrative hard to explain except as a device to remind Murasaki of her insecurity vis-à-vis Genji and so to prepare for "repositioning" her (suenaoshi) in the tale. He argued that Genji is upset over the way he failed to resist trying to seduce Akikonomu ("Usugumo"), the daughter entrusted to him by Rokujō, and over the way he now cannot help pursuing Asagao; and he suggested that, thanks to Genji's preoccupation with Fujitsubo, these tensions are resolved for him in the snow scene. When Genji sees Murasaki as Fujitsubo, the "repositioning" is complete. Murasaki is no longer a substitute for Fujitsubo, but herself, and once the chapter is over Fujitsubo will all but disappear from the tale.

Suzuki Hideo continued this line of thinking in a further attempt to define the significance of the chapter. Taking Genji's reassurances to

---

55 Akiyama, *Genji monogatari no sekai*, 93-113.

Murasaki ("There is nothing serious to any of this")[56] at face value, he proposed that the author contrived the "device" of the closing passage about the snow and the moon in order to settle Murasaki's fears. Rejecting Imai's understanding of Murasaki's poem, he wrote that in this scene Genji successfully draws Murasaki into harmony with his own attunement to the "nature surrounding their solitude." He held that when Genji sees Murasaki as Fujitsubo, "and his heart...turned again to her alone," she becomes for him, and will remain thereafter, what Fujitsubo had been.[57]

Shimizu, Akiyama, and Suzuki held that in the snow scene Genji renounces his attachment to Fujitsubo in favor of Murasaki and that thereafter Fujitsubo ceases to figure in the tale.[58] Even in the closing lines of "Asagao," however, Genji longs to share Fujitsubo's lotus throne in paradise. She and Murasaki still do not seem to be identical, and Genji's attachment to her memory does not seem to have been ended by that single rush of feeling. The Shimizu reading, in particular, has Genji's interest in Asagao extinguished by that moment under the winter moon, when it is not. At the beginning of the next chapter ("Otome"), the following spring, Genji is still writing to Asagao and sending her gifts, the narrator is still claiming that he has never meant to force her, the Fifth Princess (Asagao's aunt) is urging her to marry him, and Asagao herself is still afraid that her gentlewomen will take things into their own hands. In fact, eight years later (early in "Wakana One"), bystanders are still saying, "One gathers that [Genji] deeply desires a lofty alliance, and that he has so little forgotten the Former Kamo Priestess that he still corresponds with her."[59] They assume that

---

56 TTG, 372; GM 2:490.

57 Suzuki Hideo, "Fujitsubo kara Murasaki no Ue e," 140, 144. As evidence Suzuki cited the way Murasaki keeps her peace even after Genji's marriage to Onna Sannomiya, and the admiration her silence arouses in Genji. He concluded that Murasaki's suffering turns her definitively into Genji's ideal and that this transformation takes place in "Asagao," under the winter moon.

58 Akiyama, *Genji monogatari no sekai*, 112; Suzuki, "Fujitsubo kara Murasaki no Ue," 144.

59 TTG, 580; GM 4:28.

Genji's preoccupation with Asagao remains unresolved because he still does not have a proper wife.

None of the readings just outlined acknowledges what would happen in practice if Genji were to succeed with Asagao. Both his life and Murasaki's would change. In getting behind her curtains—those of a princess of unassailable standing—he would marry her, and he would then have to treat her properly as his wife. At his age and with his experience he could not doubt this or hope to get away with less. (The disasters associated with Rokujō stem from his having tried to do just that with her.) No wonder Murasaki is apprehensive. She understands the gravity of what he is up to, and his silence, far from sparing her feelings over an affair of no lasting importance, confirms that he understands it, too. The truth is too awful to confess. He must want to marry Asagao.

Rumor supports Murasaki's fears. "He is courting the Former Kamo Priestess," people said, "and the Fifth Princess has no objection. Those two would not go at all badly together."[60] This is how Murasaki first hears about Genji and Asagao: from her gentlewomen. Those spreading the rumor approve the match, as does the Fifth Princess, because Asagao, unlike Murasaki, has the rank to be worthy of Genji.

The Fifth Princess explains her position near the beginning of "Otome":

> "I gather that [Genji] has been keen on you for ages," she observed to her niece [Asagao] when they met; "it is not as though this were anything new for him. [Your late father] regretted your life taking another course, so that he could not welcome him; he often said how sorry he was that you ignored his own preference, and there were many times when he rued what you had done [in becoming the Kamo Priestess]. Still, out of respect for [Aoi's mother's] feelings I said nothing as long as [Aoi] was alive. Now, though, even she, who commanded great consideration, is gone, and it is true, I simply do not see what could be wrong with your being what [your father] wished,

---

60 TTG, 368; GM 2:478.

especially when [Genji] is again so very eager that this seems to me almost to be your destiny."[61]

In other words, Asagao's father wanted to marry his daughter to Genji and did not consider Genji's existing marriage to Aoi an obstacle. The Fifth Princess agreed, although she refrained from seconding him aloud. Both assumed that Asagao outranked Aoi, even if the prestige of Aoi's mother and the power of Aoi's father (the left minister) might have made the marriage politically tricky to achieve.[62] Meanwhile, the Fifth Princess says nothing at all about Murasaki, who for her does not count. Social "common sense" does not give Murasaki the weight to be taken seriously as Genji's wife. The same will be true later on, when Suzaku ponders marrying his Third Princess to Genji. Murasaki does not count then, either.

Surely this is the problem that Genji knows he can no longer ignore,[63] and his reason for courting Asagao. Perhaps Asagao's prestige even partly explains why he began courting her in the first place, all those years ago. Now, his long relationship with her makes it easier to seek in her the solution to his difficulty. She has the rank, and he likes her. She is an old friend. He therefore moves quickly to court her when she returns from Kamo not because she reminds him of Fujitsubo, but because she is now there to be courted, as she had not been before.

Long ago Genji chose Murasaki himself, without reference to social convention, although he then found her birth adequate. She is the emblem of the private autonomy on which he insists. However, he realizes as he rises that autonomy outside the accepted social structure is not enough, and he comes to wish to conform to this structure in order turn it to the ends of his own sovereignty. Therefore, if "Asagao" marks a change, that change is not in Genji's view of Murasaki but in his view of himself and of what his position requires.

---

[61] TTG, 380; GM 3:19.

[62] Could it be that Asagao's appointment as Kamo Priestess was engineered by Aoi's father in order to remove this threat, and that the reason given in the text (no other suitable princess was available) is only an excuse?

[63] Only Tanabe Seiko (*Genji monogatari kami fūsen*, 145) attributed Genji's interest in Asagao to social pressure and observed that he is "a little bothered by not having a proper wife."

The death of Fujitsubo and the reappearance of Asagao in private life wean him from the idea that to make one's own way one must break the rules, as he did before with Murasaki and Fujitsubo, and persuade him to act. That moment before the snowy, moonlit garden may remind him that in Murasaki he has Fujitsubo after all and so console him for his failure with Asagao. However, his love for Fujitsubo, too, was irregular, and having Murasaki is still not enough. That is why he will eventually marry the Third Princess.

Asagao: the scene between Genji and Murasaki

Genji says nothing to Murasaki about his pursuit of Asagao in part because, for him, his ambition to marry Asagao is unrelated to his love for Murasaki, and in part because he knows that this time he is in earnest. Murasaki, who learns what he is up to only through rumor, says nothing either. Her silence measures the seriousness of the matter. She is not just hurt but frightened. Noticing her changed mood, Genji reproaches her as before, although with sharper deceit.

> One evening, overcome by the empty hours, Genji decided on one of his so-called visits to [Asagao's aunt].... "I gather that the Fifth Princess is unwell, and I thought I might pay her a call," he said, on one knee before [Murasaki]; but she did not even look at him. Her profile as she played instead with her little girl suggested that something was wrong. "You are looking strangely unlike yourself these days," he said. "I have not done anything. I have been staying away a bit because I thought you might find the same old salt-burner's robe dull by now. Now what can you possibly have been making of that?"
>
> "Familiarity often breeds contempt," she replied and lay down with her back to him....She lay there thinking how naive she had always been, when such things as this could happen...As she watched him go,...she ached unbearably to think that he might really be leaving her.[64]

---

[64] TTG, 368-369; GM 2:480. "The same old salt-burner's robe" (a poetic allusion) means, roughly, "the same old me."

The way she turns her back recalls the *ware wa ware* of three years ago. His conduct is beyond words. She can hardly speak to him.

Further rebuffs from Asagao leave Genji undaunted, but when Murasaki's continuing torment troubles him and draws him back towards her after all, at first reluctantly, this crisis, too, begins to pass.

"You are looking curiously unlike yourself—I cannot imagine why," Genji said to her, stroking her hair.... "You are quite grown up now, but you still think seldom of others, and it is just that way you have of getting their feelings wrong that makes you so dear." He tidied a wet lock of hair at her forehead, but she turned further from him and said not a word.

"Who can have brought you up to be such a baby?" he asked. It was such a pity, when life was short anyway, to have her so upset with him! But then daydreams would sweep him off again...."Please understand that you have no need to worry." He spent the whole day trying to make her feel better.[65]

That night a brilliant moon illumines the snow, and Genji waxes eloquent as he strives for reconciliation.

"More than the glory of flowers and fall leaves that season by season capture everyone's heart, it is the night sky in winter, with snow glittering under a brilliant moon, that in the absence of all color speaks to me strangely and carries my thoughts beyond this world..."[66]

Although justly famous, his praise of winter is not a good sign. He is becoming overwrought.

Keen to act and to be amused, Genji sends the girls down to the garden to roll their snowball, while exaltation sweeps him on to dream aloud about Fujitsubo. It is not that the thought of Fujitsubo, having filled his mind all the time he courted Asagao, her stand-in, has at last spilled over into words. His thoughts of Fujitsubo and his interest in Asagao are unrelated, belonging as they do to the realms of private feeling on the one hand and of public ambition on the other. Having failed with Asagao, he seeks solace and reassurance in memories of

---

[65] TTG, 372; GM 2:489.
[66] TTG, 373; GM 2:490.

Fujitsubo, and he also seeks to bring Murasaki closer to him by confiding in her. Thus he flirts not only with betraying what Fujitsubo was to him but with taking her name in vain, so to speak, by putting her memory to the ends of his own self-satisfaction. "The smallest thing she did always seemed miraculous," he says. "How one misses her on every occasion!...She made no show of brilliance, but a talk with her was always worthwhile....No, we shall never see her like again." He then goes straight on to compound his fault towards her and Murasaki by comparing Murasaki explicitly, and unflatteringly, to her and then to Asagao.

> "For all her serenity, [Fujitsubo] had a profound distinction that no other could attain, whereas you, who despite everything have so much of the noble *murasaki*,[67] have a difficult side to you as well and I am afraid you may be a little headstrong. The Former Kamo Priestess's [Asagao's] temperament seems to me very different. When I am lonely, I need no particular reason to converse with her, and by now she is really the only one left who requires the best of me."[68]

A discussion of Oborozukiyo and others follows, without comparisons. In the guise of confiding in Murasaki, Genji has complacently reviewed his secure emotional assets while simultaneously placating her and reminding her that she depends on his indulgence. Nonetheless, her protest has worked as a loyal wife's was supposed to in the "rainy night conversation": it has convinced him of his folly and returned him to her. After a day spent talking her round, he has come round himself. Having indulged in calling up the image of Fujitsubo, he sees that Murasaki, there before him, has exactly her quality. This is not a new discovery for him. He has made it before when failure to grasp some petty prize has opened his eyes again to the treasure he already has. Disappointment with the Third Princess will affect him the same way, but by then it will be too late.

Later that night Genji falls asleep thinking of Fujitsubo, and his performance earns its reward when "he saw her dimly—it was not a

---

67 "Who are so much like her."
68 TTG, 373-374; GM 2:492.

dream—and perceived her to be extremely angry. 'You promised never to tell, yet what I did is now known to all. I am ashamed, and my present suffering makes you hateful to me!'"[69] He awakes with a pounding heart to hear Murasaki crying out, "What is the matter?"

Murasaki's challenge to his willful ways has provoked a play of ambition, treachery, love, conceit, cajolery, and contrition with an eerie outcome, and this pattern will recur in connection with the Third Princess. Murasaki's open unhappiness over Asagao recalls her behavior as a girl, when her sulking persuaded him to stay home instead of going out for the night. While her conduct then appeared wanton, she was really only an innocent child, and her feelings in "Miotsukushi" or "Asagao" are natural to any wife. Still, to Genji's mind, especially when he compares her to Fujitsubo or Asagao, the sharpness of her temper is a flaw, even if an attractive one. It is the inner counterpart, and perhaps the consequence, of her flawed origins. "Who can have brought you up such a baby?" he asks. The girl he reared himself, hoping to form her entirely to his will, has a will, an "I" of her own. She has "a difficult side to her" *(sukoshi wazurawashiki ki soite)* and is "perhaps, alas, a little headstrong" *(kadokadoshisa no susumitamaeru ya kurushikaran).* That could not be said of Fujitsubo, who despite her great depth "never put herself forward" *(moteidete rōrōjiki koto mo mietamawazarishikado).* Supremely distinguished, she betrayed no sharp glint of wit or temper. No more does Asagao who, apart from her stubborn refusal to engage with Genji, seems to be utterly bland. These two great ladies do not have Murasaki's "prickles." Murasaki is too proud, cares too deeply for Genji, and depends on him too much to hold her peace; while Genji, more headstrong even than she, loves her too much either to ignore her or to scold her outright. It is the exceptional strength of the bond between them that allows their story to grow through crises like these towards real disaster.

---

[69] TTG, 374-375; GM 2:495.

Suzaku's daughter: preliminary remarks

The disaster comes in the opening pages of "Wakana One," which in character and quality, as well as in narrative content, represent a new departure for the tale.[70] It is as though the author paused after the preceding chapter ("Fuji no Uraba") to look back over what she had done, reflect on her future purpose, gather all her skill, and then re-launch her work.

Feeling that he has little longer to live, Retired Emperor Suzaku seeks for his favorite daughter, the Third Princess, the "protector" (husband) she needs, and his choice settles on Genji. Genji's acceptance culminates the series of Murasaki's "three perils." The danger does not pass this time. Neither her life nor his will ever be the same again.

In her thirteenth or fourteenth year, the Third Princess is still a child. Like Murasaki she is a niece of Fujitsubo. Unlike Murasaki she is, in her own person, a nonentity, but her father loves her extravagantly. Before leaving the world to prepare for death, he gives her almost everything of value that he owns. Rank and wealth make her a prize coveted by many ambitious gentlemen of the court. One of them is Genji.

In this connection it is worth reflecting on what Genji is really like. Whether hero or villain he is to most readers the lover, the man of endless charm and wandering fancy, whose unerring style and taste define a courtly age. However, he is also a man of ambition, power, and pride. For example, after returning from exile he spares none of those who had earlier turned their backs on him. The author only rarely and briefly evokes him as statesman or political patron, a maker and breaker of men, but he is that, too. Early in "Wakana One," Retired Emperor Suzaku puts it lightly but well.

"Yes," he said, "it is true, [Genji] was exceptional [in his youth], and now, in his full maturity, he has a charm that reminds one

---

[70] Ōasa Yūji, Akiyama Ken, and others have noted that the writing in the "Wakana" chapters is qualitatively new (Ōasa, "Onna Sannomiya no kōka," 75; Akiyama, *Genji monogatari no sekai*, 150).

still more of just what it means to say that someone shines. When grave and dignified he has so superbly commanding a presence that one hardly dares to approach him, and when relaxed and in a playful mood he is sweeter and more engagingly amusing than anyone in the world."[71]
The enchanting lover and host can also inspire awe.

The reader glimpses this Genji directly in "Wakana Two." Aware of Kashiwagi's transgression with the Third Princess, Genji has nonetheless been expressing publicly the most generous affection for him; but the reader also knows that he, who is now an honorary retired emperor, is outraged beyond forgiveness. Genji then hosts a party that the frightened Kashiwagi must attend and singles him out for attention with a venomous show of friendly banter.

"The older you are, the harder it gets to stop drunken tears," Genji said. "Look at [Kashiwagi], smiling away to himself—it is so embarrassing! Never mind, though, his time will come. The sun and moon never turn back. No one escapes old age." He peered at [Kashiwagi], who seemed far less cheerful than the others and really did look so unwell that the wonders of the day were lost on him...

Kashiwagi goes home ill, thinking, "I am not that drunk, though. What is the matter with me?"[72] He soon takes to his bed, and few months later he is dead. As *Mumyōzōshi* puts it, Genji has "killed him with a glance."[73] One does not trifle with such a man.

Hikaru Genji's "light" *(hikari)* therefore suggests not only beauty, grace, and so on, but also danger. Kashiwagi is already dying when he confides to Kojijū, the gentlewoman who knows his secret, "Now that [Genji] knows what I did, I shrink from the prospect of living—which I should say only shows what a special light he has....As soon as I met his gaze that evening my soul fled in anguish, and it has never come back."[74] Genji has extraordinary potency and charisma. However, that

---

[71] TTG, 579-580; GM 4:26.
[72] TTG, 669; GM 4:280.
[73] Higuchi and Kuboki, *Mumyōzōshi*, 199. For this the text calls Genji "despicable" *(muge ni keshikaranu ōnkokoro)*.
[74] TTG, 677; GM 4:295.

does not shield him from error. He may simply err more gravely than lesser men.

He does so in marrying the Third Princess, as once he had wished to marry Princess Asagao. The error springs from ambition and pride. Genji believes that he can successfully achieve perfect prestige by adding to his panoply the last ornament that it lacked (a suitably exalted wife), while at the same time keeping the unreserved love of the only woman who really matters to him. In acquiring the first he begins to lose the second, and as he does so he begins to lose himself. He soon compromises himself in the eyes of both Suzaku and society at large, for despite his decision to marry Suzaku's daughter, his love for Murasaki will prevent him from honoring the Third Princess as he should. Then his inability to tear himself away from Murasaki when at last she becomes ill leaves the door open for Kashiwagi to violate the Third Princess. That incident, which remains secret, nonetheless leads to the Third Princess becoming a nun, which reveals to all the failure of her life with Genji. Genji's marriage is therefore a private disaster with respect to Murasaki and a public failure with respect to the Third Princess.

The Third Princess and Murasaki

Murasaki and the Third Princess make a contrasting pair, as many scholars have noted. The circumstances of the Third Princess's birth and upbringing, described early in "Wakana One," also suggest a mirror-image contrast with Genji himself. Suzaku's daughter is visibly conceived as, so to speak, an anti-particle dangerous to both.

Most Japanese scholars, and all writing in English,[75] agree that Genji accepts the Third Princess because of her link to Fujitsubo. Some also

---

[75] Haruo Shirane *(The Bridge of Dreams*, 39) wrote that "ultimately it is Genji's amorous ways, particularly the memory of the Fujitsubo lady, that lead him to marry the young lady;" Norma Field *(The Splendor of Longing*, 25) called the Third Princess "a hoped-for Fujitsubo substitute"; Doris Bargen *(A Woman's Weapon*, 128) held that "Genji is attracted to the idea of becoming her guardian because of her blood relationship to Fujitsubo"; and Charo d'Etcheverry *(Love after* The Tale of Genji, 95) described the Third Princess as "Genji's own final substitute for Fujitsubo."

point out an element of pity for Suzaku. Ōasa Yūji even suggested that Genji hopes for a new Murasaki and called the marriage a mistaken attempt on Genji's part to relive the past. Fukasawa Michio, who saw the key theme of the tale in the stark contrast between the glory of Genji's Rokujō estate and the miseries caused by the arrival of the Third Princess, held that the "occasion" of these miseries is none other than Murasaki's jealousy.[76]

It is Genji's acceptance of the Third Princess, not Murasaki's jealousy (her growing wish to disengage herself from Genji) that causes the misfortunes of "Wakana One" and beyond. However Murasaki's feelings are certainly central to these misfortunes. Akashi was no threat, even if the inexperienced Murasaki thought she was. Asagao resembled distant storm clouds that melted into the sky. However, the Third Princess actually moves into the Rokujō estate, and she far outranks even Asagao. "By birth [Asagao] is worth what I am," Murasaki assures herself in "Asagao" (in other words, "My father is a prince, too!"); but she knows that that is not the whole truth and must conclude, "I shall be lost if his feelings shift to her."[77] The Third Princess allows not even that spark of hope. Insignificant in her person, she is of crushing rank. Murasaki yields in silence. Senseless protest would only demean her further.

Decorum and discretion concerning Genji's motives

Concerning Genji's motives in general, the narrator of the tale is not necessarily as frank as she sometimes seems to be. For example, to excuse or explain his behavior she may cite his "peculiarity" *(kuse)*, as she does in the opening passage of "Asagao." The word resembles a wry apology, as though to say, "No, one cannot approve, but on the subject of so great a lord I can hardly say more, and besides, the things he does make such a good story." When the narrator represents Genji himself, she may allow him to acknowledge a "warped and deplorable

---

[76] Ōasa, "Onna Sannomiya no kōka," 85, 88; Fukasawa, "Murasaki no Ue: higekiteki risōzō no keisei," 20.
[77] TTG, 368; GM 2:478.

disposition," but the effect is similar. The author of *Mumyōzōshi* likewise remarked that it is not for her to criticize Genji, even though there are many things about what he does that one might wish otherwise.[78]

What are these things? Every reader can imagine some, and the Genji narrator certainly spells some out, to a degree. It appears early that Genji's *kuse* is in the realm of *irogonomi* (gallantry, a penchant for lovemaking). It is romantic—a compelling urge to seek to make love to certain women. However, the subjective content of that urge in particular cases remains undisclosed. Why, really, does Genji (or would a living man in Genji's place) find Akikonomu or Tamakazura all but irresistible? How does he weigh the attraction of each and the consequences of success? Both are daughters of former lovers, which suggests the erotic nostalgia stressed by Ōasa Yūji.[79] Still, other motives are possible as well: for example, a wish in the case of Akikonomu secretly to appropriate yet another woman destined (like Oborozukiyo, but higher in rank) for the emperor, or in that of Tamakazura to leave his mark less on Yūgao's daughter than on Tō no Chūjō's. The narrator could not possibly attribute such thoughts to him. Then there is Utsusemi, a provincial governor's wife. Genji was experimenting after the "rainy night conversation," and he took Utsusemi's flight from him as a challenge. Naturally he felt driven to win, especially since he had nothing at stake in the matter except his self-esteem. However, talk of his *kuse*, or the claim that "[Asagao's] coolness maddened him, and he hated to admit defeat,"[80] does not suffice fifteen years later, when Asagao is a respected princess and he has recently been offered the office of chancellor. Discretion seems to have restrained the author from attributing to him the ambition, and the maneuvering to achieve that ambition, without which his actions make little sense.

A classic study of court society by Norbert Elias shows that discretion, reticence, and caution are essential to the courtier's failure

---

[78] Higuchi and Kuboki, *Mumyōzōshi*, 198.
[79] Ōasa, "Onna Sannomiya no kōka," 87.
[80] TTG, 372; GM 2:488.

or success.[81] Court society is a network of hierarchical relationships sustained by a sophisticated etiquette that is not vain show. Instead it is the substance of each courtier's (male or female) legitimate concern, since skill yields heightened prestige and a lapse can mean social ruin. The courtier strives to divine the motives and feelings of others while studiously avoiding betraying his own.

The veil, or filter, that intervenes between Genji and the reader is therefore double. First, Genji veils himself from others. Nothing in the tale contradicts Elias on this point. He is also likely at times to veil his motives even from himself. Second, the narrator of the tale, and even the author of an appreciation of the tale *(Mumyōzōshi)*, protect him because, fictional or not, he is a great lord in the very court society to which they themselves belong. The representation of Genji, as of everyone else in the tale who "is anyone," is therefore bound to be compressed in dynamic range and painted in permissible colors. The earlier chapters relate about Genji all sorts of more or less scandalous stories of which the narrator often claims to disapprove, but these do not actually breach decorum because Genji at the time is relatively junior and because in any case it is made clear from the beginning that they do not impugn his essential dignity. Later, when he rises to palace minister (in "Miotsukushi") and beyond, his risk-taking will cease as far as the audience knows. Most of those who write on the tale would then have it prolonged not by continuing maneuvers to enhance his prestige, as Elias leads one to expect of the successful courtier, but by nostalgic pursuit (Asagao) or acceptance (the Third Princess) of only coincidentally prestigious women—women who merely represent someone else for whom he felt passion in the past.

Suzaku's daughter: Genji's motive

Decorum and discretion are vital to the negotiations conducted between Genji and Suzaku over the marriage of Suzaku's daughter. That is because Genji's deeper motives have to do with the kind of self-interest that a skillful courtier, particularly one of Genji's exalted rank,

---

[81] Elias. *The Court Society*, 78-116.

prefers to keep out of sight. As Mitoma Kōsuke recognized unequi-vocally from his perspective, that of the study of myth and folklore, Genji wants the Third Princess above all because of her rank and wealth, and he therefore maneuvers to obtain her.[82] The Introduction notes the significance of this reading, which affects any conception of Genji's character, ability, and role in the tale. It rests on the direct testimony of the Third Princess's senior nurse, in conversation with Suzaku, and of this nurse's report to Suzaku concerning what she has heard from her brother, a left controller *(sachūben)* in Genji's service.[83]

If Genji is to marry Suzaku's daughter for her rank and wealth, he must nonetheless be seen by the audience to do so without compromising his dignity. The way the negotiations are narrated, without comment and almost entirely in the words (voiced or unvoiced) of the concerned parties themselves, helps to achieve this goal. Genji never expresses himself plainly to Suzaku on the issue and may even say the opposite of what he thinks. This sort of thing is surely typical of sensitive negotiations anywhere.

Suzaku believes that Genji is the only suitable match for his daughter. However, he cannot invite Genji straightforwardly to marry her without risking the embarrassment of being refused. He cannot safely approach Genji unless he already knows that Genji will say yes. For this reason he needs intelligence on the matter from informed bystanders (the nurse and her brother) who can speak plainly. Meanwhile Genji, who wants the Third Princess, cannot ask for her without lowering himself to the level of all the others, far beneath him, who have already done the same. He must therefore maneuver Suzaku into offering her to him. For this reason he needs a back channel (the nurse and her brother) that can convey his real wishes to Suzaku. Throughout these negotiations Genji has ample opportunity to let Suzaku know that, if asked, he would refuse. Since he does not, the process continues. The weight and delicacy of these negotiations for both men can be gauged from the way they end. Even when the two at last discuss the matter face to face (by which time Suzaku knows

---

82 Mitoma, "Suzaku-in ron," 364.
83 TTG, 581; GM 4:29.

Genji's likely response), Suzaku still does not dare to ask Genji openly to marry his daughter. He only asks him to take on the responsibility of finding her a suitable husband, and on the surface that is all Genji agrees to do. However, the narrator immediately confirms that each man knows exactly what the other means. "With these words," she says, "Genji accepted."[84] Things then move quickly.

Nowhere in these pages, in speech or thought, does Genji mention any scruple toward Murasaki. She does not figure in his calculations. Suzaku's only concern about her is that she might make local trouble for his daughter. She does not count, either, for the nurse, her brother, or the retainers whom they represent.

Speaking for herself and her brother, the nurse reports to Suzaku that everyone in Genji's household recognizes the close relationship between Genji and Murasaki, but that they also take for granted Murasaki's inadequacy as Genji's wife and so would gladly see him properly married. Similar people were saying similar things ("Those two would not go at all badly together") when Genji courted Asagao. The nurse also tells Suzaku that Genji himself "deeply desires a lofty alliance, and that he has so little forgotten [Asagao] that he still corresponds with her."[85] She further reports that, according to her brother, "[Genji] would undoubtedly welcome the idea [of marrying the Third Princess], since it would mean the fulfillment of his own enduring hopes."[86]

All this makes sound, if heartless, social sense. It illustrates the practical truth that underlings know about their masters many things their masters do not want spread abroad. However, it is so incompatible with accepted views of Genji that few writers on the tale in Japanese, and none in English, even mention it; and those who do, do so only to dismiss it. According to Ōasa Yūji, the reader understands that Genji's courtship of Asagao sprang from a "retrospective passion," and the nurse's report is therefore a "petty, irresponsible assumption." "Ordinary people," he wrote, "are hardly capable of understanding

---

[84] TTG, 587; GM 4:49.
[85] TTG, 580; GM 4:27.
[86] TTG, 581; GM 4:29.

Hikaru Genji's inner feelings."[87] Similarly, Akiyama Ken doubted that the nurse could possibly believe what she says, and he refused to take her brother's words seriously.[88] No two readings of the same material could diverge more completely, in the absence of explicit authorization for one of them by the text itself. Without the nurse's testimony Suzaku might never resolve to approach Genji, but the reader remains free to dismiss it because the narrative never confirms it.[89] Fortunately, it is not really necessary to argue that the Third Princess's connection with Fujitsubo plays no role in Genji's thoughts. It would naturally intrigue him, although his failure to inform himself about her as a person suggests that his determining interest in her is elsewhere. As in the case of Asagao, the old tie might make her seem somehow familiar and accessible. It might even tip the balance for him after a period of thoroughly justified hesitation. However, that would still not make it his main reason for accepting to marry her.

Murasaki's initial reaction

Murasaki first hears the news from rumor, but she who objected to Akashi and feared Asagao does not believe it. "He had seemed in earnest when he was courting the Former Kamo Priestess, too, she told herself, but he avoided taking courtship to its extreme conclusion. She did not even bother to ask him about it."[90] After all these years, she finally trusts him.

---

[87] Ōasa, "Onna Sannomiya no kōka," 76.

[88] Akiyama, *Genji monogatari no sekai*, 165 and 183, n. 4.

[89] Bitterly disappointed by the Third Princess, Genji eventually blames himself in an interior monologue passage for having "allowed a wanton weakness to get the better of him" (TTG, 593, SNKNZ 4:64). This "wanton" seems to confirm an erotic motive, but whether the original term *(adaashiku)* actually does so remains a matter of interpretation. "Frivolous" might be more accurate. While the note to the SNKBT edition (3:240, n. 9) specifies that Genji laments his excessive erotic susceptibility, the GM note (4:64, n. 2) explains that he regrets having been drawn by foolish curiosity to the idea of marrying a princess and then having been unable to refuse Suzaku's request. The idea of marrying her for her rank, too, would now undoubtedly look frivolous to him.

[90] TTG, 588; GM 4:50-51.

Genji, who surely knows this, still does not understand the gravity of what he has done. He thinks that he will manage to redeem himself yet again, sooner or later. Nonetheless, he lets a night go by without a word to Murasaki and brings the matter up only the next day, in the voice of the man who once claimed to be bored by the birth of his daughter at Akashi.

> "[Suzaku] is not at all well," he remarked, "and I called on him yesterday. It was all very touching, you know. The thought of leaving Her Highness his third daughter has been a great worry to him, and he told me all about it. I felt so sorry for him that I simply could not refuse. I suppose people will make quite a thing of it. It is all rather embarrassing by now, and unbecoming as well..."[91]

He watches her as he speaks, wondering "how she would feel—she who, with her quick temper, objected to the least of his little amusements" and assuming that she is still as she was long ago, before weightier anxieties taught her silence. Murasaki does not react. She only says, "What an extraordinary thing for him to ask of you! For myself, why should I wish to dislike her? I shall be perfectly happy as long as she does not find my presence here offensive..." Disconcerted, he lectures her anyway on the wisdom of taking "things the way they really are."[92]

All on her own, Murasaki then struggles to take herself in hand and salvage her dignity. "This came on him out of the blue, she said to herself, and he could hardly avoid it; I refuse to say an unkind word in protest...and I will not have people gather that I am sulking." Yet the shock reminds her after all of her own misfortune, and she remembers her father's jealous wife. "His Highness of Ceremonial's wife is forever calling down disaster on me," she reflects. "How she will gloat when she hears about this!"

On this turn in her thoughts the narrator comments:

> Hers was no doubt a heart without guile, but of course it still harbored a dark recess or two. In secret she never ceased

---

[91] TTG, 588; GM 4:51.
[92] TTG, 589; GM 4:53.

grieving that her very innocence—she way she had proudly assumed for so long that his vagaries need not concern her—would now cause amusement, but in her behavior she remained the picture of unquestioning trust.[93]

Demeaned by Genji's betrayal, Murasaki masks her resentment. He has at last driven her, too, to dissemble. Once the undoubted mistress of Rokujō-in, she must now defer to one who is hardly more than a child, and she does so with perfect attentiveness and grace.

"I was wrong after all to be so sure of him, and I shall never be able to trust him again," Murasaki says to herself. When the disappointed Genji clings to her instead of returning to the Third Princess, as duty requires, she cries, "No, no, I will not let you do this to me!" (since people may blame her for detaining him) and sends him on his way. To her gentlewomen she dismisses any worry that something might spark an incident between her and the Third Princess. "It is just as well that Her Highness has come," she insists, since he wanted her. "People seem to be talking as though there were a gulf between us. I wish they would not...and I do not see how anyone could disapprove of her." In response her women whisper to each other that their mistress is "being much too nice."[94] That night, while she lies sleepless but painfully still, lest her women note her restlessness and understand, Genji (with the Third Princess) dreams of her and wakens in alarm, his heart pounding.

The Third Princess is so small and immature that one wonders about Genji's dutiful nights with her. There cannot be much to them. Meanwhile his relations with Murasaki are cool as well. His frustration soon shows when Suzaku's departure for his mountain temple leaves Oborozukiyo her own mistress again. All at once, after long years of separation, Genji is desperate to see her, and nothing, least of all her own objections, stands in his way.[95] He is extraordinarily tactless toward Murasaki in the matter. Despite his fibs and evasions she

---

[93] TTG, 589; GM 4:54.

[94] TTG, 593-594; GM 4:66-67.

[95] Apart from renewing a passionate relationship at a stressful time, Genji might also have in the back of his mind reasserting ownership of Oborozukiyo and so scoring off Suzaku, whose favorite she always was.

knows what he is up to. "Why, you are quite the young gallant again!" she says when he returns from his night with Oborozukiyo. "There you are, reliving your past, only to leave me wondering what will become of me."[96]

Murasaki wishes to become a nun

The contrast between Murasaki, Genji's private treasure, and the Third Princess, his public prize, shows the folly of vain ambition. However, when the narrative returns to Murasaki after a gap of several years ("Wakana Two"), it begins by affirming that all is well.

> [The Third Princess] had never surpassed [Murasaki], despite the widespread esteem that she enjoyed. The months and years only brought those two more perfectly together, until nothing whatever seemed to come between them.

However, the old tension remains, despite lasting affection on both sides. The narrator immediately raises a grave issue.

> "I would now much rather give up my present commonplace existence and devote myself instead to quiet practice," [Murasaki] quite seriously said to Genji again and again. "At my age I feel I have learned all I wish to know of life. Please give me leave to do so."
>
> "You are too cruel," he would reply. "I could not consider it! That is exactly what I myself long to do, and if I am still here, it is only because I cannot bear to imagine how you would feel once I had left you behind, and what your life would be then. Once I have taken that step, you may do as you please." He would not have it.[97]

The religious life has attracted Genji ever since his youth, at least from a safe distance, but by now Asagao and Oborozukiyo have both done what Murasaki wishes to do, and the reader has already heard him fret that he is falling ignominiously behind. Nonetheless, when Murasaki opens the door for him to do what he claims to have long wanted to do, he accuses her of cruelty, and he will do so again whenever she

---

[96] TTG, 600; GM 4:85.
[97] TTG, 632; GM 4:167.

broaches the subject. He clings to this world far more stubbornly than he would have even himself believe.

The matter continues to weigh on Murasaki's mind, and evidence of Genji's continuing favor does little after all to calm her fears for the future.

> Seeing her own prestige rise in time so high above that of all others at Rokujō, [Murasaki] continually reflected that although the personal favor she enjoyed was equal to anyone's, age by and by would dull her in his eyes, and that she preferred to leave the world on her own before that should happen; but she found it impossible to say so clearly, for she feared that he might condemn her for being too forward.[98]

He has chided her before, and the topic is no doubt an especially sore one for him now, not only because of his complex feelings about leaving the world himself, or about allowing Murasaki to do so, but because by this time the Third Princess has been promoted still higher in rank. People had already been whispering that he did not honor her enough, and this promotion has placed him under a still heavier obligation to put her visibly above Murasaki. Despite his struggle to resist while seeming to comply, he has had to make a show of spending more time with the Third Princess; and Murasaki, who knows that he cannot countenance her desire to become a nun, must sense also that tension over the Third Princess may sharpen his reaction to any expression of her desire to do so. Meanwhile, Genji begins to divide his nights equally between the two. "[Murasaki] accepted and understood this, but it confirmed her fears, although she never allowed them to show."[99]

Soon Genji must begin teaching the Third Princess the *kin*, to please her father, and the "women's concert" *(onnagaku)* follows. The lady from Akashi, her daughter (the heir apparent's consort), Murasaki, and the Third Princess perform at Rokujō for Genji and Yūgiri, his guest. The Third Princess does well, thanks to Genji's patient instruction, but

---

[98] TTG, 636; GM 4:177.
[99] TTG, 636; GM 4:177.

Murasaki plays the *wagon* more beautifully than Genji ever imagined, since he has never even heard her before on this instrument.

The next morning, Genji begins the day with a tactless remark.

"It is remarkable how well Her Highness does at the *kin*, isn't it!" Genji observed. "How did it strike you?"

"I wondered about her when I first heard her play a little, over there, but she has become very good now. How could she fail to, when you have been giving all your time to her lessons?"[100]

Murasaki is hurt that he hardly taught her music at all. He explains that he had to teach the Third Princess because Suzaku and the emperor both expected it of him, and he goes on to assure Murasaki that her own performance, and the degree to which it impressed Yūgiri, made him extremely proud. This is poor consolation. After all, Akashi (Murasaki's old rival), too, played superbly, and Murasaki knows as well as Genji that in her case as in others mastery of music has nothing to do with a lady's real weight in the world.

Murasaki asks again to leave the world

As Murasaki's weariness and anxiety mount, the narrator pauses to reflect with Genji that her very quality puts her in the way of misfortune.

With such accomplishments as these, and the authority with which she looked after His Majesty's children, [Murasaki] was a success in every way, so much so that Genji even feared for her, remembering the example of others, equally perfect, whose lives had not been long, for she was that rarity: someone who in every single thing she did remained beyond cavil or reproach....She was thirty-seven this year.[101]

Many passages in the tale express a similar fear that someone too beautiful will not live long. Besides, as Genji soon reminds her, the almanac warns that a woman in her thirty-seventh year is particularly

---

[100] TTG, 644; GM 4:204.
[101] TTG, 645; GM 4:205.

prone to calamity.[102] His thoughts announce imminent sorrows. The way he seems to attribute these to the agencies of fate hint that he is either blind (if he does not suspect that he is to blame) or patronizing (if he does but dismisses the idea); but these opening lines concern less him than her. They evoke the flower's full beauty just before the wind and rain, and they gently introduce a very dark passage.

Having apparently lost touch with Murasaki, Genji now goes on to muse aloud to her about the course his life and hers have taken, contrasting his sorrows and hardships with her sheltered tranquility. His uncomprehending tactlessness is a shock, considering Murasaki's distress and anxiety over the Third Princess, and her efforts to betray neither. He has never before spoken to her from so false a height.

> "For you, though, it seems to me that apart from that time when we were separated there has been little either before or after it really to cause you serious unhappiness. The greatest lady in the land, all the way up to the Empress herself, is certain to have reason to be anxious. One is never at ease in exalted company, where the spirit of rivalry is a constant torment, but *you* have always lived with your father, as it were, and you have had less of that than anyone, ever. Do you see how in that sense you have been more fortunate than others? I am sure that it was difficult for you to have Her Highness turn up here suddenly, but since it directly affects you, you cannot have failed to notice how much more devoted I am to you since she came. You who understand so many things must have grasped that."[103]

Genji's dramatic, relatively unfettered life, one that could only be a man's, is not comparable to Murasaki's, restricted as it has been by all that a woman must uphold and endure. He seems to imagine that, even now, she will believe she has no troubles just because he tells her so. His speech, which may also owe something of its tone to the pressure he himself feels, is a provocation that Murasaki cannot let pass without renouncing her own integrity and even her identity. The reader

---

[102] Fujitsubo died in her thirty-seventh year.
[103] TTG, 645; GM 4:207.

learned long ago that she will not do that and may feel that Genji should have learned the same.

"As you say," she replied, "I expect that in others' eyes I enjoy favor beyond what I deserve, but by now more sorrow than I can bear has entered my life, and that is what has inspired all my prayers." She seemed to have much more to say but to be too shy to do so. "Seriously, though," she continued, "I feel as if I have little time left, and the thought of spending this year, too, pretending otherwise worries me very much. If you would kindly permit what I once asked..."[104]

She knows that she cannot safely raise, again, the subject of becoming a nun, but she does so nonetheless. Genji's response is predictably sharp.

"That is out of the question, I tell you. What would my life mean without you? My greatest joy over all these years has always been simply to be with you day and night. What I feel for you in extraordinary. Please see my devotion through to the end!"
That was all he said, which hurt her, since she had heard that much before; meanwhile he was moved to see her eyes fill with tears, and he talked on so as to turn her mind to other things.

He concedes nothing. Instead, to distract her, he begins again to muse out loud. His earlier talk to her, about how lucky she was, did him no good. This time, with his judgment impaired by emotion, he tries something worse. The situation resembles the one near the end of "Asagao." As though to reassure her by censuring others, and perhaps even covertly to get back at her for contradicting his belief that she should be content, he launches into reminiscences about Aoi and Rokujō, and to these he adds the lady from Akashi as a model for Murasaki. This is an affront and also dangerous. When he reminisced about Fujitsubo for the same purpose, under similar but more benign circumstances, Fujitsubo came to him in a dream and reproached him bitterly. This time the result is disaster.

After discussing Aoi, remarking that she was "so terribly proper that one might say she overdid it a little," Genji continues,

---

[104] TTG, 645-646; GM 4:207-208.

"[Rokujō] comes to mind as someone of unusual grace and depth, but she made painfully trying company. I agree she had reason to be angry with me, but the way she brooded so interminably over the matter, and with such bitter rancor, made things very unpleasant. There was something so intimidating about her that I could never enjoy with her the daily intimacies of life; I could never drop my guard, lest informality invite her contempt, and so she and I soon drifted apart. I regretted her distress when scandal touched her and her good name suffered, and in fact, considering who she was, I felt in the end that I was to blame; but to make it up to her I insured that her daughter (who of course was so destined anyway) rose to be Empress, ignoring by the way a good deal of slander and bitterness, and I expect that by now, in the afterworld, she has come to think better of me."[105]

Of this Tanabe Seiko wrote only that, as earlier in "Asagao," Genji's reminiscing about his women successfully restores harmony with Murasaki. She did not add that Rokujō soon possesses a girl of the household to pour out her complaint against Genji. Norma Field noted the parallel with "Asagao" (reminiscences followed by supernatural visitation) only in passing. [106] The parallel is seldom mentioned elsewhere. However, Genji's speech is unwise.

The least of his sins is that in response to Murasaki's anguish he can do little more than talk about himself, which he does under the guise of confiding to her reflections on several of his other women. Nothing in the tale suggests that Murasaki fancies gossip, and although his remarks may interest her superficially, they could hardly bring her closer to him. A greater sin is turning the name and memory of the dead to one's own selfish purposes and disclosing their secrets. But that is not all. Genji actually speaks ill of them: first of Aoi and then of Rokujō. He who twenty-five years ago saw what Rokujō's spirit could do, when it possessed Aoi, still has the face to "treat her," as his father put it to him reproachfully then, "as casually as [he] might any other

---

105 TTG, 646: GM 4:209-210.
106 Tanabe, *Genji monogatari kami fūsen*, 165; Field, *The Splendor of Longing*, 59.

woman."[107] Fujii Sadakazu wrote that Genji built his Rokujō estate to pacify *(chinkon)* Rokujō's spirit, and others have agreed,[108] but there is another way to look at the matter. Genji built his estate on the site of Rokujō's residence, and no doubt in part with resources that passed from her to him when he undertook to see to her daughter's future; but the place is Genji's dream and Genji's glory, not a gesture towards a late lover who "made painfully trying company." Genji's building of his estate is consistent with his attitude towards Rokujō both twenty-five years ago and now. He still takes her for granted. In fact, he not only takes her for granted, he also self-righteously claims to have bought her off by doing the right thing (in the end, after perilous wavering) by her daughter. The Rokujō whom the reader knows could never let this pass.

Genji's talk turns next to Akashi, whom he praises now as in the past for a personal quality out of keeping with her station. "On the surface she yields and seems mild," he says, "but within she has such imposing dignity that she can be quite forbidding." To this Murasaki responds so self-effacingly that Genji is

> greatly moved to reflect that she who once had sharply resented the lady in question, now, out of pure devotion to the Consort, admitted her so indulgently to her presence. "You are not without your dark recesses," he said, "but it is a wonder how well you adapt your feelings to person and circumstance."[109]

He is condescending to her. A short while ago he reminded her that she had always lived, as it were, with her father, as though both were still caught in that passage of their youth, and now he talks to her as though she were still the Murasaki who protested his affair with Akashi. He also makes her only a backhanded compliment when he praises her ability to feel, as appropriate, otherwise than she really feels in the "dark recesses" where she upholds her own worth and dignity against his slights.

---

[107] T 166; GM 2:18.
[108] Fujii, *Genji monogatari: shigen to genzai*, 157-160; Shirane, *The Bridge of Dreams*, 116; Bargen, *A Woman's Weapon*, 120.
[109] TTG, 646-647; GM 4:211.

The sentiments highlighted by this discussion have made Genji sound more sharply arrogant and patronizing than he does in the original. He really loves Murasaki, but other imperatives, as well as the passage of time and gradually failing judgment, have drawn him away from her. This essay may seem sometimes to set the two against one another in a sort of modern confrontation, but one should never forget the grace of the original and its measured pace; and the grace, too, of the picture that Genji and Murasaki always make.

Murasaki's illness

That night Genji goes to the Third Princess, and to pass the lonely time Murasaki has her gentlewomen read her tales. The atmosphere is heavy with a crisis that comes quickly.

> These old stories are all about what happens in life, she thought, and they are full of women involved with fickle, wanton, or treacherous men, and so on, but each seems to find her own in the end. How strange it is, the unsettled life I have led! Yes, it is true, as he said, that I have enjoyed better fortune than most, but am I to end my days burdened with these miseries that other women find hateful and endurable? Oh, it is too hard![110] She went to bed very late and as dawn came on, she began to suffer chest pains. Her women did what they could for her. "Shall we inform His Grace?" they asked, but she would not have it and bore her agony until it was light. She became feverish and felt extremely ill, but no one told Genji as long as he failed to come on his own.[111]

Once, long ago, Murasaki thought, "I am I!", turned away from Genji, and sighed. A few years later she said, "Familiarity often breeds contempt" and lay down with her back to him. This time, when he has

---

[110] The passage on tales in "Hotaru" deserves its fame, but the way Murasaki turns to tales here, in despair, is very moving. They are her only resource. She cannot seek solace and guidance from the histories of China and Japan, as Reizei did after learning that he was Genji's son.

[111] TTG, 647; GM 4:212.

really done what she feared, and she is sick with hurt and anger, she will not even tell him. Let him return when he pleases!

Murasaki's illness will last off and on until her death four years later. Soon Genji moves her to Nijō, where they had first lived together, and all but abandons the Third Princess (at Rokujō) in order to be with her while the priests pursue their rites.

> In lucid moments Murasaki only spoke to reproach him, saying, "You are so cruel not to grant me what I ask!"; but for Genji the sorrow and pain of seeing her one instant, with his very eyes, wearing by her own wish the habit of renunciation, rather than parting from her at the end of life itself, would be more than he could ever bear. "It is exactly what *I* have always longed to do," he said, "but worry about how you would feel, once you were left alone, has constantly detained me. Do you mean to say that you would now abandon *me?*" That was his only response...[112]

Nothing has changed. What she asks is more than he can give. He cannot allow her an independent existence and feel that he remains himself. For love of her he cannot bear her to have a will, a life of her own. At least her illness has led Genji for now to forget the duties of his political marriage, which would be all very well, were it not that during his absence from the Rokujō estate Kashiwagi violates the Third Princess and precipitates another tragedy.

The possession

Genji has at last left Murasaki to spend some time with the Third Princess when word reaches him that Murasaki has died. He rushes back to Nijō and summons the most powerful healers. In response to their prayers the afflicting spirit suddenly "moved into a little girl, in whom it screamed and raged while his love began at last to breathe again."[113] It is Rokujō.

---

[112] TTG, 648; GM 4:214-215.

[113] TTG, 654; GM 4:234. The influence of this spirit has been assumed from the start, since it begins its speech to Genji by saying, "For months you have cruelly confined me and inflicted on me such pain that I had thought I might teach you a proper lesson..."

Many studies of Murasaki and issues affecting her have neglected the dramatic scene that follows, and those who mention it may still dismiss it. Tanabe Seiko found it "tacked on" and recalled Shimizu Yoshiko saying that the author must have written it only because her readers liked the counterpart scene in "Aoi" and wanted more. For Kojima Yukiko, the text makes it perfectly clear why Murasaki falls ill: she is unhappy about the Third Princess. The possession scene, Kojima wrote, is simply a "device" to explain how the dying Murasaki can unaccountably revive and regain Genji's attention.[114]

Doris Bargen rightly treated the scene at length,[115] but her conclusions amount to a denial that it represents what the text says it does: a renewed intervention in Genji's life by a personage known as Rokujō. Bargen contended that the Rokujō who possesses the medium is not an autonomous entity but Murasaki's own image of a woman whose "charisma" Murasaki appropriates to "empower herself";[116] and she charged "critics" with mistakenly adopting Genji's own, biased "preoccupation with identifying the possessing spirit,"[117] when here and in the earlier possession scene in "Aoi" they and Genji should both know that the real speaker is Genji's possessed wife. However, it takes no preoccupation with anything to accept that the spirit is Rokujō. In "Aoi" the reader already knows that the spirit is Rokujō, and Genji recognizes her instantly. In this one, Genji behaves normally for someone addressed by a medium in a trance: he seeks to verify who the speaker is. His fear that he knows the answer already is all the more reason to make sure. To agree that the speaker is Rokujō is not to take Genji's side. It is simply to read what is there.[118]

---

[114] Tanabe, *Genji monogatari kami fūsen*, 130; Kojima, "Murasaki no Ue," 68.

[115] Bargen, *A Woman's Weapon*, 124-144.

[116] Bargen, *A Woman's Weapon*, 124, 27.

[117] Bargen, *A Woman's Weapon*, 26.

[118] Bargen's reading requires a strange understanding of Rokujō. No degree of admiration or sympathy for Rokujō can explain why Murasaki or any other woman in the tale, however desperate, would seek the authority of someone so ill-used by Genji. Bargen described Rokujō as "a proud, dissatisfied, and demanding woman who knew how to gain control over a man" (*A Woman's Weapon*, 136). However, Rokujō never gained control over Genji. If she had, he would have recognized his relationship with her publicly, as she wished. His failure to do so brought her years of intense suffering.

There are three possible ways to explain the possession: Murasaki somehow provokes her relapse and Rokujō's outburst in order to get Genji's attention and rebuke him, as Bargen would have it; the author arbitrarily does it for her, as Kojima suggested; or Genji's absence removes his protection from Murasaki, and Rokujō seizes the opportunity to capture his attention herself. Only the third follows from the narrative itself, even if it does not make modern, rational, or psychological sense. The spirit says:

> I kept my eye on you from on high, and what you did for Her Majesty [Akikonomu] made me pleased and grateful, but perhaps I do not care that much about my daughter now that she and I inhabit different realms, because that bitterness of mine, which made you hateful to me, remains.

The spirit's remark that in the afterworld she cares less about her daughter than Genji assumes has a ghastly plausibility. The spirit also confirms that Genji's indiscretion is the immediate reason for her renewed reproach:

> What I find particularly offensive, more so even than your spurning me for others when I was among the living, is that in conversation with one for whom you do care you callously made me out to be a disagreeable woman.

That is just what Genji did. The spirit continues:

> I had hoped, as I did then, that you might at least be forgiving towards the dead and come to my defense when others maligned me; and that is why, since I have this shocking appearance, things have come to this at last. I have little enough against this woman, but *you* are strongly guarded. I feel far away and cannot approach you, and even your voice reaches me only faintly.

None of this has anything obvious to do with Murasaki, although in this scene Murasaki and Rokujō certainly are briefly and eerily superimposed—superimposed, not merged. That this superimposition resists explanation neither diminishes its power nor authorizes the

---

To propose Rokujō as an inspiration to Murasaki is cruel to Rokujō and denies Murasaki any sense.

suppression of one of the pair. To accept it is to feel doubly the heart-rending force of this, the height of Rokujō's speech:

> The weeping figure, her hair over her face, resembled the spirit he had seen then [in "Aoi"]. Shuddering with the same fear and astonishment, he took the girl's hands and held her down lest she embarrass him. "Is it really you?" he asked...." Say plainly who you are! Or else, tell me something to make it obvious, something no one else could know. Then I will believe you, at least a little."
> The spirit sobbed loudly.

> > *"Yes, as I am now,*
> > *my form is one new and strange,*
> > *but plainly the while*
> > *you are still just the same you,*
> > *who always refuse to know.*

> Oh, I hate you, I hate you!"[119]

The voice speaks the truth. Genji refuses to know. Murasaki, who does not hate him, could still say the same thing, but she does not.

Murasaki's *ware wa ware* ("I am I") long ago, over Akashi, was akin in spirit and rhetoric to love poems that set "I" against "you." Rokujō's utterance, which does so, too, belongs to the same family: I am no longer what I was, she says, but you are you *(kimi wa kimi nari):* you are just the same as ever. It is the classic lover's reproach become a nightmare voice, but Genji, who has no ears with which to heed it, will let this rebuke, too, pass.

Murasaki's death

Murasaki survives another four years of crisis, weakness, and reprieve. Filled though they are with sad or tender scenes and reflections, the distance between her and Genji remains. When the worst of the possession crisis seems over, Genji, "cut a token lock of her hair to give her the strength to observe the Five Precepts, and he allowed her to

---

[119] TTG, 654-655; GM 4:235-236.

receive them."[120] However, this tiny concession, made under duress, changes nothing.

Murasaki therefore does what the unhappy Rokujō could never do: she gathers herself to rise above her situation. Komashaku Kimi wrote, "It is certain that, contrary to worldly appearances, Murasaki no Ue died still burdened by her misfortune, a 'woman's' misfortune."[121] This is not untrue. In "Minori" Murasaki, who still hoped to leave the world, felt "angry with him because it would so obviously be unkind and contrary of her to act on her own, without his permission; but she feared, too, that her own sins might be weighing her down." Her *ware* is not yet gone, and she still suffers. However, she who "asked nothing more of this life and, having no fond ties to detain her, did not particularly wish to stay" is also thinking of Genji, to whom the very thought of outliving her is appalling; for "at heart she regretted only what he would suffer when the bond between them failed."[122] Meanwhile, she seeks to make peace with her life as well as she can under the circumstances. She has herself in hand.

Most of those who have written on the end of Murasaki's life have preferred to see her this way, and some have found her example inspiring. She has taken the difficult path of generosity, as her nature from the beginning disposed her to do. Feeling death approaching,

> She hastened to dedicate the thousand copies of the Lotus Sutra that she had had made as prayers for herself over the years. The event took place at Nijō, which she considered her own home....She had never told him that it was to be so solemn, and so he in turn had offered her no particular advice. The excellence of her judgment, and even her knowledge of Buddhist things, impressed him profoundly; his only role was to look after quite ordinary matters of altar adornment and so on.[123]

---

[120] TTG, 656; GM 4:241.

[121] Komashaku, *Murasaki Shikibu no messēji*, 152.

[122] TTG, 755; GM 4:493.

[123] TTG, 755-756; GM 4:495. She had probably had these copies made to pray for permission to leave the world.

She has never done anything like this before, and she does it entirely on her own, in the house she considers her own; and she does it magnificently. Kurata Minoru justly observed that with this event she achieves independence, and that the court's full attendance makes her true standing plain. Yes, in the eyes of all she really is the wife of the honorary retired emperor.[124] One thinks back to Fujitsubo's magnificent rite of the Eight Discourses on the Lotus Sutra, at the end of which she became a nun ("Sakaki").

With this Murasaki therefore rises at last to join Fujitsubo on the same high plane of perfect simplicity that Genji recalled admiringly when he described Fujitsubo to Murasaki in "Asagao." "Although she displayed no extraordinary brilliance," he said, "a talk with her was always worthwhile, and she did the smallest thing exactly right. We shall never see her like again." He then looked at Murasaki and rightly saw Fujitsubo, but in those days he could not yet honor her as she deserved, and he never learned really to do so. She lacked the world's unreserved approbation, and in any case he clasped her, like everything else, too jealously to himself. It is only in setting out on her own, within the confines of compassion towards a deeply loved but failing man, that she becomes at last in simple reality what he saw then, and the woman who by natural gift she had always been: like Fujitsubo, a born empress. Some have praised her "self-transcendence" at the end,[125] but really she transcends nothing. Instead, thoughts of herself drop away—even the wonderful gifts (music, calligraphy, skill at dyeing, freshness of taste, beauty, quick wit) that she enjoyed even more abundantly than Fujitsubo. An empress has no "I," no "prickles"; she does not deign to commit herself to personal traits. Only sorrow remains, and concern for others.

> Lady Murasaki had many things on her mind, but wisely she never spoke of when she would be gone. She confined herself to a few, quiet remarks about the fleeting character of life, but the conviction in her voice conveyed her desolation better than

---

124 Kurata, "Murasaki no Ue no shi to Hikaru Genji," 331.
125 Shigematsu, "Murasaki no Ue no ningenzō," 22-23; Maruyama, "Murasaki no Ue shōron," 50.

any words....When the conversation took such a turn that her remarks need not sound ill-omened, she mentioned those who had served her well through the years and who invited pity because they had nowhere else to go. "Do give them a thought after I am gone," she said. That was all.[126]

She is beyond rank. Soon the present empress, her adopted daughter, will come to her while she lies dying to say good-by, as naturally as any daughter would come to her mother. There is nothing for Genji to do, nor will he ever do anything again.

Conclusion

This essay has sought to acknowledge that the *Genji* text conveys after all, through its wit and grace, some of the major realities of life. Haruo Shirane wrote, in agreement with many others:

> In the *Genji* it is not the fulfillment or frustration of desire that becomes the focus of the narrative so much as the elegant and elaborate process of courtship....Almost every aspect of social intercourse is transformed into an aesthetic mode.[127]

A good deal of the narrative indeed concerns courtship, and perhaps some of this courtship really is "elegant and elaborate." Some of it, however, is other things first. Genji's pursuit of Utsusemi is more naively brazen than intrinsically elegant, his pursuit of Suetsumuhana more comical, and his abduction of the child Murasaki more racily dramatic (or, as some now say, criminal). His conquest of Oborozukiyo is far from elaborate, and his courtship of Asagao, so unrelenting that she fears betrayal by her own women, lacks any elegance at all beyond the civilized forms that Genji still upholds. This is not to criticize the tale or its hero. Rather, it is to insist that, even in the realm of courtship, less rarified realities show plainly through the tale's "aesthetic mode."

Moreover, much of the tale is not about courtship at all. Shirane continued:

---

[126] TTG, 758; GM 4:502.
[127] Shirane, *The Bridge of Dreams*, 30.

Genji becomes a great lover-hero not simply because he conquers women but because he has also mastered the "arts"—poetry, calligraphy, music—of courtship. The same applies to Genji's political triumphs, which are measured by a cultural and aesthetic code that transcends the usual notion of power and influence.[128]

Genji's mastery of the arts—assisted by his wealth, rank, skill, looks, and charm—undoubtedly makes him a cultural paragon in his world. However, his ambitions and triumphs, as well as his slow disintegration, also involve aspirations and personal maneuvering unrelated to any particular "cultural and aesthetic code." Nothing in the narrative except its supernatural elements suggests that this aspect of Genji's experience "transcends the usual notion of power and influence." Far from being unusual, except in the degree to which he is gifted, Genji succeeds by the methods of any courtier and fails as might anyone whose extravagant success impairs his judgment.

Some writers on the tale have taken it for granted that Genji represents an "ideal." Murasaki, too, has been seen as an "ideal woman." However, this view seems to put beyond question certain things that, when examined, enrich the work and give Genji and Murasaki fuller life.

The notion of "ideal" associated with Genji is probably summed up by his peerless looks and grace, which the narrator evokes repeatedly, but his enchanting quality also diverts the audience's attention from what he is up to. Many more or less troubling passages end when the narrator turns the scene into a beautiful tableau, or the gentlewomen, watching him leave, whisper to each other what a wonder he is to behold. He also has superb intellectual and artistic gifts, as well as the personal charisma that gives him, in Kashiwagi's words, such a "singular light." He is never ordinary. It is this quality that gives him in all circumstances a dignity commensurate with his exquisitely ambiguous proximity to the throne. However, while his beauty in this broad sense makes him fascinating, it does not make him a model of laudable thought or behavior. His "light" is not a sign of goodness. On

---

[128] Shirane, *The Bridge of Dreams*, 30.

the contrary, it lends grace and style to that in him which may not be laudable at all. At each moment the audience sees of him what the narrator wishes to show, but in the imagination the reader puts these moments together, looks beyond the words, and sees more or less distinctly a man. No one could think, talk, or write about "him" otherwise. This man is like other men, even if his gifts lift him above all others.

Naturally Genji has always stirred readers' dreams, but Murasaki lives with Genji the man. It is he who claims her, tests her, hurts her, cajoles her, lies to her, loves her, and even against her wishes never lets her go. Some have described their love, too, as "ideal" and called its story "the fulfillment of ideal love."[129] However, their fate is not a happy one.

Genji alone provokes this fate, moved by ambition that requires more of Murasaki than she can give him. After the abdication of Emperor Reizei ("Wakana Two"), his secret son, he entertains before the reader thoughts if not of empire, then at least of dynasty. Already the grandfather of a future emperor in the female line, he nonetheless regrets not being the same in the male:

> Genji, at Rokujō, nursed his disappointment that Retired Emperor Reizei had no successor of his own. The Heir Apparent was his direct descendant too, it was true, but no trouble having ever arisen to disturb His Retired Majesty's reign, Genji's transgression had not come to light and now would never be known; and as fate would have it, that line was in any case not to continue. Genji regretted this very much, and since he could hardly discuss the matter with anyone else it continued to weigh on his mind.[130]

Thus Genji, who would really have reigned if his father had not refrained from naming him heir apparent, has long wished to correct this error and, so to speak, to rewrite history. Dare one imagine that he made love to Fujitsubo with that, too, in mind? At any rate, it is to this

---

129 Wakashiro, *Genji monogatari no onna*, 223.
130 TTG, 631; GM 4:165-166.

sort of desire—one his gifts allowed him the hope of fulfilling—that he sacrifices with deep but blind sorrow the woman he really loves.

Murasaki may understand little of this, but there is much that he does not understand about her, either. She has her own destiny. If he, in a truer world than the flawed one they inhabit, is a born emperor whom only fortune has cheated of his realm, she in that truer world is his equal, and in this one suffers a counterpart misfortune. Her resistance to his three infidelities proceeds from no intrinsic trait, but only from the predicament of a flawed birth that does not match her nature. For him, reclaiming what should have been his requires such manipulation of persons and circumstances that despite both genius and supernatural favor he falls short after all. He wanted too much. Reizei has no heir, the Third Princess slips from him, and these two great transgressions (against his father and against Murasaki) cost him the substance of what he is and has.

Murasaki, as beautiful as he, has never for a moment been ordinary either. Still, she is a woman, and her different destiny depends on his. Despite her repeated affirmations of distinctness, she does not free herself from his appetites until his powers begin to fail and her own death approaches; and if she were not thanks to him an empress's adoptive mother, that empress's last visit to her could not seal her life. Yet in rising at the end above happiness or unhappiness she achieves something that he does not; for until lost to view he remains, like many another great man, entangled in the complexities of an extravagant pride.

GENJI AND SUZAKU:
THE DISASTER OF THE THIRD PRINCESS

The preceding essay followed the evolving relationship between Genji and Murasaki, from Genji's first discovery of Murasaki until her death. Its extended discussion of Genji's marriage to the Third Princess, the favorite daughter of his elder brother Suzaku, emphasized Genji's reasons for accepting this marriage and the ways in which it affected the relationship between him and Murasaki. However, it also prepared the ground for a further treatment of the relationship between Genji and Suzaku himself.

"The Disaster of the Third Princess" focuses on that relationship. It argues that tension between Genji and Suzaku, whether or not consciously acknowledged, provides the framework for a core plot through the tale. The plot has four stages. These are rivalry, at first political rather than personal, between the brothers; the younger brother's supernaturally-aided victory over the elder; the younger's moment of vainglorious folly, exploited to disastrous effect by the spirit of a woman he once wronged; and the elder brother's efforts as an angry ghost to torment the younger's descendants. The essay therefore examines critical issues in Part One, connects Part One to Parts Two and Three, and in this way proposes a link between the end of the tale and the beginning.

The reading presented in "The Disaster of the Third Princess" will invoke internal, psychological motives to explain the characters' thoughts, actions, and experiences. However, the recurring emphasis will be on external forces devised by the author, presumably in consonance with reader expectations and her own ideas. The essay therefore assumes authorial intention and invention: a conception of the tale's long-range trajectory and the use of devices to move it along that path. In the initial phase Genji struggles against the political advantage enjoyed by Suzaku and his supporters, especially Suzaku's mother and her father, the right minister. His allies in the contest are his father-in-law, the left minister, and his father, the Kiritsubo Emperor. This phase ends after the crisis of Genji's exile, during which the Sumiyoshi deity, assisted by the late Kiritsubo Emperor's spirit, intervenes to assure Genji's triumph. Genji then comes to tower over the court. This phase ends when both the reigning emperor (Reizei, Genji's secret son) and the emperor who abdicated in Reizei's favor (Suzaku) pay Genji, now an Honorary Retired Emperor, a formal visit at Genji's recently completed Rokujō-in estate. This triumph then seduces Genji into marrying the Third Princess. The domestic consequences lead him to gossip foolishly about the Rokujō lady, a particularly dangerous woman from his past. Her spirit, provoked anew, strikes back, setting in motion a chain of events that ruins Genji's later years and destroys the peace Suzaku that has made with his own defeat. Suzaku then has reason to die detesting Genji. In the final phase (so this essay ventures to suggest) Suzaku's angry spirit pursues Kaoru, Genji's alleged son, through the women whom Kaoru loves.

Genji and Suzaku

Genji's birth and childhood are fundamental to the rest of *The Tale of Genji*. His extraordinary gifts cannot outweigh his mother's weak social standing, and his father understands the impossibility of appointing him heir apparent, as he would like to do. The Kiritsubo Emperor therefore gives him a surname, so that he should be able eventually to serve the realm in such weighty commoner offices as minister or regent. In this way the author spares her hero the strictures that confine a ranking prince and gives his future experience maximum scope. She also endows him with unlimited material means. It is significant as well that his surname allows him over time to live on both sides of the line that separates common from imperial.

Genji and his allies have the reader's full attention from the start. The spotlight is always on him, while Suzaku remains forever in shadow. No wonder Suzaku's mother complains bitterly, at the end of "Sakaki," "My son may be Emperor, but no one has ever granted him any respect."[1] However, the younger Genji, who enjoys every gift, lacks political backing, while the elder Suzaku, who has none, enjoys powerful support. Considering what is at stake—the succession—this pervasive contrast invites tension and conflict in one form or another. Genji is very young when their father bows to necessity and appoints Suzaku heir apparent, but he could hardly help feeling more deserving; and although he might seem better off in the end with his greater, commoner liberty, the narrative continually evokes the overwhelmingly desirable prestige of the imperial.

By the end of the first chapter the author has established a political struggle surrounding succession to the throne and factional dominance over the court, and she has left no doubt about the incumbent emperor's feelings on the subject. An example discussed further in "The Possibility of Ukifune" illustrates an analogously dangerous situation in real life. Political pressure forced Ichijō (r. 986-1011), under whose reign *The Tale of Genji* was written, to bypass a son he favored and appoint instead, as heir apparent to his successor, Sanjō, a grandson of Fujiwara no Michinaga (966-1027). This seems to have embittered him. The decisive intervention of the Kiritsubo Emperor's spirit ("Akashi"), in Genji's favor and against Suzaku and his side, can therefore be seen as furthering a plot established in the book's opening pages.

Anger and resentment are unworthy of an emperor, and the narrative refrains from attributing any such feelings to Suzaku. In Part One he need not even be aware of them. However, several developments in the narrative might cause any man in his place to resent not only the esteem enjoyed by his younger brother, but also Genji's repeated, personal victories. The first of these, described in "Kiritsubo," involves his marriage to Aoi. The narrator says,

> By Her Highness his wife the sponsoring Minister had a beloved only daughter [Aoi] in whom the Heir Apparent [Suzaku] had expressed interest, but whom after long hesitation he felt more inclined to offer to Genji instead. When he had sounded out the Emperor's own feelings on the

---

[1] TTG, 219; GM 2:148.

matter His Majesty replied, "Very well, she may be just the companion for him, now that he seems no longer to have anyone looking after him"; and this had encouraged His Excellency to proceed.[2]

The sponsoring minister of the left and Suzaku's grandfather, the minister of the right, are political rivals, and the former means to strengthen his hand by securing the emperor's favorite son. Normally he would give his daughter to the heir apparent, as both she and Suzaku's mother (the Kokiden Consort) expect him to do. However, he judges that the emperor will agree out of a desire to secure Genji the most promising possible future; if he did not, he would hesitate to raise the subject at all. In this way Suzaku, who has already let it be known that he wants Aoi, loses her, and Genji gets her instead.

Suzaku's mother is furious. After complaining that no one has ever respected him, she continues, "That Minister of the Left did not offer his precious only daughter to *him,* the elder brother and the Heir Apparent; no, he gave her to the younger, a commoner and a stripling not yet even of age." She continues, "And when we were so hoping to send our girl into palace service, did anyone object to the ridiculous position this Genji had left her in?"[3] She refers to Oborozukiyo.

Kokiden once planned to marry her much younger sister Oborozukiyo to her son, then still heir apparent. Before she could do so, however, Genji made love to the young woman himself ("Hana no En"), striking up with her a passionate, lasting affair. Genji knew at the time that she was one of the right minister's daughters, although not which one, and he certainly understood the risk he was taking. Apparently he took it deliberately, because later in the same chapter he accepted her father's invitation to a party and arrived ostentatiously late, dressed (unlike anyone else present) in the manner of a prince. By then he suspected that his conquest might be the sister destined for Suzaku, and at the end of the evening he confirmed this with outrageous nonchalance, having meanwhile, by his entrance, flaunted his contempt for his host and all his host's faction.

---

[2] TTG, 16; GM 1:46.
[3] TTG, 219; GM 2:148.

Oborozukiyo goes to Suzaku in the end, but her affair with Genji makes her unappointable as *nyōgo* ("consort"), the title that the Kokiden Consort expected for her. Then Genji carries on with her so rashly ("Sakaki") that her father discovers them together in his own house. Kokiden, who happens then to be at home, is enraged. Convinced as she is already that Genji is plotting to overthrow Suzaku, she vows to bring him down, and he has to retreat to Suma.

The narrator never has Suzaku express hostility toward Genji over Oborozukiyo, but Suzaku knows that the two remain in touch even after his accession, and because he loves Oborozukiyo, the difference between possessing her person and her heart torments him. The opening passage of "Miotsukushi" makes these feelings clear. Genji has returned from exile and is about to sweep Suzaku aside, together with everyone who ever supported him.

> With his planned abdication rapidly approaching, [Suzaku's] sympathy went to [Oborozukiyo], whose experience of life had been so painful. "His Excellency the Chancellor [the former minister of the right] is no more," he said to her, "the Empress Mother's [Kokiden's] health gives every cause for concern, and now that I feel my own time is coming, I am afraid of leaving you sadly on your own in a very different world. You have never thought as well of me as of a certain other, but my greater affection has always moved me to care for you above all. The one you prefer may take pleasure in you too, but I do not think that his feeling for you approaches mine, which is far stronger, and this alone is very painful." He began to weep.
>
> She blushed scarlet, in all the full, fresh ripeness of her beauty, and her tears spilled forth until he forgot her transgressions and looked on her only with pity and love. "I wonder why you would not even give me a child," he said. "That is a very great regret. I know you will have one for him, with whom your tie is so much stronger, and the thought makes me very sad indeed. After all, he is what he is, no more, and your child will have a commoner father."[4]

---

[4] TTG, 281; GM 2:280.

His moving gentleness could hardly exhaust any man's sentiments on such a subject. His loss of Aoi to Genji cannot have been anywhere near this personally bitter. Moreover, there remains Rokujō's daughter, Akikonomu. Suzaku was smitten by her when he sent her off to Ise as High Priestess ("Sakaki"), and for years thereafter he dreamed of having her when she returned. Unfortunately Genji, who knew perfectly well how he felt about her, gave her instead to Reizei, his secret son and Suzaku's successor.

Genji's destiny

Twenty years later Genji is the grandfather of a future emperor in the female line and can look forward to the greatest distinction possible for a commoner. However he remains unsatisfied, and the reader overhears him nursing his disappointment that Reizei has no male heir ("Wakana Two").[5] In other words, Genji once aspired to found a line of emperors through his son, which only an emperor could do. And since he would have reigned if the Suzaku faction had not thwarted his father's wishes, his thoughts suggest that he resented this injury done to his father and wished to redress it. Certainly, Reizei's conception and birth set him on the path toward a hidden sovereignty of his own.

Suzaku has no son when Reizei is born, and Genji's father (who ostensibly believes the child to be his) therefore has no difficulty appointing him as Suzaku's heir apparent. However, he recognizes the threat to the boy's future and does all he can to help Genji and Fujitsubo protect him. Then he abdicates and, roughly two years later, dies. The Suzaku faction's victory, culminating in Genji's exile, is now so complete that it is hard to imagine Reizei surviving long as heir apparent. Genji returns, however, and Suzaku's abdication allows Reizei to succeed him after all. The path toward Genji's destiny is now open.

From the start, Genji is so obviously the hero of the tale that he is bound somehow to succeed in the end, and Kokiden is such an ill-tempered villain that she is certain to fail. Moreover, the author has a

---

[5] TTG, 631; GM 4:165-166.

Korean physiognomist predict in "Kiritsubo" that while Genji exhibits the signs of a born emperor and can also be seen as a "future [commoner] pillar of the court," neither role fits him well.[6] Something rarer awaits him, something that must still have to do with the throne.

After making love to Fujitsubo, Genji has a strange dream, of which a dream reader gives him "an interpretation beyond the bounds of all plausibility." Next he hears that Fujitsubo is indisposed, understands that she has conceived, and understands too, thanks to the dream, that he will become the father of an emperor. The dream reader's interpretation was shocking because a commoner cannot do that. The dream reader had also said, "I see too, my lord, that you are to suffer a reverse and that something will require the most urgent caution."[7] The "reverse" is presumably the Suzaku faction's temporary victory and Genji's exile, and the matter requiring caution must be Genji and Fujitsubo's new secret. If that secret comes to light, their son will never be the emperor that, for Genji's sake, he is destined to be.

Many readers have taken Genji's affair with Fujitsubo, and Reizei's resulting conception, as a self-evident sin. Certainly, no one could condone a young man's wronging his father, still less his sovereign, this way. Reizei's birth and accession may even seem to cast doubt on the integrity of the imperial line.[8] Seen from this perspective, his conception is less a step forward on the path of Genji's destiny than a crime that must be purged before any such step can be taken. However, the narrative leaves room for other readings as well. Richard Okada suggested that Genji's father may have known, and that if he did, he probably was neither surprised nor displeased.[9] This essay proposes that the Kiritsubo Emperor did indeed know and approve what Genji has done, and that the Sumiyoshi deity, the guardian of the throne, considered Reizei rather than Suzaku to be the Kiritsubo Emperor's

---

[6] TTG, 13; GM 1:39-40.

[7] TTG, 98; GM 1:234.

[8] Andō Tameakira (1659-1716) wrote in 1703 that, for some, Reizei's conception made the entire work too repellant even to touch ("Shika shichiron," 220), while in the 1930's Genji's behavior was widely condemned as constituting high treason. At times the issue has placed readers sympathetic to the tale in a serious quandary.

[9] Okada, *Figures of Resistance*, 358, n. 45.

legitimate successor. Seen this way, Genji's offense is the occasion for his rise.[10]

The Kiritsubo Emperor's Silence

The narrator makes it clear that Genji and Fujitsubo both feel intensely guilty about Fujitsubo's pregnancy, and the child so astonishingly resembles Genji that no one privy to the secret could imagine anyone else failing to notice it. Fujitsubo is terrified. However, in "Momiji no ga" the Kiritsubo Emperor sees the resemblance only to dismiss it.

> When Genji visited Her Highness's residence as usual, to join in music making, His Majesty appeared with the child in his arms. "I have many children," he said, "but you are the only one I have seen day and night since you were this small. I expect it is the way he reminds me of those days that makes him look so very like you. Perhaps all babies are like that." He simply doted on his little son.[11]

The emperor claims to believe that the resemblance is no more than a figment of his fond imagination, and perhaps the author really meant her audience to take him at his word. However, this passage is so far out of keeping with similar ones from *Genji* and elsewhere that the reader is not obliged to do so. The emperor may recognize whose child this is and simply let the matter pass.[12]

---

[10] The author of *Sagoromo monogatari*, which varies on many *Genji* scenes and themes, interpreted Genji's experience this way and transposed the pattern of transgression and divine favor into her own work. (See the conclusion of "Two Post-*Genji* Tales on *The Tale of Genji*.")

[11] TTG, 142; GM 1:329.

[12] The baby could just as well look like Genji because he and Genji are both (ostensibly) the Kiritsubo Emperor's sons and because, in addition, their mothers closely resemble each other. However, the narrative never suggests any such possibility and so appears to offer less real conjecture than a set motif. Examples from *Sagoromo monogatari* as well as *Genji* support this idea. In *Sagoromo* the empress has no idea who violated her daughter, but when the baby is born she instantly recognizes Sagoromo's features, and so does the emperor when he eventually sees the boy. Other passages in *Genji* (Genji pleading to Tamakazura that she looks exactly like her mother, Yūgao) and *Sagoromo* (Sagoromo seeing the deceased Asukai's face in her daughter's) suggest that seeing the parent's face in the child's is a convention that may have

As Okada noted, the Kiritsubo Emperor purposefully brought Genji and Fujitsubo together during Genji's late childhood ("Kiritsubo").[13]

> His Majesty, who cared so deeply for both [Genji and Fujitsubo], asked her not to maintain her reserve. "I am not sure why," he said," but it seems right to me that he should take you for his mother. Do not think him uncivil. Just be kind to him. His face and eyes are so like hers that your own resemblance to her makes it look quite natural." Genji therefore lost no chance offered by the least flower or autumn leaf to let her know in his childish way how much he liked her...
>
> Genji's looks had an indescribably fresh sweetness, one beyond even Her Highness's celebrated and, to His Majesty, peerless beauty, and this moved people to call him the Shining Lord. Since Fujitsubo made a pair with him, and His Majesty loved them both, they called her the Sunlight Princess.[14]

Thus Genji's father once encouraged such intimacy between Fujitsubo and his favorite son that Genji fell in love with her; and this in a tale in which Genji himself, thinking later on about Yūgiri and Murasaki, and Tō no Chūjō thinking about Yūgiri and Kumoi no Kari, know very well where such permissiveness may lead. He even allowed the two to seem a pair in the eyes of the world. No doubt Suzaku's appointment as heir apparent, and his subsequent accession, weighed on the Kiritsubo Emperor not only as personally disappointing but also as detrimental to the realm. Then came the confusion over Fujitsubo's pregnancy, since her real date of conception—obscured as thoroughly as possible by her women—made his paternity unlikely. Perhaps he began then to suspect a truth that the child's face confirmed: this boy was not his son, but instead his beloved Genji's. Through this child, and for the good of all (as confirmed later by the success of Reizei's

---

prepared the original audience to doubt the Kiritsubo Emperor's candor. Tanizaki Jun'ichirō certainly did. In "Yume no ukihashi," which he presented as a comment on *Genji*, he had the narrator's father (the Kiritsubo Emperor) purposely encourage a scandalously intimate relationship between the narrator's stepmother (Fujitsubo) and the narrator himself (Genji).

13 Okada, *Figures of Resistance*, 195-196.
14 TTG, 15; GM 1:44.

reign), his own choice for the succession could still be restored and Genji could play a role commensurate with his merit. To encourage this happy outcome the Kiritsubo Emperor had only to remain silent. So he did.

Some twenty years later, after Kaoru's birth ("Kashiwagi"), Genji reflects that he once did to his father with Fujitsubo what Kashiwagi has now done to him with the Third Princess, and he wonders whether his father knew after all.[15] If his father did not, then Genji's suffering in this case makes sense as retribution for his undetected crime. However, if the Kiritsubo Emperor not only knew but also silently condoned an act that promised to rectify the injustice Genji had suffered, then for him as for the Sumiyoshi deity, what seemed to be a crime was not one after all.[16]

The Will of Sumiyoshi

Having decided to leave the capital in advance of the decree of exile soon to be issued against him ("Suma"), Genji visits his late father's tomb. There he reports his departure and, before leaving, "shiver[s] to behold a vision of his father as he had seen him in life." However, the figure remains silent. This eerie moment foreshadows the Kiritsubo Emperor's active intervention later on. At last, near the end of "Suma," the great drama of Genji's exile begins: the storm that seems to threaten the whole world and that will bring about his move to Akashi.

The storm begins when, at his companions' urging, Genji goes to the shore to commission a purification rite from a visiting yin-yang master *(onmyōji)*. The rite involves infusing evil influences into a doll that is then sent drifting out to sea, or, if the purification takes places inland,

---

[15] Genji's inability to forgive Kashiwagi is repellant in comparison, but it is also true that, in violating the Third Princess, Kashiwagi yielded less to sanctioned destiny than to pathetic folly.

[16] Norma Field suggested something similar when she wrote *(The Splendor of Longing*, 29), "For instance, it is possible that Genji's violation of the imperial succession does not ultimately constitute a transgression, for according to a higher principle, he was born to rule, if not directly, then through his enthroned children."

down a river or stream. Genji feels kinship with the doll and likens himself to it in a poem:

> *I, sent running down*
> *to the vastness of a sea*
> *I had never known,*
> *as a doll runs, can but know*
> *an overwhelming sorrow.*

The plight of the doll, intrinsically innocent but made to bear off the evil of others, reminds him of his own. The narrative continues,

The ocean stretched unruffled into the distance, and his thoughts wandered over what had been and what might be.

> *"Myriads of gods*
> *must feel pity in their hearts*
> *when they look on me:*
> *there is nothing I have done*
> *anyone could call a crime,"*

he said. Suddenly the wind began to blow, and the sky darkened. The purification broke off in the ensuing confusion.[17]

The storm certainly begins in response to Genji's declaration before the gods that he has done nothing that deserves to be called a crime, but his words remain hard to interpret. Is he lying, is he deluded, or is he right? Perhaps he is even quibbling: No, he has never been guilty of sedition, the crime with which Kokiden charges him, and his intercourse with Fujitsubo can have nothing to do with his exile since it remains unknown. However, the gods must know what happened even if the humans do not, and the latter issue is probably what interests them most. Perhaps his false claim to innocence provokes the powers of sea and rain to chastise him on the spot, but if so, it is unclear why the storm should launch him in the end toward a triumphal rise.

---

[17] TTG, 252-253; GM 2:217-218.

In *The Bridge of Dreams,* Haruo Shirane discussed various responses to the problem of Genji's poem and the consequent storm. A common approach is to see the storm as punishment and purification for Genji's misconduct, as well as his lying poem about it, but some have suggested a rite of passage from youth to adulthood or even a sort of death and resurrection.[18] So wide a range of readings highlights the difficulty of the issue, but one possible interpretation is consistent with this essay. The storm is indeed a purification, but punishment is a minor issue. While the higher powers sanction Genji's lovemaking with Fujitsubo, that lovemaking is a still a transgression that must be cleansed before Genji can follow his destiny. More importantly, the ordeal purges Genji of evil heaped unjustly on him, as upon a purificatory doll, by others (the Suzaku faction) of warped intent. Perhaps that is why Genji likens himself in his poem to the purificatory doll *(hitokata)* before him and insists that he himself is guilty of no crime. The real crime is that of the people who have driven him out of the city so as to be able to enjoy, undisturbed, power and prosperity never granted them by the gods. Their intent is warped because it violates, in particular, the will of the Sumiyoshi deity.

The storm rages through the night, until at last Genji's companions rest.

> When Genji, too, briefly dropped off to sleep, a being he did not recognize came to him, saying, "You have been summoned to the palace. Why do you not come?" He woke up and understood that the Dragon King of the sea, a great lover of beauty, must have his eye on him. So eerie a menace made the place where he was now living intolerable.[19]

This dream suggests that the powers of the sea are intensely interested in Genji's fate and mean to guide it. The dragon king's call "to the palace" foreshadows the Akashi Novice's divinely-inspired invitation to his magnificent establishment at Akashi, as the author of *Kakaishō* (1367) seems to have recognized when he observed in this connection that the dragon king desires Genji as a beautiful son-in-

---

[18] Shirane, *The Bridge of Dreams*, 14-16.
[19] TTG, 253; GM 2:219.

law.[20] The dragon king's desire for Genji is related to his well-attested appetite for priceless jewels. Apparently he sees Genji as such a jewel. In the supernatural realm, Genji's conduct with Fujitsubo was therefore no crime. Instead it endowed him with new potency.

After the storm has raged for days, Genji prays to Sumiyoshi, the dragon king, and other divinities for help, and his companions pray on his behalf; whereupon "the heavens redoubled their thunder and a bolt struck a gallery off his own rooms." Only then, after a few more hours of terror, does the sky clear at last. Genji contemplates his narrow escape and expresses in a poem his gratitude to the divinities of the sea.

> Had I not enjoyed
> divine aid from those great gods
> who live in the sea,
> I would now be wandering
> the vastness of the ocean.[21]

He then dozes off and has another vision of his father.

> He was so exhausted after the endless turmoil of the storm that without meaning to he dropped off to sleep. While he sat there, propped upright...[his father] stood before him as he had been in life, took his hand, and drew him up, saying, "What are you doing in this terrible place? Hasten to sail away from this coast, as the God of Sumiyoshi would have you do."
>
> Genji was overjoyed. "Since you and I parted, Your Majesty, I have known so many sorrows that I would gladly cast my life away here on this shore."
>
> "No, you must not do that. All this is simply a little karmic retribution. I myself committed no offense during my reign, but of course I erred nevertheless, and expiation of those sins now so absorbs me that I had given no thought to the world;[22] but it

---

[20] Tamagami, *Shimeishō, Kakaishō*, 320. See also the discussion of this topic in Shirane, *The Bridge of Dreams*, 77-80, as well as the beginning of "Genji and the Luck of the Sea."
[21] TTG, 259; GM 2:228.
[22] Emperor Daigo, to whom Genji's father corresponds, was reputed to have suffered in hell for his misdeeds, which included exiling Sugawara no Michizane in 901. In a

was too painful to see you in such distress. I dove into the sea, emerged on the strand, and despite my fatigue I am now hurrying to the palace to have a word with [Suzaku] on the matter." Then he was gone.[23]

The Kiritsubo Emperor's words, too, suggest that Genji did no wrong with Fujitsubo. He comments on Genji's plight and compares it to his own, distinguishing between personal karma (in life he acted in some matters as a man among other men should not) and right conduct for an emperor. For a man subject to considerations of common morality, certain of his deeds require expiation, but these do not concern the powers that protect the imperial line. As an emperor he was blameless. So, too, is Genji, who likewise bears an imperial responsibility.

In urging Genji to leave Suma the Kiritsubo Emperor repeats the dragon king's invitation to the undersea palace, although in terms more practically intelligible to a living person. He also speaks for the Sumiyoshi deity, since he presumably "dove into the sea" to consult with its deities and then "emerged on the strand" to represent them to Genji. His "word with [Suzaku] on the matter" goes as follows.

On the thirteenth of the third month, the night when lightning flashed and the wind roared, His Majesty dreamed that [his father] stood below the palace steps, glaring balefully at him while he himself cowered before him in awe. His [father] had much to say, and no doubt he spoke of Genji. His Majesty described his dream in fear and sorrow to [his mother, Kokiden]. "One imagines all sorts of things on a night when it is pouring and the skies are in tumult," she said. "You must not allow it to disturb you unduly."

Something now went wrong with His Majesty's eyes, perhaps because he had met his father's furious gaze, and he suffered unbearably.[24]

---

famous vision recorded in 941 the monk Nichizō saw him there, "squatting on glowing coals" (Tyler, *Japanese Tales*, 148).

[23] TTG, 259; GM 2:230.
[24] TTG, 267; GM 2:251.

The Kiritsubo Emperor's personal intervention on Genji's behalf takes time to succeed because Kokiden continues to resist. Unbowed by this demonstration that her son, the elder brother, is no more than an obstacle in the way of his own father's will, she silences Suzaku as before, whenever he suggested pardoning Genji. Next, her father dies and she herself becomes ill, but still Suzaku is prevented from recalling Genji to the city until he is gravely ill himself.

In the meantime, the Akashi Novice gives the Kiritsubo Emperor's injunction "to sail away from this coast" immediately realizable expression when he arrives by boat through the last of the storm to invite Genji to Akashi. The dream that prompts him to do so matches Genji's own, and the narrative leaves no doubt that he, too, speaks for Sumiyoshi.[25] His successful passage to Suma suggests divine aid, and his return journey, with Genji aboard, goes so swiftly that "one could only marvel at the will of the wind."[26] Sumiyoshi has taken control of Genji's fate.

"Genji and the Luck of the Sea" discusses the nature and history of the Sumiyoshi deity in detail. Suffice it to write here that the origins of Sumiyoshi have to do with Jingū Kōgō and her son Emperor Ōjin, the deity of the Usa Hachiman shrine. In time the Minamoto (Genji) claimed Ōjin as their patron. The figure of Hikaru Genji therefore evokes a sacred lineage that goes back through Ōjin to Jingū Kōgō and Sumiyoshi. Perhaps this explains why Ashikaga Yoshimitsu (1358-1408) looked to Genji as the founding head of the Minamoto *(Genji no chōja)*[27] and claimed the same title himself. He also coveted Genji's title of honorary retired emperor and sought to emulate Genji in his repeated assumption of a retired emperor's prerogatives. Just after

---

[25] The "strange being" who speaks in the Akashi Novice's dream (TTG, 260) represents Sumiyoshi, as the Novice knows, since he thanks Sumiyoshi as soon as Genji disembarks at Akashi; and the being who speaks in Genji's counterpart dream (TTG, 253) therefore does so, too.

[26] TTG, 260; GM 2:233.

[27] By the Kamakura period the *Genji no chōja* was indeed a senior Minamoto, but for Murasaki Shikibu the notion of "Genji" seems to have included, at least under some circumstances, any high-ranking non-Fujiwara, even an emperor's daughter (TTG, 631; GM 4:166).

Yoshimitsu's death, Emperor Gokomatsu (r. 1382-1412) finally awarded him the title *daijō hōō* (cloistered retired emperor), thus completing Yoshimitsu's assimilation of himself to Genji.[28] The *Genji* author seems therefore to have derived from the story of Jingū Kōgō and Ōjin an ideal Minamoto, at once commoner and imperial, whose secret kingship, conferred on him by Sumiyoshi, lifts him to a height beyond the reach of any mere Fujiwara like his friend Tō no Chūjō.

The succeeding chapters of the tale bear out this understanding of the Sumiyoshi deity's intention. In response to the Akashi Novice's prayers for his daughter's future and to the Kiritsubo Emperor's hopes for Genji, and in agreement with his own purpose, he spirits Genji away to Akashi, where the Novice's establishment corresponds in the tangible world to the palace of the dragon king. If Sumiyoshi had not done so—if the Kiritsubo Emperor's glare had forced Genji's immediate recall to the city—Genji would never have met the lady from Akashi, never had a daughter by her, and never become the father of a future empress. The astrologer's prediction reported in "Miotsukushi," just after his daughter's birth, could not have come true:

> An astrologer had foretold that Genji would have three children, of whom one would be Emperor and another Empress, while the third and least among them would reach the highest civil rank of Chancellor.[29]

Genji's first two children (Reizei and Yūgiri, his son by Aoi) already meet the prediction, and he therefore knows from the start what this, his third and last child, will be.

One may wonder whether Genji himself understands his exceptional destiny. In the course of the tale he sees specters and hears spirits speak, but such things seem generally to engage his thoughts—at least the ones to which the reader is privy—only when

---

[28] Hyōdō, *Heike monogatari no rekishi to geinō*, 89-90. *Kakaishō,* completed in 1367 by a member of the entourage of Yoshimitsu's father (the shogun Ashikaga Yoshiakira) interprets many matters in the tale as precedent for later practice, and it particularly highlights Genji's standing as honorary retired emperor (Yoshimori, "*Kakaishō* no Hikaru Genji").

[29] TTG, 283; GM 2:285.

they are directly before him. He is a man of this world, not another: an enterprising lover, an accomplished artist, and a master politician. However, dreams, prophesies, his father's blessing, and his own faith in himself give him reason to believe in a special destiny, one upheld by the power of the sea.

Genji's father wanted to see him come into his own, and during Genji's exile, if not before, Sumiyoshi joins the Kiritsubo Emperor as a patron to assure that outcome. Their success yields a dual triumph, one aspect of which is common and one imperial, one bright and one in shadow. Genji's Akashi daughter makes him the grandfather of an emperor in the female line, while secretly Genji is also the next emperor's father, hence the potential grandfather of an emperor in the male line as well. Three years after his accession ("Usugumo"), Reizei learns whose son he really is, and his first thought is to abdicate in Genji's favor. Genji forbids him to do so, but Reizei's wish to honor his father moves him to award Genji the title of honorary retired emperor ("Fuji no uraba").[30] Thus Genji attains heights never reached before and, properly speaking, impossible, thanks above all to two irregular episodes in his life (his affair with Fujitsubo and his exile) and to the supernatural powers, associated with the imperial line, who support him in his struggle against the Suzaku faction. At his peak he comes to enjoy what one might even call supra-imperial power and prestige.

Boundaries and sexual transgression: patterns of great success

Japanese scholars have discussed Genji's extraordinary rise under the heading of "kingship" *(ōken)*. Kawazoe Fusae, for example, argued that Genji's exile at Suma, his move to Akashi, and his triumphal return follow the ritual pattern of the Daijōsai (the imperial enthronement ceremony)[31] and therefore amount to an assumption of hidden

---

[30] This extraordinary honor amounts almost to a public declaration that Genji is Reizei's father. Together with the *Sagoromo* author's adoption of the pattern of Genji's rise (see n. 17), it suggests that the issue of Reizei's paternity itself, hence the idea of a perturbation on the imperial line of succession, may not have been as serious for the author and her original audience as it came to seem later.

[31] Kawazoe, "Suma kara Akashi e," in *Genji monogatari hyōgen shi: yu to ōken no isō.*

kingship. This approach rightly highlights Genji's quasi-sovereign standing, but it does not fully account for the process of Genji's rise as the tale conveys it. In particular, it does not recognize the motif of transgression. Several myths or legends give this motif a central role, in a context compatible with what is at issue in Genji's case. The material falls into two categories. The first, which includes two stories involving the boundary between land and sea, relates to the birth of Genji's daughter, while the second consists of two stories that underlie esoteric initiations given a new emperor. In the former case the "transgression" crosses a line between physical realms, but in the latter it is sexual.

The *Kakaishō* gloss about the dragon king desiring a beautiful son-in-law also links the dragon king's call to the myth of Hikohohodemi, which is widely acknowledged to underlie the story of Genji's exile. "Genji and the Luck of the Sea" discusses it in detail. The aspects of the myth most relevant here are the hero's crossing of the land-sea boundary (approximated for Genji, a mortal man, by descent to the sea's edge); his union with a sea-woman who bears him a child; the sea-woman's disappearance from the main line of the story; and the child's rise. The significance of this pattern in Japan can be gathered from its presence also in a legend that explains the rise of the Fujiwara.[32] According to *Sanshū Shido Dōjō engi*, Fujiwara no Fuhito's (659-720) younger sister was so beautiful that the Chinese emperor sent for her and gave Japan great gifts in return. However, he withheld his most precious treasure, a jewel imbued with the Buddha's full presence. His wife wheedled it out of him on behalf of her native land, but during a great storm off the north coast of Shikoku the dragon king, who coveted it, stole it from the ship carrying it to Japan. Fuhito went down to the nearby shore to get it back, stayed three years, married a sea-woman, and had a son by her. He then persuaded her to dive for the jewel, which she retrieved from the dragon palace at the cost of her life. Fuhito returned to the capital, where his son, Fusazaki (681-737), became the founder of the dominant "northern house" of the

---

[32] Wada, *Setonai jisha engi shū*, 52-65; Abe, "Taishokan no seiritsu"; Tyler, "The True History of Shido Temple."

Fujiwara. Meanwhile, the jewel went to Kōfukuji in Nara, where it magically guaranteed Fujiwara power. The author of *The Tale of Genji* may not have known this story, which Abe Yasurō dated speculatively to the mid-Kamakura period,[33] but it is in the same vein as her own.

However, the pattern of these stories accounts only for Genji's daughter. It sheds no light on the transgression that makes Genji an emperor's father. That matter can be viewed in the light of two stories that purport to explain the origin of esoteric Shingon and Tendai enthronement rites *(sokui hō)*. The Tendai rite is particularly suggestive.

The Shingon story says that when Fujiwara no Kamatari (614-669) was still a baby the Kashima deity came to him in the form of a fox (Dakini); took him round the four directions; put him on its belly, where, according to variant texts it "enjoyed" or "violated" him; and returned him to his parents with a wisteria-wrapped sickle *(fuji, kama)*, saying, "With this you will rise to be the emperor's teacher."[34] The story of Genji and Fujitsubo is plain in comparison, but both share the motif of a transgressive sexual encounter followed by the acquisition of extraordinary power and prestige.

The Tendai story is the so-called *Jidō setsuwa* ("The Story of the Youth"), which tells how the Buddha on Vulture Peak personally transmitted to the line of Chinese and then Japanese emperors two empowering verses from the Lotus Sutra. In time these verses, the substance of the Tendai accession rite,[35] passed to Jidō, the favorite of the First Emperor of China. According to the treatise *Tendai-gata go-sokui hō*, Jidō "crossed the emperor's pillow" *(mikado no on-makura no ue o koetari)*, which presumably means that he made love to the

---

[33] Abe, "Taishokan no seiritsu," 133. Abe suggested that the legend was inspired by, among other things, the *Gangōji engi* story *(Konjaku monogatari shū* 11/15). Anything like it in the *Genji* author's day would have been current in oral form among low-ranking practitioner monks *(dōshu)* and, like fiction itself, would have been formally frowned on by the scholar-monks *(gakusō)* and their relatives in the higher civil nobility.

[34] *Tenshō Daijin kuketsu*, 499-500; *Shun'ya jinki*, 191. See Abe, "*Iruka* no seiritsu," 16-38.

[35] Itō, "Jidō setsuwa kō," 1-32; Abe, "Jidō setsuwa no keisei," part 1, 1-29; and part 2, 30-56.

empress. The court demanded Jidō's death for this offense, but the emperor merely exiled him and, before he left, taught him the two verses. The exiled Jidō then wrote them on chrysanthemum leaves, from which dew flowed into a nearby stream and changed the water to an elixir that made Jidō immortal. Eight hundred years later he taught his secret to Emperor Wen of Wei. "Forever after," the treatise says, "the heir apparent has received [these verses] when he receives the imperial dignity from Heaven."[36] The text calls this initiation "the rite of sovereignty over the four seas" *(shikai ryōshō no hō):* a sovereignty therefore founded ultimately on violation of an empress, to which the injured emperor responds by complying with the court's demand in such a manner as to favor the offender. Whether or not the *Genji* author could have known the Jidō story, its resemblance to Genji's experience needs no emphasis. Perhaps Genji's transgression with Fujitsubo sounded more familiar, more acceptable, and more intelligible to the author's original audience than it did to later readers. They might have understood that it assured his later glory.

Genji's flaw, Rokujō's anger

Whatever heights a man may achieve in his life, not even the gods can make him invulnerable. Time and his own failings assure decline. The theme of time in the tale is well recognized. The characters age, their sorrows build, and the narrator's repeated evocations of Genji's beauty, in defiance of time, only remind the reader that he, too, is mortal. Meanwhile, personal flaws and weaknesses shape his governing sorrows. One flaw is vanity, and another—more a weakness than a flaw—is his love for Murasaki. That love, with its increasingly clear element of blind clinging, makes him vulnerable, and to one character the author gives the reason, the will, and the occasion to hurt him. Rokujō, whom his vanity and carelessness injured so deeply in the early chapters, strikes when that vanity places him in harm's way.

"Genji and Murasaki" suggested that Genji's rise in the world causes a mismatch between what Murasaki means to him privately and the

---

[36] Quoted in Itō, "Jidō setsuwa kō," 10.

way she appears in relation to his public self; sought to explain in that light Genji's motive for accepting the Third Princess; and argued that in doing so Genji overreaches his good fortune. Rokujō precipitates the disaster that follows.

Genji's thoughts about many women in the tale betray vanity, but Rokujō's case is special. It also illustrates a difference between Parts One and Two. Her relationship with Genji in Part One takes such a dramatic course that no reader could forget her. However, her role in Part Two, this time as an angry spirit, has a more obviously calculated character. The living Rokujō of Part One is fascinatingly complex, but after her death ("Miotsukushi") there is no reason to believe that she will play any further role in Genji's life. When she reappears after all ("Wakana Two") it is nineteen years later, and she serves a clear purpose in the plot. Certainly she moves the story forward in Part One as well, but this part, although richly suggestive, does not feature the long chain of demonstrable causation that characterizes the central drama of Part Two. Rokujō's two interventions as a spirit are critical links in this chain.

The gifted and high-strung Rokujō (the living woman) is a minister's daughter and the widow of an heir apparent. Nothing about her encourages anyone, even Genji, to take her lightly, but Genji does. It is one thing for him to visit this daunting woman when he pleases, but he suspects that being committed to her for life would be a different experience. His inner conflict over her appears first in comparison with the undemanding Yūgao, whom a jealous spirit then kills. Is it a phantom of the living Rokujō? Intentionally or not the narrative diverts the reader from any certain conclusion, but most assume a connection with her.

Genji's relationship with Rokujō properly requires him, considering who she is, to marry her (that is, to acknowledge her publicly), regardless of his private feelings on the matter. In the tale, rank above all governs a man's treatment of a woman. If he is high and she low, he can treat her more or less as he pleases; but the higher she is, and the better supported, the more respect she commands. Although a fatherless widow, Rokujō means a good deal to the Kiritsubo Emperor himself. When she decides to accompany her daughter (the new High

Priestess) to Ise, so as to remove herself from her excruciating impasse with Genji, Genji's father rebukes his son.

> "His Late Highness thought very highly of [Rokujō] and showed her every attention, and I find it intolerable that you should treat her as casually as you might any other woman. I consider the High Priestess my own daughter, and I should therefore appreciate it if you were to avoid offending her mother, both for her father's sake and for mine. Such wanton self-indulgence risks widespread censure." The displeasure on his countenance obliged Genji to agree, and he kept a humble silence.

> "Never cause a woman to suffer humiliation," [Genji's father] continued. "Treat each with tact and avoid provoking her anger."[37]

This pointed warning foreshadows the "carriage quarrel" and its aftermath, as well as Rokujō's role in Part Two. Soon her living spirit attacks Genji's wife, Aoi, and eventually kills her. The obvious thing for Genji to do after Aoi's death is finally, after a period of mourning, to recognize Rokujō. Rokujō's women assume that he will do so, and no doubt their mistress entertains the same hope. Instead, Genji avoids her and secretly consummates his marriage with Murasaki. After long and acute mental suffering, Rokujō leaves at last for Ise, shamed and defeated.

The operations of Rokujō's living spirit allow the author to remove the excessively respectable Aoi from the narrative, establish Rokujō as a potential threat to Genji in the future, and seal the long intimacy of Genji and Murasaki's married life. Rokujō therefore plays a vital role even early on, but the author will not call on her again for twenty-five chapters and many hundreds of pages. When she does, it is less Rokujō's spirit that starts the trouble than Genji's ill-judged self-satisfaction.

---

[37] TTG, 165; GM 2:18.

The course of the narrative

After Rokujō's death Genji adopts her daughter, Akikonomu, who apparently brings with her the land for Genji's Rokujō-in estate. The estate is finished in "Otome," and in "Fuji no uraba" Genji becomes honorary retired emperor. To celebrate he invites Emperor Reizei to visit him, as no commoner could do. Reizei then invites Suzaku, and "Fuji no uraba" closes with an account of the wonders of a day in which nothing seems amiss, except that near the end Suzaku, in a poem, "sound[s] perhaps a little piqued."[38] The next chapter ("Wakana One," the first of Part Two) begins, "His Eminence Suzaku began feeling unwell soon after His Majesty's visit to Rokujō."[39] This opening may hint that the magnitude of Genji's triumph has dealt his brother a blow.

Feeling death approaching, Suzaku longs at last to act on an old desire to leave the world, but he cannot bring himself do so until he has found a suitable husband for the Third Princess. "Genji and Murasaki" covers this subject in detail. After long and delicate negotiations Genji accepts her, only to be brought up short by the discovery of what she is really like.

This marriage upsets Murasaki, and a rift opens between the two. She asks him to let her become a nun, but he refuses, apparently aware that he really and truly cannot live without her. In time, his failure to comprehend her feelings leads to a scene of palpable estrangement that takes place in "Wakana Two." Instead of sympathizing, he lectures her on her good fortune and goes on to compound his blunder by musing to her aloud about some of the women he has known. The first of these is Rokujō, of whom he speaks disparagingly. "She was someone of unusual grace and depth," he says, "but she made painfully trying company. I agree that she had reason to be angry with me, but the way she brooded so interminably over the matter, and with such bitter rancor, made things very unpleasant." [40] In closing he

---

[38] TTG, 574; GM 3:462.
[39] TTG, 577; GM 4:17.
[40] TTG, 646; GM 4:209.

congratulates himself on having made Rokujō's daughter empress, and in that connection he remarks complacently, "I expect that by now, in the afterworld, she has come to think better of me."

This is dangerous gossip. Quite apart from what Rokujō once did to Aoi, the "Asagao" chapter ends with a precisely parallel passage in which Genji reminisces to Murasaki about Fujitsubo and then has a dream in which Fujitsubo (who died in the preceding chapter) reproaches him angrily. It is surprising that he should do it again, especially about Rokujō. Retribution comes swiftly. By dawn Murasaki is seriously ill, and some months later the report goes out that she has died. Genji rushes to her side and orders one last, desperate exorcism. Finally the afflicting spirit moves into a medium, through whom it says to Genji,

> I kept my eye on you from on high, and what you did for Her Majesty made me pleased and grateful; but perhaps I do not care that much about my daughter now that she and I inhabit different realms, because that bitterness of mine, which made you hateful to me, remains. What I find particularly offensive, more so even than your spurning me for others when I was among the living, is that in conversation with one for whom you do care you callously made me out to be a disagreeable woman.[41]

The speaker is Rokujō, provoked by Genji's chatter to Murasaki and far less interested than he supposed, now that she is dead, in all he has done for her daughter. Below, and only for the purposes of this essay, this scene will be called Possession One.

In Possession One Rokujō's target is Genji, whom she attacks through his beloved Murasaki. However, the exorcism blunts her effort, and Murasaki revives. Rokujō then bides her time, and events elsewhere during this acute phase of Murasaki's illness give her a new opening to act. Six years ago (in "Wakana One") the young Kashiwagi caught a glimpse of the Third Princess and remained obsessed with her. He now steals in and makes love to her while Genji is away nursing Murasaki. She conceives. Genji soon discovers the affair. The

---

[41] TTG, 655; GM 4:235.

frightened Kashiwagi avoids him until, at a party that he cannot avoid attending, Genji taunts him and looks into his eyes. Genji's glance drives the spirit from his body. At last Kashiwagi dies, just after learning of the birth of Kaoru, his son by the Third Princess.

After the birth, the shamed and terrified Third Princess believes herself to be dying. She says to Genji, "in a much more grownup manner than usual,"

> "I still doubt that I will live, and they say that sort of sin [dying as a consequence of childbirth] is very grave. I think I shall become a nun, because that might help me live longer, or at least it might lighten this burden of sin if I am to die after all."

He answers,

> "You will do nothing of the kind. It is out of the question. What you have been through has frightened you, I imagine, but it hardly threatens your life."

Privately, however, he wonders whether that might not be a good idea.

> The poor thing is all too likely to come under a cloud again if she goes on with me this way. I doubt that with the best will in the world I can change my opinion of her anymore, and there will be some difficult times; people will note my indifference, and that will be unfortunate, because when [Suzaku] hears of it the fault will appear to be entirely mine. Her present indisposition makes a good excuse to let her do it—I might as well.[42]

He hopes above all to avoid Suzaku blaming him for neglecting the Third Princess, and he assumes that Suzaku does not know the truth. Allowing her to become a nun might achieve that, even though at heart "the idea repelled him," as it did in Murasaki's case as well. His calculations are pointless, however, because Suzaku has already blamed him repeatedly and has even taken countermeasures against Genji's neglect of his daughter.[43] Suzaku also suspects that his

---

[42] TTG, 679; GM 4:302.

[43] Suzaku had the reigning emperor (his son) raise the Third Princess's rank, which then placed still greater and thoroughly unwelcome pressure on Genji to treat her properly.

daughter's child is not Genji's, having worked this out when he learned of her pregnancy:

> His Eminence, cloistered on his mountain, heard about her condition and thought of her with tender longing. People told him that Genji had been away for months and hardly visited her at all, at which he wondered despairingly what had happened and resented more than ever the vagaries of conjugal life. He felt uneasy when [Murasaki] was seriously ill and Genji, so he heard, spent all his time looking after her. Moreover, he reflected, [Genji] seems not to have changed his ways since then. *Did* something unfortunate occur while he was elsewhere? Did those hopeless women of hers take some sort of initiative without her knowledge or consent?[44]

That is exactly what happened. Genji is wrong to imagine that he can escape Suzaku's informed censure. It is already upon him.

A few days after the birth, the Third Princess cries out in despair that she may never see her father again. Genji informs Suzaku,

> who was so devastated that he set forth under cover of night, despite knowing full well that he should not. His sudden, completely unannounced arrival took Genji by surprise and covered him with confusion.[45]

The Third Princess immediately begs her father to make her a nun, which he does over Genji's protests:

> [Suzaku] silently reflected that after accepting the daughter offered him with such boundless trust, Genji had failed in his devotion to her, as [Suzaku] himself had been greatly disappointed to learn over the years, although he had never been able to voice his reproaches and so had been reduced merely to deploring what other people thought and said. Why not take this opportunity to remove her from [Genji], he thought, without exposing her to ridicule by leaving the impression that she had merely despaired of him?[46]

---

[44] TTG, 665; GM 4:267.
[45] TTG, 680; GM 4:303.
[46] TTG, 680-681; GM 4:306.

At last Suzaku's dissatisfaction with Genji is explicit. He makes his beloved daughter a nun to save her from him.

Now Rokujō's spirit speaks (through an unidentified medium) in order to claim victory ("Kashiwagi").

> The spirit afflicting Her Highness came forth during the late night prayers. "Take *that*, then!" it ranted. "You thought you were ever so clever getting the last one back, and that so annoyed me that I just kept lying in wait. Now I can go." It laughed aloud.[47]

"The last one" is Murasaki. This speech (Possession Two) is strange, but it defines a critical articulation point in the plot.

The significance of Possessions One and Two

Possessions One and Two have received varied treatment in studies of the tale. Some readers dismiss one or both. For example, Ikeda Kikan called them a "failure" in the author's attempt to achieve large-scale coherence between Parts One and Two.[48] Other, similar views are cited in "Genji and Murasaki." Such criticism probably has to do with notions of psychology and with sympathy for Murasaki. Compelling psychological reasons seem already to explain her illness (she can no longer bear the way Genji treats her), and the idea of attributing it to spirit possession may seem feeble, even irritating, in comparison.

Another psychological approach has been to see Possession One, especially, as a projection of Genji's own guilty conscience *(kokoro no oni)* towards Rokujō, even though the narrative never suggests that he has one. Fujimoto Katsuyoshi invoked Genji's "deep psychology" to this end and suggested that Rokujō's appearance in both instances is essentially a "hallucination" *(genshi)* on Genji's part.[49]

The diversity of reactions to Possessions One and Two, and the ingenuity of the explanations proposed for them, suggest the presence of a particularly difficult problem. No understanding of them may ever

---

[47] TTG, 682; GM 4:310.
[48] Ikeda Kikan," "Genji monogatari no kōsei to gihō," quoted in Ōasa, *Genji monogatari seihen no kenkyū*, 531.
[49] Fujimoto, *Genji monogatari no mono no ke*, 67, 76.

seem quite convincing, but at least it is possible to view them from a different perspective.

Possessions One and Two certainly tie this part of the tale back into the earlier chapters, since they prolong a theme already established there. As for what might have prompted the author to bring Rokujō back this way, Ōasa Yūji emphasized the calculated character of both possessions as plot devices. He also observed that Rokujō's possessing spirit is the only one identified in the tale.[50] Elsewhere, illness arouses suspicions of spirit possession,[51] but these may be wrong (as when Genji is ill after Yūgao's death); and even when they are right (as in the case of Princess Ochiba's mother), it seems not to matter much who or what the spirit is. The dying Kashiwagi even scoffs at the idea, confirmed nonetheless by the best diviners, that a woman's spirit has possessed him. In contrast, the author presents Possession One and Two without qualification. Ōasa therefore suggested that they are less examples of the supernatural in the tale *(kaii no mondai)* than evidence of plot construction *(kōsō no mondai).*[52] He wrote: "If viewed simply as a *mono no ke,* this one['s appearance] is merely unnatural and abrupt; but that probably means that its nature is not to be sought by analyzing *mono no ke.*" He concluded that Rokujō's interventions are devices intended to further the development of the plot.[53]

Ōasa then observed that by attributing Murasaki's illness and the Third Princess's retirement from the world to the workings of Rokujō's spirit, rather than to the affected women's own feelings, the narrator keeps the emphasis solely on Genji. Nothing untoward would happen if the spirit did not wish it, and the spirit wants only to make Genji suffer. These two women's plight is a matter entirely of Genji's fate, not theirs.[54] Ōasa's insight sheds new light on a passage of Rokujō's speech in Possession One. Her spirit says, "I have little enough against [Murasaki], but *you* are strongly guarded. I feel far

---

[50] Ōasa, *Genji monogatari seihen no kenkyū,* 533-534.
[51] The only exception is the final "illness" (due to self-starvation) and death of Ōigimi in "Agemaki."
[52] Ōasa, 535.
[53] Ōasa, 539, 541.
[54] Ōasa, 545.

away and cannot approach you, and even your voice reaches me only faintly."[55] Perhaps the protector is Sumiyoshi, to whose shrine Genji has just made an elaborate pilgrimage. However, the narrative has said nothing about divine protection since "Akashi," nor will the subject come up again. The spirit's words apparently serve in this context to reaffirm the focus on Genji. His women may languish, suffer, take holy vows, or even die, but nothing must make him falter until his own time (defined by the author) has come.

Possession One therefore seems not to invite the reader to sympathize with Murasaki against Genji, although the reader may well do so anyway. Instead the narrative purposely exonerates Murasaki as the cause of her own illness, for the likely reason that her giving in to her feelings would constitute an unbecoming and uncharacteristic affirmation of self. She herself would then become the reason Genji's absence allows Kashiwagi access to the Third Princess. Possession One instead makes this misfortune the fault of Rokujō, who has been provoked by Genji's foolish talk. Genji has slighted her again, as in Part One, and once more with dire consequences.

By reintroducing Rokujō into the tale at this point, the author has reaffirmed the plot centrality of pride, anger, and the will to revenge. In the pages and chapters that follow, she will demonstrate more impressively than ever what havoc these can cause. As Ōasa observed, Rokujō's "curse" removes the "linchpin" from Genji's world, causing it to crumble around him. However, Ōasa nonetheless accorded Possessions One and Two significance different from the one suggested here. By this time, he wrote, Rokujō has "no particular, individual motive to harm Genji." Instead her spirit represents "Genji's generalized past" and therefore functions toward him as a "literal ghost of the past," the aim of which is to avenge his violation of Fujitsubo.[56] This does not work, partly for reasons already explained and partly because an angry spirit can represent only itself; it cannot act for another power unrelated to it in life, still less for an abstraction like Genji's past. Rokujō's interventions in Part Two may or may not

---

[55] TTG, 655; GM 4:237.
[56] Ōasa, *Genji monogatari seihen no kenkyū*, 602-604.

strike the reader as successful, but her spirit, once invoked by the author, certainly has reason to act as the author requires.

According to Possession Two, one of the oddest passages in the tale, the spirit attacks Genji through the Third Princess after failing with Murasaki. As a significant possession event it is strikingly short, and the spirit's brusque, excited tone little resembles Rokujō's previous utterances. The spirit seems to address Genji directly, as usual, but the narrative devotes only a few words to his reaction.

> Genji was horrified. Why, has that spirit been here, too, all the time? He felt pity and dismay. [The Third Princess] seemed to have revived a little, but she did not yet look out of danger.[57]

It is hard to gauge the content of his feelings. Is he so exasperated that he no longer cares what the spirit does? Does the spirit so frighten him by now that nothing more need be said? Moreover, as in the case of Possession One, the spirit's declaration of victory may seem pointless. Having just given birth, the Third Princess is far more likely to be ill for natural reasons, especially considering her painful relationship with Genji. Fujimoto Katsuyoshi remarked that although Genji seems to take the spirit seriously as the cause of her desire to become a nun, Suzaku never even mentions it, and he described it more or less as a fake that Genji's guilty conscience predisposes him alone to take seriously.[58] Given these complexities, it is unlikely that many readers even remember Possession Two for long. It seems to make little useful sense. It might even be a remnant left over from some process of editing.

However, Possession Two can also be seen as critical. Possession One initiates the long illness that will eventually cause Murasaki's death and destroy Genji, and it also sets in train the disaster of Kashiwagi. Possession Two then involves Suzaku in that same disaster. It therefore marks the point at which the tension between Genji and Suzaku tips toward catastrophe for Suzaku as well, and perhaps also

---

[57] TTG, 682; GM 4:310.

[58] Fujimoto, *Genji monogatari no mono no ke*, 88-89. Fujimoto suggested that the medium is a highly suggestive girl of the Third Princess's household, one who already knows about Rokujō, and who then appropriates Rokujō's persona to sum up the household's and even her mistress's feeling toward Genji.

toward the strangeness of the Uji chapters and the darkness that engulfs Ukifune.

Suzaku's fate

The Third Princess's becoming a nun is a blow for Genji. By doing so immediately after bearing a son believed by everyone to be Genji's, she declares that her marriage has gone disastrously wrong and that Genji has failed her. Moreover, by giving her the precepts her father shows that he agrees. None of this redounds to Genji's credit.

More significantly, Rokujō's second intervention brings Genji and Suzaku into direct confrontation. Dazzling gifts have always so favored the younger Genji that Suzaku has had little reason to expect anything good from him personally, but in "Wakana One" he pins all his hopes on him as a husband for his favorite daughter, both for her sake (a secure, worthy future) and his own (peace of mind). However, Genji has now betrayed him in that, too, and Suzaku has acted rashly in response. Having entered religion as soon as his daughter was married, he should have renounced all profane cares, but over the succeeding years his anxiety about her has haunted him repeatedly, disrupting his practice and turning his thoughts back to worldly sorrows. Then her piteous call reaches him, and he comes down to her from his temple under cover of night. His helpless, fatherly response compromises his vows, his practice, and even his dignity. He cannot doubt for a moment that the fault is Genji's.

It is one thing for a father to bear his own trials patiently, but quite another for him to suffer while a beloved daughter, whose future he has done everything to assure, nonetheless suffers misery and humiliation because of a villain whose identity is all too plain. Suzaku's plight is even worse than that, since by now he is properly no longer a father at all, but instead a monk who has severed all profane ties. His only desire, after a troubled life, should be for a peaceful death and the Pure Land at last. The undeserved torment inflicted on him by Genji's betrayal is the sort of thing that could turn a monk at his death into a *tengu,* or a great courtier, not excluding an emperor, into an angry spirit *(onryō).* "The Possibility of Ukifune" argues that this outcome can be imagined for Suzaku, after his death during the eight-year gap between Parts Two and Three of the tale.

A glance back over Parts One and Two

The argument so far can be summed up as follows. In Part One Genji and Suzaku act out a story pattern from Japanese myth, in which a younger brother triumphs over his elder. The pattern involves a trial (Genji's exile) and supernatural assistance (Genji's father and Sumiyoshi). Genji's rise culminates in "Fuji no uraba," when he is appointed honorary retired emperor and plays host to both Reizei (the reigning emperor) and Suzaku (retired).

It has often been suggested that the story originally ended with "Fuji no uraba." If Part Two was indeed conceived and begun later, a simple editorial touch at the end of "Fuji no uraba" (Suzaku feeling "perhaps a little piqued"), combined with the opening line of "Wakana One" (Suzaku becoming "unwell soon after His Majesty's visit to Rokujō"), sufficed to link the two. The theme in Part Two is the younger brother's fate after his triumph.

Having gained every advantage open to him, the man of uncontested power loses his way in consonance with his own characteristic failings. Tempted in passing by the knowledge that the Third Princess, like Murasaki, is Fujitsubo's niece (his erotic weak spot), and attracted above all by the idea of adding the last touch to a public glory that is already complete, Genji yields to vanity and accepts her. He assumes that Murasaki will understand and resign herself in the end, but she cannot. He assumes that the Third Princess will have something of the personal quality he imagines, but she does not. Worse, he takes it for granted that, once Suzaku has entered the religious life, no father-in-law will trouble him with reproaches or demands; but Suzaku cannot give up caring about his favorite daughter. Murasaki sickens and eventually dies, Kashiwagi deals Genji a stinging blow, the Third Princess rejects Genji to become a nun, and her plight drags her father down as well.

No wonder the precipitating agent for all this, Rokujō's spirit, is supernatural. A thousand years later, the hero of a novel would follow a natural path to success, but the *Genji* author appealed to the supernatural instead. Then she did the same to achieve Genji's decline. To a degree, Rokujō's spirit indeed functions as the ghost of Genji's past. Its influence arises from Genji's past misdeeds and enduring failings, as summed up in his treatment of Rokujō, and it acts in Part Two as a destructive counterpart to Sumiyoshi in part one. In effect it is an agent of karma, just as Sumiyoshi and the spirit of Genji's father were when they furthered the destiny of a man visibly favored even from birth by the gods.

Part Three: the gloom of Uji

Genji and Suzaku both die during the eight-year gap between Part Two and Part Three of the tale, rendering perhaps fanciful any idea that the break between them, over the Third Princess, colors the narrative further. Nonetheless, "The Possibility of Ukifune" suggests that it may conceivably do so. The rest of this essay will present some preliminary arguments.

Part Three consists mainly of the Uji chapters, which evoke a mood of gloom, frustration, isolation, and failure in a setting far removed from court and city. The shadow lying over these chapters may to do with the influence of Suzaku's angry spirit.

"Hashihime," the first of the Uji chapters, begins:

> There was in those days an aged Prince who no longer mattered to the world. Of extremely distinguished birth on his mother's side as well, he had seemed destined for great things, but then times changed, and disgrace brought him a downfall so thorough that for one reason and another everyone who upheld his interests renounced the world, leaving him completely alone in both public and private.[59]

This prince (the Eighth Prince) is a younger brother of Genji and Suzaku. He was once destined to become heir apparent, but the attempt to have him appointed failed. This can only have happened during Genji's exile. The Suzaku faction wanted the Eight Prince to

---

[59] TTG, 829; GM 5:117.

replace the heir apparent (Reizei) appointed by the Kiritsubo Emperor. However, the intervention of this emperor's spirit on Genji's behalf, the death of the minister of the right, the Kokiden Consort's illness, and Genji's triumphant return then drove him instead into lonely obscurity.

The Uji narrative therefore begins by linking the Eighth Prince's current plight, hence that of his daughters, to the great power struggle that took place over forty years ago. In "Hashihime" he is a widower and lives at Uji with two of his daughters, Ōigimi and Nakanokimi. Ukifune, a third, unrecognized daughter of whom the reader will not hear until several chapters later, has grown up in the provinces.

In "Tenarai," the tale's next-to-last chapter, a healer attempts to exorcise the spirit that for the past two months or so has possessed Ukifune. Once induced to speak, the spirit says enough to suggest that it is Suzaku's. ("The Possibility of Ukifune" discusses this subject in detail.) It also talks of having "settled in a house full of pretty women."[60] These are the Eighth Prince's two recognized daughters, of whom it then claims to have killed one: Ōigimi, Kaoru's great love. After Ōigimi's death Nakanokimi, whom Kaoru had never courted, married Niou and moved to the Capital. Eventually, thanks to Nakanokimi, Kaoru discovered Ukifune, saw how closely she resembled Ōigimi, and moved her to the house at Uji. There the spirit possessed her.

However, the Eighth Prince's daughters (Suzaku's nieces) are not the direct objects of the spirit's animus. The spirit seems instead to want to harm Kaoru through his attachment to them. Kaoru, who is Suzaku's grandson, also passes for Genji's son. Apparently the spirit wants to torment Kaoru through Ōigimi and Ukifune, because of his relationship to Genji and because he embodies Genji's ruin of the Third Princess.

Literarily, Uji makes an appropriate setting for the dark story that these chapters tell, with or without the involvement of Suzaku's spirit. Its poetic reputation rested on a word play exploited repeatedly in the Uji chapters and found canonically in *Kokinshū* 983, a poem by Kisen

---

60 TTG, 1083; GM 6:295.

Hōshi. Kisen's almost untranslatable poem superimposes the adjective *ushi* ("dreary," "hateful") on the place name and suggests that the poet is a bitter man. In "Hashihime" the Eighth Prince uses the same device in his reply to a poem from Retired Emperor Reizei:

> It is not, alas,
> that I am lost forever
> in enlightenment;
> I only deplore this world
> from here in the Uji hills.

The narrator adds, "To [Reizei]'s regret, his modesty about his accomplishment as a holy man betrayed a lingering bitterness against the world."[61]

Uji was therefore an obvious refuge for such embittered figures as Kisen Hōshi, the Eighth Prince, or, perhaps, Suzaku's spirit. Kisen Hōshi being the poetic spirit of the place, the spirit that possesses Ukifune can also be seen as continuous with his, although with a specific role to play in a specific story. Furthermore, the Uji of the tale is itself *ushi*: a dreary place, especially for anyone who, like the Eighth Prince, lived beside the Uji River. Already forgotten in the city, he had to move there when his city house burned down.

> The place was near the weir, and the loud noise of the river ill suited his longing for peace, but there was nothing else to do. Blossoms, autumn leaves, and the flowing river: these were his solace in the gloomy reverie that now more than ever was his only refuge.[62]

The noise of the river is heard often in the succeeding chapters, sometimes in association with the sound of the wind. Endless mists, too, shroud the Uji hills. The place is thoroughly gloomy, as Kaoru observes when he first visits the Eighth Prince there:

> It was a sadder place than he had been led to imagine...There are other, quiet mountain villages with an appeal all their own, but here, amid the roar of waters and the clamor of waves, one

---

61 TTG, 834; GM 5:130.
62 TTG, 832; GM 5:126.

seemed unlikely ever to forget one's cares, or, amid the wind's
dreary moan, to dream at night a consoling dream.[63]

Kaoru turns against Uji after Ōigimi's death, but he remains
sufficiently under its spell to install Ukifune there as his mistress. Then
he hears that she, too, has died ("Kagerō"). "What a pathetic end!" he
exclaims to himself. "...And what an awful place it is! There must be a
demon living there."[64] The spirit that speaks in the next chapter
confirms his suspicion. The Uji chapters resemble an immense
elaboration on Kisen Hōshi's poem.

Kaoru's burden of karma

In Parts One and Two the long-term focus of the narrative is on Genji,
while in Part Three it is on Kaoru. The uniqueness of both men is
summed up by an attribute peculiar to each: Genji shines, while Kaoru
gives off an exquisite perfume. In Japanese literature, *Taketori
monogatari* provides the classic example of personal radiance like
Genji's, but the motif is limited neither to literature nor to Japan.
Kaoru's scent is exotic in comparison.

Two passages in Part Two ("Kashiwagi," "Yokobue") evoke Kaoru
as a baby, but, as Konishi Jin'ichi observed,[65] neither mentions his scent.
It first appears in "Niou Miya," the first chapter of Part Three, when
Kaoru is in his mid-teens.

One could hardly say of his features just what distinguished
them or made them especially worthy of admiration; he simply
had superb grace and was at heart unlike what appears to be
the common run of men. He gave off a delicious smell, an
otherworldly fragrance...[66]

This fragrance is ambiguous in meaning. Readers have often
associated it with Kaoru's otherworldly (Buddhist) aspiration and
taken it as suggesting a kind of sanctity, but despite his professed piety
he is no holier by the end of the tale. Since Genji's light links him to

---

[63] TTG, 834; GM 5:132.

[64] TTG, 1052; GM 6:215.

[65] Konishi, "Genji monogatari no imejerî," 218.

[66] TTG, 788; GM 5:26.

something beyond the human world, Kaoru's fragrance may do so too, but in his case the link seems to be to darkness and the gloom of Uji.[67] Kaoru sometimes complains that he feels singled out for misfortune, and with respect at least to his private life he may be right. His troubles seem connected, as he himself vaguely believes them to be, with the irregular circumstances of his birth. In that sense, the spirit's appearance in "Tenarai" only gives an outline identity to a problem that has weighed on him ever since.

The nature of that problem is elusive, but at first glance it seems clear enough. Kaoru began early to suspect that there was something irregular about his birth and that Genji was not his real father. "Takekawa" mentions "rumors that chanced to come his way" and the resulting "constant anxiety."[68] He felt somehow apart from others and longed to know the truth. In "Hashihime" he hears the whole story at last and receives a collection of letters between Kashiwagi and his mother. Contrary to what the reader might have expected, however, this revelation makes no difference. The subject never comes up again, and Kaoru's anxiety and vague aspiration to religion continue as before. He never even reflects that as Kashiwagi's son he is a Fujiwara, not a Minamoto, and that for all these years he has therefore been honoring the wrong clan deity—an issue that does not escape Tamakazura when the world learns in "Miyuki" that she is Tō no Chūjō's daughter, not Genji's. Something else must be wrong.

Kaoru's existential discomfort remains unchanged when a passage in "Kagerō" casts doubt on the very idea that it has something to do with his birth. After the empress (Genji's daughter) has spoken of him to one of her women, the narrator continues, "It was true that she and [Kaoru] were brother and sister [harakara], but she was still somewhat in awe of him..."[69] The narrator in the original may

---

[67] Konishi ("Genji monogatari no imejerî," 226-227) cited several *Kokinshū* poems that associate the scent of plum blossoms, to which Kaoru's own is linked repeatedly, with the darkness of night.

[68] TTG, 787; GM 5:23.

[69] TTG, 1066; GM 6:256. The author of the apocryphal *Genji* chapter *Yamaji no tsuyu* (attributed to Kenreimon'in Ukyō no Daibu, 1157?-1233?) described Kaoru in her

conceivably be speaking from the empress's point of view, and if so the passage may mean only that the empress *believes* Kaoru to be her brother. However, this remark, unqualified by any other, rings strangely enough to remind one that in this chapter Kaoru behaves toward the empress exactly as though he were her brother, which would be improper, hence unlike him, if he were not. The passage suggests a link between Kaoru's state of mind and the miasma of Uji— a miasma associated in the next chapter with a possessing spirit.

The spirit that speaks in "Tenarai" therefore resembles Rokujō's as an agent of karma, or fate. In pursuing its own ends, which is all that such a spirit can do, it subjects Kaoru to miseries earned before he was born—miseries visible in germ in the tale's first chapter. As for Genji himself, many people in the tale have reason sooner or later to be grateful to him, but he causes others grievous harm. Yūgao is an example, and yet she never haunted him after her death. That would have been out of character for her, but she also did not matter enough to be able to do so; besides, he never insulted her as he insulted the proud Rokujō. In his world, slights inflicted on the great were especially dangerous, after the victim's death as well as before. Thus it is indeed Rokujō and Suzaku whom Genji most grievously and most dangerously wrongs. With these two, especially, he loses his footing and provokes an enmity beyond his control, one that will haunt him and his descendants, and wear down even beyond his death the greatest heights of good fortune.

---

opening sentence as *Kano Hikaru Genji no on-sue no ko,* "the Shining Genji's last child" (Yamagishi and Imai, *Yamaji no tsuyu, Kumogakure rokujō*, Shintensha, 24, 31.)

GENJI AND SUZAKU:
THE POSSIBILITY OF UKIFUNE

This essay continues the preceding one by suggesting that Suzaku's bitterness toward Genji, precipitated by the misfortune of his daughter, may affect even the tale's last heroine, Ukifune, through the mechanism of spirit possession. It also discusses more generally the nature and significance of Ukifune's experience. Nearly all Genji readers have long taken it for granted that she throws herself into the nearby river in order to drown, but that she is instead swept downstream and washed ashore at the spot where she is then found.[1] However, the narrative does not confirm that assumption. Instead, it suggests that a spirit carries her: the spirit exorcised in "Tenarai," and the one perhaps associated with the memory of Suzaku.

Ukifune's reputation

Ukifune is the last major female character in the tale, and the final chapters ("Ukifune" to "Yume no ukihashi") tell the most striking part of her story. In "Ukifune" Kaoru and Niou, the young men most prominent in the Uji chapters, pursue her, and the success of both places her in an agonizing dilemma. She could save herself by choosing one over the other, but she remains unable to do so. Instead she sinks into paralyzing despair, and, living as she does beside the Uji River, decides to drown herself. At the end of "Ukifune" the reader knows what she is about to do, and the next morning (the start of the next chapter, "Kagerō") she has indeed disappeared. However, early in the chapter after that ("Tenarai") she is found alive under a tree. Her rescuers take her home to Ono, on the western slopes of Mt. Hiei, where to sever all connection with her old life she has herself ordained as a nun. Late in "Tenarai" Kaoru hears of her, and in "Yume no ukihashi" he discovers where she is. Desperate to meet her again, he

---

[1] Kinugasa Teinosuke's 1957 movie *Ukifune* and Hōjō Shūji's play *Ukifune* both illustrate this assumption, and a video currently sold by the Tale of Genji Museum in Uji shows Ukifune leaping off the Uji Bridge. Such evidence is endless.

sends her younger half-brother to her with an appeal. However, in the book's final passage she refuses either to accept Kaoru's letter or to recognize her brother. The closing lines evoke Kaoru's chagrin.

The author of *Sarashina nikki* (mid-11th c.) described dreaming in her youth of languishing in romantically melancholy isolation, like Ukifune at Uji;[2] but the *Mumyōzōshi* author, although sympathetic to Ukifune's plight, described her personally as a "tiresome character" *(nikuki mono to mo iitsubeki hito)*.[3] Since then Ukifune has continued to arouse pity and admiration in some, mixed feelings in others. Sakamoto Tomonobu struck an often-heard note when he identified the theme of Ukifune's story as that of "the establishment of self *(jiga no kakuritsu)*."

> Alone [Ukifune] decides to die; alone she sets out toward the place of her death. She sets out to part from all those whom she loves, all those close her. She keeps the sorrow of parting sealed in her breast, where she strives to bear it. Ukifune is strong. She is not swept on by fate; she decides her own fate...The movements of her own heart, the situation in which she has been placed: these things she can observe coolly, objectively...She certainly deserves pity, but the death that awaits her is a death that she has chosen herself, and the appearance of a young woman who can in this way, on her own, choose her own fate, suggests new possibilities for women.[4]

Many readers have particularly emphasized Ukifune's Buddhist aspiration. *Yamaji no tsuyu*, an "apocryphal" *Genji* chapter attributed to Kenreimon'in Ukyō no Daibu (1157?-1233?), likewise credits her with

---

[2] Akiyama Ken, *Sarashina nikki*, 36, 75; Morris, *As I Crossed a Bridge of Dreams*, 57, 87.

[3] Higuchi and Kuboki, *Mumyōzōshi*, 197. The *Mumyōzōshi* author placed her under the heading of "unfortunate women" *(itōshiki hito)* in *The Tale of Genji*. For more on the early reception of Ukifune, see Mostow, "On Becoming Ukifune: Autobiographical Heroines in Heian and Kamakura Literature."

[4] Sakamoto Tomonobu, "Ukifune monogatari no shudai," 347-348. A similarly lyrical appraisal appears in Ino, "Kakusu/kakureru: Ukifune monogatari," 127-142. Reviewing evaluations of Ukifune, Sakamoto cited in dissent only Shimizu Yoshiko ("Yo o ujiyama no onnagimi"), who saw her as "characterless" and with a "foolish heart," and who wrote: "It is not possible to take her suicide as a self-determined act."

steadfast courage in the pursuit of her chosen path in life.[5] Some have seen in Ukifune the author's meditation on the weakness of the human heart—a weakness that she resolutely overcomes.[6] Her passage to a new life, through her failed drowning attempt, has also been described as a passage through death to rebirth.[7] Nagai Kazuko connected all these themes when she wrote that to develop a full "self" Ukifune must pass the boundary between birth and death, and that after her rebirth she transcends the self in a quest for the very source of her existence: the "other shore" *(higan),* or enlightenment, symbolized for her by the mother whom, at the end, she still longs to meet once more.[8] Her example has even been called an inspiration for Kaoru, whose longing for the religious life remains unrealized at the end of the tale.[9]

Ukifune's journey to the Uji Villa

Ukifune, the unrecognized daughter of the late Eighth Prince, lives in a house beside the Uji River. Once her father lived there with his two recognized daughters, Ōigimi and Nakanokimi, but then he died, and Ōigimi after him. Nakanokimi moved away, leaving the house empty. In "Azumaya" Kaoru installs Ukifune there as his mistress.

In "Ukifune," Kaoru's great friend Niou tracks her down to Uji and impersonates Kaoru in order to make love to her. Thereafter she is torn between the two men. Propriety and good sense commend Kaoru, who knew her carnally first and who is also endlessly dignified and responsible. However, he is also a little dull. Pure pleasure commends Niou.

Ukifune's mother lives with her husband and her other children (Ukifune's half siblings) in the city, but she sometimes visits Uji. On one such occasion Ukifune is already in black despair when she overhears her mother chatting with the other women of the household. Her mother knows about Kaoru but not about Niou, and she remarks

---

[5] *Yamaji no tsuyu,* in Yamagishi and Imai, Yamaji no tsuyu, Kumogakure rokujō.
[6] Enomoto, "Ukifune ron e no kokoromi," 44-45.
[7] Hinata, "'Genji monogatari' no shi to saisei: Ukifune o chūshin ni," 48-53.
[8] Nagai, "Ukifune," 290-291.
[9] Washiyama, Genji monogatari shudai ron, 216.

that if Ukifune were ever to betray Kaoru, "I would want nothing more to do with her." To Ukifune this is a "devastating blow." "I wish I were dead!" she says to herself. "The awful secret will get out sooner or later!"

The narrative continues, "Outside, the river roared menacingly past." "Not all rivers sound like that," her mother remarks, deploring the dismal wildness of the spot. A gentlewoman chimes in by telling how just the other day the ferryman's grandson fell in and drowned. "That river has taken so many people!" she sighs. Ukifune has already been thinking that she wants to die. Now she realizes that she could drown herself.[10]

The tension rises as the need to decide between Kaoru and Niou becomes more pressing. Ukifune is prostrate with despair. Her two most intimate gentlewomen then remonstrate with her, and one (Ukon) tells her a cautionary tale.

> In Hitachi my sister had two lovers—this can happen to little
> people too, you know. Both were equally keen on her, and
> she could not decide between them, but she favored the
> more recent one just a little. That made the first one jealous,
> and in the end he killed the other![11]

So Ukifune realizes that Kaoru might actually harm Niou, and the fate of Ukon's sister (who was never allowed to return to the capital) confirms her conviction that nothing awaits her in any case but misery and shame. Resolved to die, she destroys all her correspondence and writes two farewell poems to her mother. Darkness is falling. The reader knows exactly what she plans to do that night. Some will also have recognized in her situation a motif established in the *Man'yōshū* and elsewhere: that of the girl who drowns herself after finding herself caught between two or more men.[12]

The next morning ("Kagerō") she is gone. To keep up appearances the household stages a false funeral. Eventually the narrative moves back to the palace and, for the most part, to other matters. Early in

---

[10] TTG, 1032; GM 6:167-168.

[11] TTG, 1037; GM 6:178.

[12] Suzuki Hideo, "Ukifune monogatari shiron," 41-44. "Two Post-*Genji* Tales on *The Tale of Genji*" discusses this subject further.

"Tenarai," however, Ukifune reappears on the very night of her disappearance.

"Tenarai" begins by introducing Yokawa no Sōzu (the Prelate of Yokawa), a senior and highly respected monk of Mt. Hiei, as well as his mother and sister. These two women, both nuns, live at Ono, but just now they are on their way home after a pilgrimage to Hasedera. When the Sōzu's mother falls ill, the worried party send for him, and he hastens to her side. Since they can now go no further, they stop at a friend's house near Uji. Unfortunately, the friend happens to be purifying himself for a pilgrimage of his own, and when he learns that one of the party is seriously ill he asks everyone to leave, lest the sick person die, pollute his house, and so render his preparations useless. The party will apparently have to go straight home after all, at whatever risk to the old lady. Suddenly a directional taboo makes that impossible. At last the Sōzu remembers a villa (Uji no In, "the Uji Villa") that once belonged to Retired Emperor Suzaku. It is nearby, it is empty, and since the Sōzu happens to know the steward, he decides to go there instead.

These zigzags of circumstance (the mother's illness, the friend's purification, the directional taboo, the Sōzu's acquaintance with the steward) suggest that supernatural influence guides the party to the Uji Villa in order to have them find Ukifune.

Many Heian nobles had a country house at Uji. For example, *Kagerō nikki* mentions an Uji no In owned by Fujiwara no Kaneie and located on the east side of the Uji River (the same side as Ukifune's house), as well as another on the opposite (Byōdō-in) side owned by Fujiwara no Morouji. Uji was a "resort area" *(yūraku no chi)* for aristocratic residents of the capital.[13] By the mid-eleventh century it offered the services of singing girls *(asobi),* who came to be associated especially with the vicinity of the Byōdō-in.[14] However, it was also associated

---

[13] Matsuda, *Genji monogatari no chimei eizō,* 51; Kubota, "Uji e no shiza: monogatari no 'ba' zenshi," 17-19, 23-26. For a further discussion of Uji in the Heian period, see Kawashima, *Writing Margins,* 224-227.

[14] Goodwin, *Selling Songs and Smiles,* 17, 21; also Pigeot, *Femmes galantes, femmes artistes,* 20-21. Both writers translate a letter in which Fujiwara no Akihira (989-1066) described the *asobi* of Uji.

with Buddhist devotion and reclusion. The preceding essay discussed the monk Kisen Hōshi's famous poem that plays on "Uji" and *ushi* ("dreary") and the echoes of that poem in one by the Eighth Prince. Some villas at Uji were even turned eventually into temples. An example is the Byōdō-in itself, built by Fujiwara no Yorimichi in 1052 on the site of a villa inherited from his father, Michinaga. As for the Uji no In of the tale, modern conjecture (perhaps influenced by the idea that Ukifune actually threw herself into the river) places it near the east bank of the river, roughly four or five hundred meters downstream from Ukifune's house. [15] However, most medieval commentaries identify it with the Byōdō-in site, directly across the river from the house.

The Sōzu and his party reach Uji no In at night. The place is so eerie that the Sōzu sends two of his accompanying monks, with a torch, to look around the deserted back of the villa for anything strange or threatening. The monks find themselves in a wood. Peering through the gloom beneath the trees, they make out what looks like a weeping young woman in white. They assume that it is a trickster fox, and so does the Sōzu when he hears their report. "I have always heard that a fox may take human form, but I have never seen one that has actually done it!"[16] he says before going to view their find himself. It is Ukifune.

Ukifune is not lying on the riverbank. The villa presumably faces the river, and she is in the woods behind it *(ushiro no kata).* While the narrative in "Ukifune" repeatedly emphasizes the river's menacing roar, the wood in "Tenarai" is silent. There might as well be no river.

How did she get there? If she was swept downstream she must have crawled past the villa to the wood, but that is impossible. Just above Uji the river emerges from a gorge. At the site of the Eighth Prince's house it is wide and fast, with presumably (in the days before riparian works) rocky banks. In 1180, six hundred men drowned here when a large Heike force swam their horses across the river to attack Minamoto no Yorimasa at the Byōdō-in. Moreover, the narrative of the

---

[15] Tsunoda and Katō, *Genji monogatari no chiri*, 129. The map locates the Uji Villa just where the river widens out into the now-drained Ogura no Ike.
[16] TTG, 1078; GM 6:282.

days preceding Ukifune's disappearance repeatedly mentions rain. The river is swollen. Ukifune could not have survived being swept down it, especially if she actually intended to drown in the first place; and if she had, she would have been bruised and half dead by the time she was washed ashore. She has swallowed no water, and as the Sōzu's sister soon discovers, she has not a mark on her. She is not even wet, since just now it is not raining.[17] Nor can she have walked to the wood, since her feet are intact. Her clothing is intact, too, perfume and all.

The two monks, who believe her to be evilly supernatural, send for their master, but the Sōzu recognizes her as human and has them carry her to the house. There his sister, now a nun, gladly takes charge of her. Having lost her daughter some years ago, she has just been to Hasedera to pray for a new one, and in a dream Kannon promised her this boon. Kannon therefore led the Sōzu's party to the Uji Villa in order to bring them to this new daughter, whose arrival there alive is also, as the Sōzu and the reader eventually learn, Kannon's work. Thus the story told in "Tenarai" begins as a typical Kannon miracle tale *(reigen tan)*. However, it soon takes on a strangely ambiguous character, almost as though it had been turned inside out.

The spirit

One scholar writing on spirits *(mononoke)* in the tale speculated that Ukifune must have walked there in a trance-like state to the spot where she was found, or that she was perhaps was kidnapped and abandoned by someone like a passing *yamabushi*.[18] Another, recognizing that a spirit took her, assumed that the spirit carried her in its arms, or that she walked beside it.[19] Still others have agreed with Nagai Kazuko that Ukifune never regained her memory of what happened while she was possessed and that "the author does not

---

[17] Iimura, *Genji monogatari no nazo*, 218-227. Iimura also showed that Ukifune's remembered sobbing when the spirit dropped her corresponds to the sobbing the monks hear when they find her.

[18] Abe Toshiko, "Genji monogatari no 'mononoke'," Part 2, 19.

[19] Iimura, *Genji monogatari no nazo*, 230.

describe exactly what happened."[20] The different descriptions of the agent involved seem to compound the difficulty. When exorcised by the Sōzu, the spirit declares itself to have been once "a practicing monk" *(okonai seshi hōshi)*. Next, Ukifune herself recalls "a very beautiful man" approaching her, inviting her to come to its home, and taking her in its arms. Later on, however, she remembers a demon *(oni)* making off with her, and later still the Sōzu tells Kaoru that "a *tengu* or a tree spirit *[kodama]* must have taken her to the spot by deceit."[21] The narrative therefore proposes six seemingly conflicting appearances or identities for the spirit: a former monk, a beautiful man, a demon, a *tengu,* a tree spirit, and the fox mentioned when the monks first find her. These seem to cancel one another out, leaving the issue imponderable.

Several medieval documents resolve the difficulty. The fourteenth-century *Genji* commentary *Kakaishō* provides the first clue. In connection with the spirit's speech to the Sōzu, in the exorcism scene, *Kakaishō* quotes *Kojidan* 211 in full.[22] This anecdote tells how a high-ranking monk conceived lust for a woman (the Somedono Empress, 829-900), died, and became a *tengu* that then possessed her. Next, *Kakaishō* cites another version of the same story, according to which a holy monk was called in to heal the same empress and desired her so intensely that he vowed to die and become an *oni* in order to possess her, which he did.[23]

These stories suggest that a ranking monk who succumbs to temptation because of a woman can become after death either an *oni* or a *tengu.* The spirit's self-description ("Once I was a practicing monk") therefore agrees both with Ukifune's memory of it as an *oni* and the Sōzu's belief that it may have been a *tengu.*

The Sōzu's other suggestion, a *kodama,* is equally plausible. Japanese folklore has long associated *tengu* with tall trees, and the

---

[20] Nagai, "Ukifune," 283.

[21] TTG, 1083; GM 6:296.

[22] Tamagami, *Shimeishō, Kakaishō*, 595-596.

[23] Later commentaries repeat these references, having nothing further to suggest. *Mingō nisso* simply quotes *Kakaishō* in full (Tanaka, *Mingō nisso*, 691-692); and *Kogetsu shō* refers to the same material (Kitamura Kigin, *Kogetsushō*, 940-941).

narrative amusingly emphasizes the tree-spirit aspect of Ukifune's abductor. Ukifune is found lying under a tree that, according to the villa's caretaker, is often haunted by supernatural creatures.

"Does any young woman live nearby?" [The monks] showed [the caretaker] what they were talking about.

"Foxes do this," the caretaker replied. "Strange things can happen under this tree. One autumn, the year before last, they made off with a little boy just a year or so old, the son of someone in service here, and this is where they brought him. It is hardly surprising."

"Did the boy die?"

"No, he is still alive. Foxes love to give people a fright, but they never actually do anything much." He had seen it all before, and the arrival of a party of people in the middle of the night seemed to preoccupy him a good deal more.[24]

The monks' discovery is old hat to the caretaker, who takes the material mischief of spirits for granted. However, his idea of a supernatural being that moves someone from one place to another is a fox *(kitsune).* Despite possible differences in degree of mischief, all these entities are continuous with one another.

The linked verse *(renga)* manual *Renju gappeki shū*, by Ichijō Kanera (1402-1481), confirms this continuity. Kanera listed both *kitsune* and *oni* as linking words for *kodama*, specifying that they refer to *Genji*, together with the place name Uji and the chapter name "Tenarai."[25] For the author as for the users of this manual, the key word associated with this episode in the tale—one that included the possibility of all the rest mentioned—was therefore *kodama*.

Ukifune's perception of the beautiful man belongs under the same heading. She first recalls him this way:

I was...rooted to the spot, when a very beautiful man approached me and said, 'Come with me to where I live!'; and it seemed to me that he took me in his arms. I assumed that

---

24 TTG, 1079; GM 6:283.

25 Ichijō Kanera, *Renju gappeki shū*, 184. For this reference, as well as those concerning other *renga* manuals and the two nō plays discussed below, see Goff, *Noh Drama and The Tale of Genji*, 80-83, 186. Kanera's entry heading equates *kodama* with *yamabiko*.

he was the gentleman they addressed as 'Your Highness', but then my mind must have wandered, until he put me down in a place I did not know. Then he vanished.[26]

He has long been identified as Niou, although in recent times some have suggested Kaoru[27] or even Ukifune's father.[28] However, these conjectures do not help because the figure is an illusion in the first place. Soon after recalling him, Ukifune says to the Sōzu's sister:

"My only dim memory is of sitting evening after evening staring out into the night and not wanting to live, until someone appeared from under a great tree in front of me and, as it seemed to me, took me away."[29]

She associates the figure explicitly with a tree. *Tengu* (to say nothing of foxes) are famous masters of illusion, and *setsuwa* literature contains many anecdotes about the elaborate hallucinations they create. An example is *Konjaku monogatari shū* 20/3 (also *Uji shūi monogatari* 2/14), in which a *tengu* appears as a buddha among the branches of a persimmon tree, shining and scattering flowers. When a suspicious minister's relentless gaze finally breaks the spell, the buddha suddenly vanishes, and a large kestrel with a broken wing falls out of the tree. Ukifune's beautiful man is a *tengu-kodama* trick that reveals nothing about the spirit's nature or identity. It shows only that the spirit knows what form will appeal to her.[30]

According to Janet Goff, medieval *renga* manuals devoted to *The Tale of Genji* (as *Renju gappeki shū* is not, being general in coverage) ignore Ukifune's exorcism scene.[31] However, at the end of their section

---

[26] TTG, 1083; GM 6:296.

[27] Ikeda Kazuomi, "Tenarai no maki mono no ke kō: Ukifune monogatari no shudai to kōzō," 166-170.

[28] Bargen, *A Woman's Weapon,* 235.

[29] TTG, 1085; GM 6: 299.

[30] In *Konjaku monogatari shū* 20/7, a third version of the story about the Somedono Empress, the demon (the former monk) rushes in and, with the empress's eager cooperation, makes love to her in the presence of the whole court. The story describes the demon as naked, bald, and eight feet tall, with black, glistening skin, eyes like brass bowls, knifelike teeth, and so on; and presumably that is more or less what the courtiers see. However, it is probably not what the empress sees.

[31] Goff, *Noh Drama and* The Tale of Genji, 80-81.

The Possibility of Ukifune

on the "Ukifune" chapter they attribute her disappearance to a *kodama*, which they then specify as a linking word for "Uji." An example is *Hikaru Genji ichibu renga yoriai no koto* by Nijō Yoshimoto (1320-1388), which states explicitly that the man Ukifune saw was a *kodama*.[32] The much larger manual entitled *Hikaru Genji ichibu uta* (1453) not only makes the same connection with a *kodama* but also has the spirit in the exorcism scene describe itself as a *kodama* rather than as a former "practicing monk."[33]

Goff examined *renga* manuals in connection with her study of nō plays based on *The Tale of Genji*. Two plays, both of which exploit these manuals extensively, concern Ukifune.[34] One is *Ukifune*, which Zeami (1363?-1443?) praised in *Sarugaku dangi* even though it is not by him. (Although still in the repertoire, it is rarely performed.) The *maeshite* is a nameless woman of Uji, and the *nochijite* is Ukifune. The text sheds little light on the matter under discussion, but it is noteworthy that, at the end of the first part, the *maeshite* describes herself as still possessed by an evil spirit *(nao mononoke no mi ni soite)*.[35] The discussion will return below to the idea that Ukifune remains at least partially possessed even after the exorcism.

The second play, *Kodama Ukifune*,[36] is not in the repertoire and appears to date from the early sixteenth century. The *maeshite* is a nameless woman at Ono. The identity of the *nochijite* is confusing, but it seems to be above all the possessing spirit itself, as the *Genji* reader knows it from the exorcism scene in "Tenarai."

Muromachi-period readers, including such authoritative literary figures as Nijō Yoshimoto and Ichijō Kanera, therefore gathered from the *Genji* narrative that a spirit transported Ukifune. The same understanding presumably underlies the gloss in most medieval commentaries, to the effect that the Uji Villa occupied the site of the

[32] Okami, *Yoshimoto renga ron shū*, 235.
[33] Imai, *Hikaru Genji ichibu uta*, 284, 288.
[34] For commentary and complete English translations, see Goff, *Noh Drama and* The Tale of Genji, 182-197.
[35] Goff, *Noh Drama and* The Tale of Genji, 190; Itō, *Yōkyoku shū*, vol. 3,131.
[36] Tanaka Mitsuru, *Mikan yōkyoku shū*, 194-200.

Byōdō-in.[37] The tale makes it clear where the house was, and the commentary authors must have known that the Byōdō-in site was directly across from it. The river could not have carried Ukifune there, nor could a living person with a boat, since the boat would have landed further downstream. The only possibility left is a spirit.

If medieval readers were more or less agreed on the subject, when did the controversy about it arise? Perhaps Edo-period Confucians like Kumazawa Banzan (1619-1691) were the first skeptics. No one will ever know what Banzan might have written about Ukifune, since he never took his *Genji* commentary *(Genji gaiden)* past "Fuji no uraba." However he believed that the tale was "written throughout with the basic purpose of the transformation of the ways [of society] *(fūka),*" and his approach to it was thoroughly historicist and rationalist.[38] James McMullen wrote, "Banzan provided rational, again sometimes psychological, explanations of the flourishing world of spirits in the novel." For example, Banzan attributed Yūgao's death to a psychological cause (fear) rather than to a supernatural one (the phantom woman seen by Genji), and he denied that Rokujō's living spirit actually left her body to torment Aoi.[39]

Banzan's emphasis on rationality and psychology is visible in modern discussions of the spirit that speaks in Ukifune's exorcism scene. Perhaps the most authoritative of these now is the one proposed by Mitani Kuniaki and adopted by Fujimoto Katsuyoshi.[40]

Mitani began by citing from Murasaki Shikibu's personal collection a poem *(Murasaki Shikibu shū* 44) that comments on a painting. According to the *kotobagaki*, the painting showed a possessed woman with a demon behind her. The exorcist held the demon bound, while a man chanted a sutra. According to the poem, the man was the husband,

---

[37] Commentaries that mention the Byōdō-in or its site confidently include *Kakaishō* (1367), *Genji taigai shinpishō* (ca. 1430), *Rōkashō* (1476), *Bansui ichiro* (1575), and *Mōshinshō* (1574). *Sairyūshō* (ca. 1528) gives it as the main possibility, but *Mingō nisso* (1598) doubts the idea. Only *Kachō yosei* (1472) omits the Byōdō-in entirely.

[38] McMullen, *Idealism, Protest, and the* Tale of Genji, 323.

[39] McMullen, 329-330.

[40] Mitani Kuniaki, "Genji monogatari daisanbu no hōhō: chūshin no sōshitsu aruiwa fuzai no monogatari," 95-99.

the possessed woman was his second wife, and the demon (the possessing spirit) was his first wife, now deceased. The poem suggests that although the husband attributes his present wife's suffering to the resentment of his first, this suffering is really due to his own "heart demon" *(kokoro no oni),* his bad conscience. Mitani concluded from this that although Murasaki Shikibu accepted the phenomena associated with spirit possession, she did not attribute them to the operations of an autonomous, external power. Instead, she saw the afflicting spirit as an expression of the guilt of the person whom its rantings addressed: in this case the husband.

Mitani linked this view to the psychology of the unconscious and then interpreted in this light the various possession events attributed in the tale to the spirit of Rokujō. Since Genji is in these cases the living person addressed, the spirit is a manifestation of Genji's own guilt and fear, whether or not he is conscious of them. The same principle therefore applies to the possession scene in "Tenarai." Since the spirit addresses the Sōzu (the exorcist), it is a manifestation of the Sōzu's guilt and fear.

The Sōzu is indeed nervous about having come down to Ono from Mt. Hiei to exorcise a young woman, since his action could suggest that he is attracted to her in an unseemly way, hence that he has broken his vows and discredited Buddhism and his fellow monks. However, these misgivings do not adequately support Mitani's argument. As noted also in the Introduction to this book, Murasaki Shikibu's poem cannot reliably explain every possession scene in *The Tale of Genji,* since one cannot be certain in what spirit she wrote it or how generally applicable she took this example to be, and especially since there is no reason to assume that, through her fictional narrator, she wrote her personal understanding into her fiction. Moreover, it is impossible to understand how a power that has carried Ukifune from one place to another and possessed her by this time for two months could be no more than a manifestation of this exorcist's guilty feelings. Mitani accorded the spirit no other significance than to reveal the unconscious preoccupations of the Sōzu and then of Ukifune who, after the exorcism, remembers seeing the "very beautiful man," while Fujimoto denied that what Ukifune sees has anything to do with what the Sōzu hears because Ukifune does not remember ever having been possessed by a monk.

Apart from the circumstances of Ukifune's disappearance and her own memories of what happened to her, the narrative repeatedly hints at possession and spirit abduction. When the women of the household see Ukifune so depressed ("Ukifune"), they immediately wonder whether a spirit is troubling her, and her nurse exclaims a little later, "The way you keep lying about, for some reason, there must be some spirit trying to spoil everything!"[41] At the end of the chapter Ukon lies down beside Ukifune and says, "They say the soul of anyone with such cares as yours may go wandering far away. Perhaps that is why your mother had those [alarming] dreams [of you]."[42] The hints grow broader in "Kagerō," which begins with a remark that Ukifune's disappearance resembled a maiden's abduction in a tale—presumably one about a maiden being taken by a demon. Ukifune's nurse is heard crying, "Whoever you are who took my darling, human or demon, oh, give her back!"; Ukifune's mother "could only suppose that a demon had devoured her or that some fox-like creature had made off with her"; and Kaoru sighs about what an awful place Uji is, speculating that "There must be a demon living there."[43]

Late in "Tenarai" the narrator actually tells the reader that a spirit took Ukifune. Having been called to the palace to exorcise the First Princess,[44] the Sōzu stays on to chat with the empress and tells her about the young woman found at Uji. All the empress's gentlewomen are asleep except one Kozaishō, who listens eagerly. When his story is over she asks, "But *why* did the spirit take a well-born girl to a place like that?"[45] The Sōzu, whose power and experience qualify him to

[41] TTG, 1038; SNKBT 6:182.
[42] TTG, 1044; GM 6:196.
[43] TTG, 1048; GM 6:205. TTG, 1049; GM 6:209. TTG, 1052; GM 6:215.
[44] The Princess who so fascinates Kaoru in "Kagerō." Her need for exorcism may be a mere plot device to bring the Sōzu and the empress together, but it may also be related to Kaoru's interest in her. If it is, then the possessing power is the same one that afflicts Ukifune, and the Sōzu recognizes this, so that in his conversation with the empress he is naturally reminded of Ukifune.
[45] TTG, 1102; GM 6:346.

know spirits, must have told the empress how Ukifune got to the Uji Villa.

The exorcism

Once found, Ukifune remains for two months or so in a sort of trance—a condition that any character in the tale would be likely to associate with spirit possession. The Sōzu's sister clearly does so. Although to all appearances dying, Ukifune never dies. At rare moments she says a word or two, once to implore the Sōzu's sister to throw her into the river,[46] but normally she is silent, still, and inaccessible, although she apparently eats enough to survive and retain her looks. She has no memory of her past or of who she is. At last the Sōzu's sister begs her brother to come down from Mt. Hiei and exorcise her.

In order to succeed, the Heian exorcist had to get the possessing spirit to move into a medium. (The Sōzu has one with him.) Once it had moved, he could make it confess who it was and why it was causing trouble; then he could admonish it and dismiss it. The spirit would naturally resist this transfer, which a particularly potent one could make very difficult. In the narrative the Sōzu attempts to follow these steps.

> The Sōzu made a mighty vow that the rite he was about to undertake would succeed, whatever it cost him, and he went at it the entire night. At dawn he successfully got the spirit to flee into the medium, whereupon he and the Adept, his disciple, redoubled their efforts to make it say what sort of power it was and why it was tormenting its victim this way.

The spirit then makes the following declaration:

> "I am not someone you may force here and subdue. Once I was a practicing monk *[hōshi],* and a little grudge against this world kept me wandering until I settled in a house full of pretty women. I killed one of them, and then this one chose to turn against life and kept saying day and night that she wanted only to die. That was my chance, and I seized her one

---

46 TTG, 1081; GM 6:288.

dark night when she was alone. Somehow, however, Kannon managed to protect her after all, and now I have lost to this [Sōzu]. I shall go."

"What is speaking?" [the Sōzu asked]. But perhaps the possessed medium was weak by then, because there was no proper answer.[47]

The Sōzu compels the spirit to speak, but he cannot make it identify itself properly or explain its motive. He also cannot dismiss it adequately, since it leaves of its own accord. All this suggests that he has not fully subdued it and that it may be back. Meanwhile, it has revealed that Kannon was responsible for Ukifune's presence at the Uji Villa: Kannon prevented the spirit from taking her all the way into death by making it drop her there. If Kannon had not done so, Ukifune would have been found dead the next morning on the veranda of her house; for this is the meaning of *moteyuku* ("take away") or *toru* ("take") when the subject is an angry spirit *(onryō)*. The person "taken" dies on the spot.

If this spirit is identifiable, it must be someone known to the reader, and the needed clues must be present in its speech. Its opening words ("I am not someone you may force here and subdue") are already a warning. Then it says, "Once I was a practicing monk." The only figure in the tale who fits this description is Retired Emperor Suzaku, who died after several years as a monk. An emperor's spirit could certainly speak this loftily.[48] Moreover, the reader has already been told that in life Suzaku owned the Uji Villa.

The idea of an imperial curse

Angry spirits were feared in Heian times, and an emperor's posthumous wrath was seen as especially dangerous. The threat was that such a spirit would "take" one or more people. *Eiga monogatari* reports that when Emperor Kazan (968-1008, r. 984-986) was gravely

---

[47] TTG, 1083; GM 6:294-295.

[48] *Hōshi* is not too modest for a monk-emperor. In "Usugumo" Emperor Reizei thinks of the ranking monk who tells him the secret of his (Reizei's) birth as a *hōshi*, and in "Wakamurasaki" the word designates Murasaki's great uncle, a monk of high rank.

ill he kept repeating, "If I die, I shall take all the Princesses with me before the end of the forty-nine days." Then he died. All four of his daughters died within that time. He had indeed taken them with him *(mote-tori-yuku)*, and that is what the spirit meant to do with Ukifune. The *Eiga* narrator remarks, "Everyone agreed that the strength of a high-born person's will is a fearsome thing."[49]

Kikki, the diary of Yoshida Tsunefusa (1142-1200) recorded an imperial curse under the date Juei 2/7/16 (1183). Retired Emperor Sutoku (1119-1164, r. 1123-1141), in exile in Sanuki, copied the *gobu daijō* ("five-part Mahāyāna")[50] in his own blood and wrote at the end, "This is so that in an unjust reign my merit for the life to come should destroy the realm" *(hiri no yo, goshō no ryō, tenka wo horobosubeki no omomuki)*. The sutras he had copied were to be sunk in the sea. However, the court obtained them and instead dedicated them at a temple "in order to bring his angry spirit to enlightenment." Tsunefusa wrote at the end, "Terrifying, terrifying!"[51]

Retired Emperor Go-Toba (1180-1239, r. 1183-1198) even left first-person testimony on the subject of angry spirits. On Katei 3 8/25 (1237), in exile on Oki, he wrote a testament in which he recorded what Emperor Go-shirakawa (1127-1192, r. 1155-1158) had once told him: that Go-Shirakawa hoped to escape the cycle of reincarnation but was also afraid of becoming a demonic spirit *(maen)*. If that should happen, Go-Shirakawa told Go-Toba, and something takes *(toru koto araba)* any descendant of mine, understand that none other than my own power will have done it. He continued,

> If I turn all my good works and merit to evil and do anything of that kind, all that good will vanish, and I will enter deeper and deeper into evil. If any descendant of mine is then ruling the realm, he must perform no rite for the gods or buddhas but to pray for my enlightenment.

Then he went on,

---

[49] Yamanaka, *Eiga monogatari* 1:388-390. McCullough, *A Tale of Flowering Fortunes* 1:265-266.
[50] The *Kegonkyō, Daihōdōdaishūkyō, Daibon hannyakyō, Hokekyō,* and *Nehangyō.*
[51] Quoted in Katō, "Shōkū kyōdan ni yoru ichinichikyō kuyō," 122.

"Alas, I acted foolishly, paid little heed to what he had said, prayed for this and that, went on pilgrimage here and there, and now it has come to this *(kakaru koto ni nariniki)*. If hereafter any descendant of mine rules the realm and performs any such rites that are not for my enlightenment, my curse will be upon him *(ikko ni on-mi no tatari to narubeki koto nari)*."[52]

Katō Gitai concluded from these examples that the greater the person's power or prestige in life, the more powerful that person's spirit will be after death, and that "When an emperor who has accumulated great Buddhist merit applies the power of that merit negatively and becomes an *onryō*, the result is a very powerful *onryō* indeed."[53]

Go-Shirakawa, Sutoku, and Go-Toba were all bitter about what they had suffered at the hands of others. Go-Shirakawa had been forced to abdicate, while Sutoku and Gotoba had been exiled.[54] No emperor faced exile in the time of *The Tale of Genji,* but forced abdication occurred (Kazan is an example), and succession issues, too, could cause acute resentment. One of these arose at the death of Emperor Ichijō (980-1011, r. 986-1011). In conformity with custom, Ichijō was to designate before he died his heir apparent's (Sanjō, 976-1017, r. 1011-1016) successor. According to *Eiga monogatari* he wanted to appoint his eldest son, a grandson of Fujiwara no Korechika (974-1010), but was obliged instead to appoint a grandson of Fujiwara no Michinaga.[55] *Eiga* also records that Michinaga disposed of Ichijō's property after Ichijō's death.[56] He was therefore in a good position to find, as *Gukanshō* reports him doing,

---

[52] Quoted in Katō, 123. Katō noted that in *Godaiteiō monogatari*, a historical tale *(rekishi monogatari)* written prior to 1327, Go-Toba plays a major role as an *onryō*.

[53] Katō, "Shōkū kyōdan ni yoru ichinichikyō kuyō," 128.

[54] *Gukanshō* describes fears that Go-Shirakawa's *onryō* had become active. Okami and Akamatsu, *Gukanshō*, 293-294; Brown and Ishida, *The Future and the Past,* 168-171.

[55] Yamanaka, *Eiga monogatari* 1:484; McCullough, *A Tale of Flowering Fortunes* 1:309-310.

[56] Yamanaka, *Eiga monogatari* 1:465-468; McCullough, *A Tale of Flowering Fortunes* 1:318.

something that looked like an Imperial Mandate written in the deceased Emperor's hand. At the beginning of the document were these words: "The sun, moon, and stars wish to lighten the world, but they are hidden by great banks of clouds and the sky is dark." Without reading further, Michinaga rolled up the document and burned it.[57]

He had probably recognized a written curse. *Eiga*'s silence about his discovery does nothing to make this unlikely. No such sentiments, written or oral, would be mentioned in *Genji,* either, but the bitter succession struggle between the factions represented by Genji and Suzaku is central to the tale. The narrative describes the spirit of Genji's father hurrying to the palace and glaring angrily into Suzaku's eyes, and it also mentions the death of Suzaku's maternal grandfather and the grave illness of his mother. Although the narrator blames neither the death nor the illness on Genji's father, people might well have feared under the circumstances that he had "taken" one and meant to "take" the other. From the standpoint of the reader, whose sympathy lies with Genji, the Kiritsubo Emperor's partisan intervention merely upholds right and justice. Seen from Kokiden's side, however, he is an *onryō*. Suzaku could therefore be one, too, as long as a reason can be found to explain his condition.

Suzaku's "little grudge"

That reason is the spirit's "little grudge." The expression *(isasaka naru urami)* is a grim euphemism. Kashiwagi similarly cites a "little matter" *(isasaka naru koto)* to explain his falling out with Genji: his violation of Genji's wife, which leads to his own death.[58] In "Hashihime," a monk tells Retired Emperor Reizei that "a trifling matter" *(hakanaki koto)* prevents the Eighth Prince from leaving the world: the fate of the Prince's two daughters, who would be alone and defenseless without him.[59] Again, in "Agemaki," Hachimiya tells the same monk in a dream, from the afterworld, that "trifling affections" *(isasaka uchi-omoishi*

---

[57] Okami and Akamatsu, *Gukanshō,* 173; Brown and Ishida, *The Future and the Past,* 58.
[58] TTG, 684; GM 4:316.
[59] TTG, 833; GM 5:129.

koto) have kept him far removed from paradise.[60] The spirit's "little grudge" therefore involves attachment to a woman, one so strong as to compromise the speaker's spiritual wellbeing. The woman may be either a lover or a daughter. If the spirit is Suzaku's, she can only be Suzaku's cherished Third Princess.

Suzaku loved this wanly appealing creature beyond all reason, and to assure her future he married her to Genji. Then Murasaki became desperately ill, and Genji spent week after week looking after her. Unfortunately, his prolonged absence in favor of another woman who ranked far below the Third Princess amounted to an insult of which Suzaku was well aware. It also left an opening for Kashiwagi to make love to the Third Princess himself. She became pregnant, and Genji soon found out what had happened. He forgave neither Kashiwagi, who died under the burden of his wrath, nor the Third Princess, who became terrified of him. The birth of the resulting child, Kaoru, made Suzaku's daughter ill.

Suzaku had not felt able to leave the world until the Third Princess was securely settled. Once her marriage to Genji was arranged he therefore entered a "mountain temple" as an ordained monk. Unfortunately, he soon began hearing rumors that Genji was slighting or neglecting her. Next came the catastrophe of Kashiwagi. Of course it was kept from him, but, as "The Disaster of the Third Princess" explains, he worked it out anyway. Genji warned the Third Princess to behave and not "stand in [your father's] way on the path towards the life to come,"[61] but when she became ill in connection with Kaoru's ignominious birth, she could no longer contain herself. "I may never see [my father] again!" she cried, weeping bitterly. Genji had to tell Suzaku.

A monk was supposed to be beyond all worldly care, but in answer to her need Suzaku came down from his mountain by night to be with her. No monk should have done such a thing, still less a cloistered emperor. His daughter immediately begged him to ordain her. The reader watches in astonishment while Suzaku and his daughter join

---

[60] TTG, 906; GM 5:320.
[61] TTG, 666; GM 4:270.

forces against Genji to make her a nun. Genji has betrayed Suzaku's hopes, and Suzaku's obsession with his daughter has compromised his dignity, his practice, his vows, and all hope of spiritual peace. No wonder his spirit is angry.

This is the "little grudge" that leads his *onryō* eventually to settle in a "house full of pretty women." It is the Eighth Prince's house at Uji, inhabited initially by him and his two daughters, Ōigimi and Nakanokimi. In "Agemaki," Ōigimi allowed herself to die rather than marry Kaoru, and at the time her desperate deed seemed entirely her own. Now, the spirit suddenly announces that it killed her.

But why? The spirit has old reasons for bitterness against Genji, but Genji is dead, and the accessible focus for its anger is Kaoru. Moreover, Ōigimi and Ukifune are both Suzaku's nieces (daughters of a half-brother), and the testimony of Goshirakawa suggests that an imperial *onryō* may have been more likely to attack a descendant. The spirit appears to have killed Ōigimi because she was the great love of Kaoru's life, and to have tried to kill Ukifune because, for Kaoru, Ukifune is an explicit substitute for Ōigimi.[62]

The Sōzu's story about the young woman found at the Uji Villa frightens the empress so much that he "remained silent about what he had not yet told."[63] What had he not yet told? Probably what the spirit had said, since its words suggest so awful a conclusion. As for the Sōzu, he may have known. His failure to get a proper answer to the question

---

[62] Suzaku may also be attracted to the Uji house by its music. In "Wakana Two" Genji observes to Kashiwagi, "[Yūgiri] is fully competent by now to serve the realm, but he seems not to have much of a gift for the finer things of life, few of which are foreign to [Suzaku]. His Eminence is particularly fond of music, at which he is expert, and I expect that despite his appearance of renunciation he is looking forward to enjoying it in peace" (TTG, 668; GM 4:277). Music seems to have been Suzaku's sole genuine accomplishment. The idea that he is "looking forward to enjoying it in peace" is probably disparaging, since its pleasures were held in principle to hinder progress on the religious path. Genji seems to doubt that Suzaku will be able to resist those pleasures even then. His remark, which may foreshadow Suzaku's inability to give up his concern for his favorite daughter, may also suggest why Suzaku's spirit settled in that "house full of pretty women," since the Eighth Prince, like Suzaku, had no other skill than music, which his daughters also favored.

[63] TTG, 1102; GM 6:345.

"What is speaking?" may be a narratorial evasion, since no one addressing the tale's original audience could have identified such a spirit clearly.

Ukifune deranged

Ukifune's dramatic passage to the Uji Villa naturally lingers in the reader's mind, but her exorcism attracts relatively little attention. As already noted, medieval *renga* manuals generally omit it. It has little to offer poetry. A modern study of spirits in the tale must discuss it, but an account of Ukifune's experience may mention it only in passing as the moment when she returns to herself and begins her new life. Mitani Kuniaki discussed it not in order to affirm its importance but to illustrate the thesis of his article, which concerns the "absence" *(fuzai)* or the "hollowing out" *(kūdōka)* of any center in the Uji narrative. Having argued that the spirit means one thing to the Sōzu and something else to Ukifune, in keeping with the unrelated, subconscious preoccupations of each, Mitani concluded that in the narrative's larger context it actually means nothing at all.[64] Some studies of Ukifune have even ignored the spirit, the exorcism, and every hint of the supernatural.[65] However, if the spirit is Suzaku's its role is surely significant, and its most obvious victim is Ukifune herself.

The narrative's portrayal of Ukifune is confusing. Although she grew up in the wilds of the East (Hitachi), Kaoru's first glimpse of her ("Yadorigi") shows him a beautiful young woman so sheltered and refined that she hardly even knows how to get down from a carriage. The day's journey from Hasedera has exhausted her, unlike her hale and hearty (hence crude) gentlewomen. Otherwise, she has little to say and few thoughts, apart from those associated with attachment to her mother and dismay over being caught between Kaoru and Niou.

Her education is puzzling.[66] Kaoru finds her acceptably ladylike, and so in time do Nakanokimi and Niou. One readily assumes that her

---

[64] Mitani Kuniaki, "Genji monogatari daisanbu no hōhō," 102.
[65] Akiyama, *Genji monogatari no sekai*, 249-269.
[66] Nagai Kazuko ("Ukifune," 287) likewise found the way Ukifune's mother had neglected her daughter's education incomprehensible.

mother, who has always longed to marry her well and who knows life among the high nobility, has taught her proper deportment. However, it appears in "Azumaya" that she cannot play a single note of music, not even on the *wagon* (the instrument characteristic of the East),[67] and in "Tenarai" that her "unfortunate upbringing" never left her "the time for such things."[68] Her mother's ambition for her makes this incomprehensible. She also has no training in poetry, since she cannot join in when the nuns at Ono amuse themselves by composing poetry. Nonetheless, she manages in practice to write for herself, and to exchange with others, poems that show adequate familiarity with established poetic diction. Perhaps the most curious detail about her is her startling skill at *go* ("Tenarai")—one that even she seems not to expect.

Ukifune is very pretty, although Kaoru and Niou both assure themselves repeatedly that she has nothing like the distinction of Ōigimi or Nakanokimi; she is susceptible to sensual pleasure, which the loftier Ōigimi shunned; and, in a dilemma that she cannot resolve, she is prone to spend more and more time lying on the floor listening to other people talk. She is passive. Her one act of resistance occurs when Kaoru sends her a letter revealing that he knows what has been going on between her and Niou: she sends it back, claiming that it has been delivered to the wrong person. Kaoru smiles at her response, reflecting that he did not know she had it in her. Still, her gesture is one of passive rather than active resistance. A more ordinary man than Kaoru might laugh, wonder what kind of fool she takes him for, and either drop her or move her elsewhere immediately.

Her attempt to die highlights her passivity. She does not think of drowning until she hears her mother and the other women talking about how many people have drowned in the river. No doubt she makes active preparations (destroying her papers, writing farewell poems), but when the moment comes she cannot go through with it, as she herself recalls after the exorcism, when her mind clears and she remembers some of what happened to her.

---

[67] TTG, 1004; GM 6:100.
[68] TTG, 1085; GM 6:302.

I threw myself into the water (didn't I?) because I could bear no more. But where am I now? She tried and tried to remember, and at last it came to her that she had been in dark despair. They were all asleep, and I opened the double doors and went out. There was a strong wind blowing, and I could hear the river's roar. Out there all alone I was frightened, too frightened to think clearly about what had happened or what was to come next, and when I stepped down onto the veranda I became confused about where I was going. I only knew that going back in would not help and that all I wanted was to disappear bravely from life. Come and eat me, demons or whatever things are out there, do not leave me to be found foolishly cowering here! I was saying that, rooted to the spot, when a very beautiful man approached me and said, 'Come with me to where I live!'; and it seemed to me that he took me in his arms. I assumed that he was the gentleman they addressed as 'Your Highness', but then my mind must have wandered, until he put me down in a place I did not know. Then he vanished. When it was over I realized that I had not done what I had meant to do, and I cried and cried. After that, though, I remember nothing."[69]

She became frightened and confused on the veranda *(sunoko)*, and she never reached the river at all.[70] Perhaps she wished to embrace death bravely, but in reality she cowered there and begged the spirits to come out of the dark and do for her what she could not do for herself.[71] So one did. She was "taken" at her own request.

---

[69] TTG, 1083; GM 6:296.

[70] A model of the Uji house, made at Chūbu University, shows the river running right past it, roughly in the place where the lake would be relative to a *shinden* dwelling in the city. A gallery broken by a "middle gate" *(chūmon)* runs from the house to where the *tsuridono* would be, but instead of a *tsuridono* there is a gate in the fence that surrounds the compound. Beyond the fence, a few steps lead down to the river. For a plan and photograph, see Tsunoda and Kanō, *Genji monogatari no chiri*, 395.

[71] Similarly, in "Yokobue" the ghost of Kashiwagi comes to the sound of Yūgiri playing the flute that Kashiwagi once treasured; and, in "Agemaki," Ōigimi implores the spirit of her father to "gather me to you, wherever you are!" Her sister then has a vivid dream of him.

It is widely assumed that after the exorcism she recovers her wits fully and permanently. However, her attitude at Ono is unusual. She displays little human affect toward the nuns (the Sōzu's sister and mother, and their women) who have gladly given her refuge, regarding them all with disdain. She who grew up in the East contemplates their drab colors and self-pityingly remembers the elegant women who used to surround her in the capital. One wonders when that can have been. Nor is she grateful to Kannon for saving her life. She refuses to accompany the Sōzu's sister on a pilgrimage to Hasedera, reflecting that she has no wish to travel that way with people she does not even know and protesting silently that, in any case, Kannon has never done anything for *her*. She seems to be elsewhere. In fact, she appears still to be under the spirit's sway and so at least partially deranged.

She and the Sōzu both continue to suspect and fear the spirit's presence. When she begs him to make her a nun ("Tenarai") the narrator remarks:

> His Reverence could not understand it. What could have caused her, with all her beauty, so profoundly to detest what she was? The spirit possessing her had talked about that, he remembered. Yes, no doubt she has good reason! Why, it is a wonder that she even survived! She is in fearful danger, now that that evil thing has noticed her.[72]

And the Sōzu says when at last he tells Kaoru about her ("Yume no ukihashi"):

> "I performed [the exorcism], and after that the young woman at last revived and became human; but she told me sadly that she felt as though the thing that had possessed her was still with her after all, and that she wanted to escape its evil influence and devote herself to praying for the life to come.[73]

The Sōzu's fear for her is one reason he ordains her, despite his doubts about the wisdom of doing so. He hopes that being a nun will help to protect her.

---

[72] TTG, 1099; GM 6:336.
[73] TTG, 1114; GM 6:377.

The wavering character of her memories recalls someone whose madness still leaves her spells of relative lucidity. She often insists that she remembers nothing, and although sometimes she seems to be lying, at other times she seems to be speaking the truth. She remembers more in her lucid moments, when the spirit's grip weakens, and less when it grows stronger.

A moment of severe fright shocks her into her clearest memories in "Tenarai." She is not yet a nun, and the former son-in-law of the Sōzu's sister is pursuing her. To escape his advances she seeks refuge in a room she has never entered before, that of the Sōzu's mother. The old nun wakes up in the middle of the night and sees her lying there. "Who are you and what are you doing here?" she demands to know. The terrified Ukifune takes her for a demon.

> "She is going to eat me! she thought. That time when the demon made off with me I was unconscious—it was so much easier! What am I to do? She felt trapped. I came back to life in that shocking guise, I became human, and now those awful things that happened are tormenting me again! Bewilderment, terror—oh yes, I have feelings! And if I had died I would now be surrounded by beings more terrifying still![74]

The elusive original suggests that the "shocking guise" she remembers is that of a body—hers—possessed by an alien power: the one the monks found at the Uji Villa.[75] She grasps that after her initial ordeal she remained in a non-human guise (since an angry spirit is not human) until the exorcism restored her sufficiently to humanity (hito to narite) that she could manage daily life; and in this moment when shock has returned her most fully to herself, she realizes that despite her usual remoteness and coldness she has human feelings after all. Her thoughts then begin to range "as never before over the whole course of her life," which she now remembers in a normal way.[76]

---

[74] TTG, 1097; GM 6:330-331.

[75] "Shocking" is imiji, the adjective used self-descriptively by the spirit of Rokujō in the possession scene involving Murasaki ("Wakana Two").

[76] In "Yume no ukihashi," Ukifune describes her wavering state of consciousness as follows to the Sōzu's sister: "You see, the reason I told you nothing is that I hated to imagine you then knowing that I had kept so much from you. The distressing spectacle

These memories convince her that Niou was a reprehensible bounder whom she should have shunned at all costs, but she feels at the same time a fond regret for Kaoru. "No, no, I *must* not feel that way!" she silently reproves herself. "I will not have it!"[77] She is determined instead to become a nun.

Ukifune first mentioned this desire after her exorcism and her recollection of the "very beautiful man." At the time the Sōzu's sister allowed her to receive the five precepts given to laymen, but no more. Later on, when this lady and most of the rest of the household are away on pilgrimage to Hasedera, the Sōzu comes to the house, and Ukifune seizes this opportunity to ask him to ordain her.

This is a strange ambition for a young woman, as the narrative has pointed out before, and the "Tenarai" chapter stresses repeatedly that such a step is an unnatural and dangerous, especially for a young woman with Ukifune's looks. Whether or not she deserves praise for wishing to take it depends on the source of her desire to do so. To be praiseworthy it must be hers, conceived in response to an inner urge all her own. However, it could just as well be her demon's, devised in the service of that demon's own purposes; and the demon has reason to force her to become a nun. Long ago, disaster and dishonor left Suzaku's daughter no other choice once she had borne Kaoru, who remains in thrall to the memory of Ukifune.

Ukifune begs the Sōzu to make her a nun immediately, pleading that she feels extremely unwell and that in fact she may be dying. "My state now is just as bad as it was last time," she says, referring to when she received the five precepts, "and I feel so ill already that if I get much worse the precepts will no longer do me any good."[78] The

---

I undoubtedly made must have offended you, but I could not remember anything of my past then, I suppose because I was not in my right mind and because my soul, if that is the word, was no longer what it had been. But then I heard the gentleman they told me was the Governor of Kii talking to you about people I felt I had once known, and it seemed to me that I was beginning to remember things. I went on thinking about it all after that, but I still could not grasp anything clearly..." (TTG, 1118; GM 6:389) This moment occurs some time after Ukifune's thoughts have ranged "as never before over the whole course of her life."

[77] TTG, 1097; GM 6:331.
[78] TTG, 1099; GM 6:337.

narrative says nothing about the nature of her illness, but since she herself associates it with a time of great physical weakness and even worse mental disturbance provoked by spirit possession, her condition now probably has a similar cause. However, Imai Gen'e suggested that in fact there is nothing wrong with her and that she is simply lying in the service of her higher aspiration.[79]

Imai did so in the context of his argument that Ukifune is "a modern version of Kaguya-hime,"[80] the heroine of *Taketori monogatari.* Early in "Tenarai" the Sōzu's sister herself made this association,[81] and Imai and others, especially Kobayashi Masaaki, have developed the idea.[82] Imai conceded that Ukifune is of the earth, unlike Kaguya-hime, whose home is the heavens, but he read her becoming a nun, hence liberating herself from the world, as a metaphorical parallel to Kaguya-hime's return to the moon.[83] Thus he accepted the fittingness of everything she thinks and does toward that noble goal, and approved her lies as skillful means.

However, Ukifune cannot really be Kaguya-hime, whose celestial nature is fundamentally different from that of the earthly couple who nurture her. Kaguya-hime is a fairy, a magical being, and it is no wonder that she should return in the end to another world. However, the Ukifune of "Ukifune" and earlier is not like that; nor is the one of "Tenarai" and later, except that the spirit seems to have separated her mind from her body. Her body remains as earthly as ever, but her mind rejects any relationship not only with her past but also with her worldly present. She refuses to recognize any relationship between herself and the Sōzu's sister or anyone else at Ono, as Imai acknowledged. He attributed this to her courage and her lofty resolve, of which he, like many others, wrote movingly.

---

[79] Imai, "Ukifune no zōkei," 62.

[80] Imai, "Ukifune no zōkei, p. 62.

[81] "[The Sōzu's sister] was as wonder-struck as the old bamboo cutter must have been when he found Kaguya-hime, and she waited apprehensively to see through what crack [Ukifune] might vanish forever." (TTG, 1085; GM 6: 302)

[82] Kobayashi, "Saigo no Ukifune" and "Ukifune no shukke."

[83] Imai, "Ukifune no zōkei," 58.

Nonetheless, despite her wish to become a nun, the narrative conveys only her dismay at having to suffer the presence of the Ono nuns. To her they are drab, officious, tedious, and crude. She has no sympathy for them and no gratitude, either. In time she becomes a nun herself, but she remains ashamed of her appearance. She may study the sutras, but there is no sign that she learns anything from them in the way of either wisdom or compassion. In her radically selfish state her thoughts are unrelated to her own circumstances. Her memories of elegant surroundings in the Capital (Kaguya-hime's palace in the moon) are hardly more than fantasies, and her conception of the religious life is so constricted that it is little more than a fantasy either. An earthly young woman whose thoughts are Kaguya-hime's is deranged, and those who care for her risk serious trouble.

The Sōzu's fall

The Sōzu is an example. Kozaishō is the only gentlewoman listening when he tells the empress about the young woman found at Uji. Kaoru, her lover, soon hears the story too and realizes who the young woman must be. By the end of "Tenarai" he is all but certain. At the start of "Yume no ukihashi" he visits the Sōzu on Mt. Hiei, questions him, and discovers exactly where she is. He also lets the Sōzu know that Ukifune is *his* responsibility. She is his, not the Sōzu's, to dispose of.

Kaoru is a very great lord, and the Sōzu, a senior and respected member of the Buddhist hierarchy, wilts before him. Upon learning the truth, "His Reverence felt as though he had committed a grave error in turning a young woman so important to [Kaoru] into someone now dead to the world."[84] Not that Kaoru flaunts his rank; it is simply self-evident. Having once removed himself entirely from the profane world, the Sōzu is now again under its sway. Like Suzaku, he has compromised himself by ordaining a young woman.

It all began at the Uji Villa, when he decided not to leave Ukifune to die, but his critical gesture was coming down from Mt. Hiei to exorcise her. After hesitating a moment, he reflected that "a tie already links me

---

[84] TTG, 1114; GM 6:377.

to her" and decided to proceed. His sister and his disciples both saw "that it might not redound to his credit if it were to be noised about that he had left deep retreat on the Mountain to pray earnestly for a woman who really meant nothing to him at all." However, he brushed their objections aside.

As a monk I am hopeless enough already," he said, "and I am sure I violate this precept or that all the time, but I have never suffered reproach over a woman, nor have I ever erred in that direction. If I do so now, when I am over sixty years old, it will only have been my destiny."[85]

The exorcism therefore commits him further to Ukifune, and when at last she begs him to ordain her he cannot refuse. Now his fate is so entangled with hers that he has no choice but to cooperate ignominiously with Kaoru in undoing what he has done.

Kaoru, who brought Ukifune's young half-brother along to use as a go-between, asks the Sōzu to give the boy a note for Ukifune. "It would be a sin for me to play any such part in bringing you to her," the Sōzu replies, but Kaoru protests immaculate intentions:

"I am mortified that my request should seem to you to carry the danger of sin. I myself hardly understand how I can have lived this long as a layman....I take care never to do what the Buddha forbids, to the extent that I understand these things, and at heart I am no less than a holy man myself. How could I possibly place myself at risk of sin in so trivial a matter?...I shall be perfectly happy if only I am able to discover her circumstances for myself and to set her mother's heart at rest."[86]

It has often been suggested that the theme of the Uji chapters is Kaoru's simultaneous preoccupation with love and renunciation,[87] and this passage has been cited to show that this preoccupation remains unresolved to the end. However, by this time Kaoru's protestations ring hollow, and his claim to be "no less than a holy man" sounds

85 TTG, 1083; GM 6:294.
86 TTG, 1115; GM 6:380-381.
87 For example, Mitani Kuniaki, "Genji monogatari daisanbu no hōhō," 87-88; and Suzuki Hideo, "Uji no monogatari no shudai," 355-391.

fanciful at best. One can hardly tell whether he means what he says, whether he is lying in order to secure the Sōzu's cooperation, or whether the narrator is simply repeating platitudes about him. In any event, the Sōzu cannot presume to press him. He must accept Kaoru's words at face value. He therefore writes the note, which is indeed a sin, and hands it to the boy, to whom he then suddenly begins making unseemly advances. Such is his fall from the venerable height that he occupied early in "Tenarai."

The ending

In the last scene of the chapter and the book, Kaoru sends Ukifune's half-brother to her with the Sōzu's note and a letter from himself, expecting that the boy will talk to her and arrange for him to do the same. Instead, Ukifune will neither acknowledge Kaoru's letter as concerning her nor recognize her brother, let alone talk to him. However, the intense pressure on her (from a brother she once liked, from her spiritual advisor, from Kaoru, from the nuns around her) rouses her to nothing resembling self-possessed refusal.

Instead it incapacitates her. The more she is pressed to respond normally (angry resistance, acknowledgment of the inevitable, affection for mother and brother, concession of fondness for Kaoru, consideration for the nuns, defense of her dignity as a nun, and so on), the more she recedes into paralyzed inhumanity. Soon, nothing is left of her but a voice repeating that she is unwell, very unwell; that a letter plainly addressed to her must be for someone else; and that *although she is trying to remember* these people who claim to know her, she remembers no one and nothing. She can only lie prostrate with her face buried in her clothes. In her story all these signs, especially her failure of memory, are symptoms of possession. Kikuta Shigeo observed that the only way for Ukifune to resist the various pressures on her, so as not to stray from the long path to salvation that lies before her, is to "disguise herself in insentience" *(hijō ni jiko o yosou);*[88]

---

[88] Kikuta, "Azumaya, Ukifune, Kagerō, Tenarai, Yume no ukihashi," 148.

but the Sōzu's sister gives the boy a better explanation. "There may be a spirit afflicting her," she says.[89] There is indeed.

Ukifune's half brother returns to Kaoru, and the lines describing his reaction close the book:

> Kaoru, who had awaited him eagerly, was confounded by this inconclusive outcome. He reflected that he would have done better to refrain and went on to ponder, among other things, the thought that someone else might be hiding her there, just as he himself had once, after full deliberation, consigned her to invisibility.[90]

Beyond the ending

Arthur Waley found this ending "perfect," and for Mitani Kuniaki the void that follows it perfectly concludes the Uji chapters.[91] Others, however, have wanted to know what happened afterwards. *Yamaji no tsuyu* therefore continues the story: Ukifune meets both Kaoru and her mother again after all. *Kumogakure rokujō* (Muromachi?) takes the story still further, in a thoroughly respectable manner. In the "Sumori" chapter Kaoru returns Ukifune to lay life and entrusts her to his wife, the Second Princess; and in the "Nori no shi" chapter Ukifune figures as Sanjō no Ue, the mother of two of Kaoru's children. She and Kaoru take the precepts together at Yokawa.

The following speculation about what happens beyond the end of the tale claims no virtue but consistency with the above discussion. It is offered only in a spirit of play.

Readers have often imagined Ukifune setting out resolutely toward a higher goal and, like the author of *Yamaji no tsuyu*, seen her continuing to do so, under her present circumstances, into the future.[92]

---

[89] TTG, 1119; GM 6:393.

[90] TTG, 1120; GM 6:395.

[91] Waley, "Review of *Ivan Morris's The World of the Shining* Prince," 378; Mitani Kuniaki, "Genji monogatari daisanbu no hōhō," 104.

[92] Imai Gen'e, for example, wrote of her finding peace in spending the rest of her life as a solitary nun ("Ukifune no zōkei," p. 61). However, Hirota Osamu cast doubt on this view when he characterized Ukifune's story as one not of salvation but of "absence of

However, it is difficult to see how she could do so. Unless she is to set out alone, begging her way along the roads and exposing herself at the same time to many obvious perils, she will continue to require the support and care of others who wish her well. For the moment these others are the Ono nuns, with whom her relationship is vital, whether she acknowledges it or not. Unfortunately, her complete withdrawal from human contact at the end of "Yume no ukihashi" leaves these nuns in an impossible position. If the Sōzu cannot defy Kaoru, the nuns can still less defy both of them. The first time Ukifune rejected a letter from Kaoru on the grounds that it was not for her, she risked provoking him either to abandon her or to reclaim her against her will. By doing so again, she abdicates any responsibility for her own fate. She can do nothing for herself, since she has removed herself completely from her own situation, and there is nothing the nuns can do for her either. They will have to yield in one way or another to Kaoru's wishes. And this is to speak only of Kaoru. How long will Ukifune's brother keep the news from his mother, and what dramatic scene will follow when she finds out? The author of *Yamaji no tsuyu* has Ukon (summoned by Kaoru) plan elaborate precautions to prevent an unseemly outburst and a dangerous failure of discretion before she and the boy tell Ukifune's mother that Ukifune is still alive.

Above all, there is Niou. Near the end of "Tenarai" Kaoru reflects:

"How strange it will feel if this young woman really turns out to be she! How can I make sure? People may well think me an idiot if I start making inquiries in person, and if His Highness [Niou] were to hear of it he would certainly do everything in his power to prevent her from following the path she has chosen. Perhaps Her Majesty said nothing, despite her knowledge of this extraordinary matter, because *he* asked her not to. If *he* is involved I shall have to consider her well and truly dead, however strongly I may feel about her.[93]

---

salvation" (Hirota Osamu, "Jusui shinai Ukifune, seichō shinai Kaoru," in Sekine Kenji, ed., *Genji monogatari: Uji jūjō no kuwadate*, Ōfū, 2005, p. 144).
[93] TTG, 1109; GM 6:366.

He can hardly think of Ukifune without fearing that Niou will find out, too, or that he may already have done so. This fear surfaces again in the book's last sentence, when Kaoru ponders "the thought that someone else might be hiding her there, just as he himself had once, after full deliberation, consigned her to invisibility."

In love and rivalry Kaoru and Niou have long been inseparable, and each in his way has been unswerving in his pursuit of Ukifune. The idea of giving up never occurs to either one. A year ago, neither knew what had happened to her, but now Kaoru has found out, and the plot mechanism of the Uji chapters makes it as certain as the orbits of the planets that Niou will soon find out, too. The author of *Yamaji no tsuyu* felt the same inevitability. By the time her chapter ends, the only question in the reader's mind is not *whether* Niou will find out, but when and how, and what will happen then.

The tale's final sentence therefore hints that Kaoru's renewed pursuit of Ukifune is about to be joined by Niou's, although in a more corrupt mood. After all, Ukifune is now a nun, living among nuns. Seen this way, the narrative stops at a brief null point in a tormented process, the progress of which beyond that point can be imagined from what precedes it. In a manner painful for all concerned, Ukifune has turned Kaoru away. Stillness and reflection follow, but surely not for long.

Once, Ukifune could have chosen Niou or Kaoru, but inability to do so delivered her instead to an evil spirit. Kannon prevented the spirit from killing her, but it was too powerful to quell. Ukifune's disappearance then suspended the rivalry between Kaoru and Niou.

The perfect way to revive that rivalry more destructively than ever is to insure that once Kaoru and Niou find her again she remains incapable of choice, fight, or flight; and that is just what the spirit does. In her condition of infinite, mesmerizing passivity—one that demands everything and gives back nothing—she resembles a vortex into which all involved with her risk falling.

Neither Niou nor Kaoru could ever visit Uji easily, but the journey was always more difficult for Niou. Each trip there to see Ukifune placed his future in jeopardy. By the end of "Ukifune," his success in escaping detection (except by Kaoru) already strains credulity. Once his rivalry with Kaoru resumes, past the end of the book, the tension between them will rise to a new pitch. One way or another the affair will come to light. There will be a colossal scandal, into which will vanish the Sōzu's reputation, Kaoru's career, the good name of Yūgiri (Niou's father-in-law), and Niou's viability as the next emperor. Niou is Genji's grandson. His downfall will discredit not only himself but also the empress (Genji's daughter) and her other children, including the current heir apparent (also Genji's grandson). The succession will shift to another line, and no grandson of Genji will ever reign. Could the angry spirit, all that remains of Suzaku, wish for more?[94]

Conclusion: Ukifune and the author

This essay has argued that Ukifune was transported by a spirit, identified that spirit as Suzaku's, and argued that the spirit continues to influence her to the end of the tale. But did the author really mean anyone to think of Suzaku? Or is the case for identifying the spirit as Suzaku's merely an accidental byproduct of the process of composition? It is impossible to say. The essay has further maintained that in the last two chapters Ukifune is deranged and that her future promises nothing good.[95] This view, which differs from the usual evaluation of Ukifune and her role, undermines the autobiographical reading that makes of Ukifune an image of Murasaki Shikibu herself.

Tomikura Tokujirō remarked in a roundtable discussion in 1948, "When we moderns read *Genji*, we feel the youth or maturity of the author's development and grasp the evolution of this great work from that standpoint."[96] He seems to have meant that the later parts of the book convey the author's increasing maturity, which, for Saigō

---

[94] Niou is Suzaku's grandson too, but nothing in the text discourages the reader from imagining the existence of another candidate for heir apparent, outside Genji's line.

[95] Mitani Kuniaki ("Genji monogatari daisanbu no hōhō," 92) seemed to share a similar pessimism when he wrote, "The fact that Ukifune was refused even death, and that even intentionally becoming a nun could not bring her salvation, is merely a repetitive variation on [the] loss of identity [that pervades the Uji chapters as a whole]."

[96] "Zadankai 'Genji monogatari no seiritsu katei'," 58.

Nobutsuna as for others, culminates in Ukifune. Saigō wrote at about the same time:

> I believe that the instant in which the author finished the Uji chapters must have been the very instant in which she plunged herself wholly into Pure Land teaching, and the instant, too, when *monogatari* literature approached complete dissolution of self *[jiko hōkai]*. One can say that the value of *Genji monogatari* lies in its critical depiction, to the extent possible at the time and thanks to trueness of spirit *[tamashii no shinjitsusa]*, of the downfall of the aristocratic class.[97]

Saigō saw in Ukifune the author's attainment of both true Buddhist devotion and clairvoyant social awareness. Akiyama Ken wrote, "The attitude reached by Ukifune, that is to say, the position reached by the author through the evolution of the world of the tale, is none other than a critical attitude toward aristocratic society";[98] and Enomoto Masazumi considered the figure of Ukifune to reflect the author's "life experience."[99] More recently, Setouchi Jakuchō and Kawai Hayao gave this kind of interpretation mass prominence. Setouchi wrote that in describing Ukifune's ordination the author was really describing her own; that through her the author expressed her own deep longing for salvation; and that by writing Ukifune's story as a nun the author herself was saved.[100] Kawai (a psychologist) meanwhile argued that through Ukifune the author herself achieved full psychological individuation.[101] For Setouchi and Kawai, Murasaki attained full mastery and wisdom by creating a character dedicated to reaching that goal.

The reading developed in this essay discourages this approach, although it does not of itself put Murasaki Shikibu's authorship in question. There is unlikely to have been any such straightforward parallel between the author's state of mind at the end of the tale and

---

97 Saigō, "Genji monogatari no hōhō," 170 (originally published in 1950).
98 Akiyama, "Ukifune o megutte no shiron," 267.
99 Enomoto, "Ukifune ron e no kokoromi," 44.
100 Setouchi, *Genji monogatari no joseitachi*, 152-168.
101 Kawai, *Murasaki mandara*, 200-233.

the one that she imagined for Ukifune. However, there actually are reasons to question continuous authorship. Some matters already discussed bring the issue into focus with respect to the last two chapters. They suggest a possible change of author, or at least a transition to a new story, between "Ukifune" and "Tenarai."

One of these matters is the way Ukifune gets from her house to the Uji Villa. Nothing remotely like this occurs earlier in the tale. Ukifune's appearance under the tree at the Uji Villa has an arbitrary, fantastic character out of keeping with anything else in the book. Another is the confusion over how she traveled. A careful *mise-en-scène* in "Ukifune" convinces readers that Ukifune is about to drown herself, but most readers miss an even more elaborate one later on, designed to reveal that she did not. No doubt rationalist prejudices encourage this error, but the error also suggests a lapse of communication between the author and the reader. With Ukifune's reappearance at the Uji Villa, the reader's assumptions about the narrative fail. All unawares, the reader, too, enters a new world.[102]

Finally, the spirit's announcement that it killed Ōigimi is surprising, when nothing in "Agemaki" suggests such a thing. Kaoru never orders an exorcism for her, although, elsewhere in the tale, that would be the obvious thing to do under the circumstances. The best one can say is that the text does not actually exclude the possibility of a spirit.[103] If the spirit was active that early it must have influenced the whole Uji story and perhaps most of Kaoru's life, making the Uji chapters a sort of black parody of the main ones, in which Genji rises to unheard-of glory

---

[102] Mitani Kuniaki ("Genji monogatari daisanbu no hōhō," 103) pointed out that "Tenarai" begins with the expression *sono koro* ("at that time"), which he held to indicate a new narrator. Suzuki Hideo ("Uji no monogatari no shudai," 390) also noted that after "Kagerō" it is no longer Kaoru but Ukifune who carries the central theme *(shudai)* of the tale. Moreover Suzuki seems to have found the post-"Tenarai" chapters so different from the earlier ones in the Uji sequence that he carried neither of his discussions of Ukifune ("Ukifune monogatari shiron" and the essay just cited) past "Kagerō." However, these are merely indicative clues. Neither Mitani nor Suzuki suggested a significant discontinuity between "Ukifune" or "Kagerō" and "Tenarai."
[103] Ikeda, "Tenarai no maki mono no ke kō, 175-176.

despite the dark workings of Rokujō's bitterness.[104] However, it is only one line (the spirit's claim to have killed Ōigimi) that suggests such thoughts, and that line could have been planted, in a stroke of editorial genius supported by minor changes in "Agemaki," to sensational effect. By whom? No one will ever know, but it does no harm to wonder.

---

[104] Mitani Kuniaki ("Genji monogatari daisanbu no hōhō," 92) observed that the Uji chapters turn the main ones "upside down," although he had a different issue in mind. He wrote that while the "central theme" of the main chapters is kingship (ōken), the key concern of the Uji chapters is disempowerment and dispossession.

GENJI AND THE LUCK OF THE SEA

Genji scholars agree that the pattern of Genji's retreat to Suma, marriage at Akashi, fathering of a daughter there, and triumphant return to the capital draws on a *Nihon shoki* (also *Kojiki)* myth best known in English as "The Luck of the Sea and the Luck of the Mountains."[1] Haruo Shirane spelled out the parallel at length.[2] The myth centers on two brothers (Yamasachi-hiko, "Luck of the Mountains," and Umisachi-hiko, "Luck of the Sea"), whom Shirane identified with Genji and Suzaku. He associated the myth's other figures (indicated below) with the Akashi Novice, the lady from Akashi, and Murasaki. "Genji and the Luck of the Sea" will develop the relationship between the myth and the tale by linking the former to the cult of the Sumiyoshi deity, who plays so essential a role in restoring Genji's fortunes. By integrating the myth further into the background of the *Genji* narrative, the essay will recognize more fully its contribution to the story of Genji and Suzaku.

The following summary includes the correspondences that Shirane noted between the characters. Yamasachi-hiko appears in it as Hikohohodemi, the name more consistently used in *Nihon shoki*, and Umisachi-hiko as Honosusori. The rest of the essay will consistently refer to the story as the myth of Hikohohodemi.

Hikohohodemi (Genji) hunts with success in the mountains, while his older brother, Honosusori (Suzaku), fishes with equal success in the sea. The two then trade places, and Hikohohodemi borrows his brother's fishhook. A fish takes the hook. Hikohohodemi offers his

---

[1] Takada, *Genji monogatari no bungakushi*, 228. Takada identified the basic study of the subject as an article by Ishikawa Tōru, "Hikaru Genji ryūtaku no kōsō no gensen," first published in 1960 and included in his *Heian jidai monogatari bungaku ron*, Kasama Shoin, 1979.

[2] Shirane, *The Bridge of Dreams*, 77-79; Aston, *Nihongi* 92-95; Sakamoto Tarō, *Nihon shoki* 1:163-188; Philippi, *Kojiki*, 148-158; Kurano and Takeda, *Kojiki,* 135-147. For "The Luck of the Sea and the Luck of the Mountains," see Keene, *Anthology of Japanese Literature from the earliest era to the mid-nineteenth century*, 54-58.

brother others, but Honosusori insists on the original. Feeling ill-used, Hikohohodemi returns to the shore to look for it. Shiotsuchi no Oji ("Old Man Spirit of the Tides") then arranges passage for him to the palace of the sea god (the Akashi Novice), who welcomes him. He marries the sea god's elder daughter, Toyotama-hime (the Akashi lady), who is pregnant when he returns to the land. As a parting gift the sea god gives him a pair of magic jewels with which, in the upper realm, Hikohohodemi subdues his elder brother. Toyotama-hime then comes up on the shore to give birth. She forbids Hikohohodemi to look at her, but he disobeys and sees her true form: that of a creature of the deep. After bearing a son (Genji's daughter) she therefore returns forever, shamed and angry, to the sea. However, she sends her younger sister, Tamayori-hime (Murasaki), to look after the boy, who eventually marries Tamayori-hime and fathers the future Emperor Jinmu.[3] The discussion below will explain why Genji's daughter is rightly accepted as corresponding to Hikohohodemi's son.

Murasaki Shikibu must have known this myth. The evidence is almost too famous to need citing. Not only was she linguistically competent to read *Nihon shoki*, which is in Chinese, but she also wrote in her diary that the emperor had remarked, while listening to someone read him the tale, "She must have read the Chronicles of Japan!...She seems very learned."[4] What the emperor had in mind remains uncertain, but Takada Hirohiko confidently connected his remark to the myth of Hikohohodemi.[5]

The point of contact between the myth and *Genji* scholarship is a gloss in the fourteenth-century commentary *Kakaishō*. The gloss comments on a sentence at the very end of "Suma": "He [Genji] woke up and understood that the Dragon King of the Sea, a great lover of beauty, must have his eye on him."

---

[3] In later versions Tamayori-hime's role was often elided, and Toyotama-hime's son, Ugaya-fuki-awasezu-no-mikoto, was understood to be Emperor Jinmu himself. An example is the medieval *Sumiyoshi engi* (Yokoyama and Matsumoto, *Muromachi jidai monogatari taisei*, 59), which on p. 43 identifies Ugaya-fuki-awasezu as the *suijaku* ("manifest trace") of the Sumiyoshi deity.

[4] Bowring, *The Diary of Lady Murasaki*, 57.

[5] Takada, "Suma, à la croisée du lyrisme et du destin," 67.

When Hikohohodemi-no-Mikoto went to the sea's edge in search of the fishhook that he had lost, the Dragon King, impressed by his beauty, married him to his daughter Toyotama-hime and detained him for three years in his sea palace. This appears in the Chronicles of Japan.[6]

This comment mentions neither the brother (Honosusori, Suzaku) nor the other figures in the story. However, such glosses are limited by nature to the content of the particular expression or line to which they attached, and it is fair to gather from this one that the *Kakaishō* compiler had the whole myth in mind.

Takada described the account of the storm in "Suma" and "Akashi" as uniquely dynamic and marked by particularly intense supernatural interventions. He continued, "Only the [Hikohohodemi] myth was charged with sufficient energy to break through all references to historical figures comparable in their experience to Genji...and to create the vital conditions for the hero's rise to unequaled glory." He thus gave the myth a role not merely plausible but necessary in the background of the tale. Affirming the author's grasp of the precision and economy with which myth conveys the essential patterns of human behavior, Takada acknowledged at the same time that her elaboration on this fundamental pattern contrasts with the strikingly subtle psychological analysis otherwise characteristic of the tale. "Nonetheless," he wrote, "these two apparently opposed modes of expression come together remarkably well in the 'Suma' chapter." One broad thesis of these essays is that they do so equally well throughout most of the tale.

This essay will briefly introduce the Sumiyoshi Shrine and then turn to the role of Akashi (the place and the characters associated with it) in the tale. After linking Akashi to Sumiyoshi, it will develop the connection between Sumiyoshi and Jingū Kōgō, her son Ōjin, and Genji's rise. It will next discuss Genji's rise from the perspective of "kingship" *(ōken),* a major theme in Japanese *Genji* scholarship in

---

[6] Tamagami, *Shimeishō, Kakaishō*, 320. *Kachō yosei* develops this comment by explicitly likening Genji to Hikohohodemi, the Akashi Lady to Toyotama–hime, and her father to the dragon king (Ii, *Kachō yosei*, 99).

recent decades. Finally, it will link Sumiyoshi to the Hikohohodemi myth itself.

The Sumiyoshi Shrine

The modern Sumiyoshi Shrine is well inland, separated from the sea by reclaimed land and surrounded by the urban sprawl of Osaka. Long ago, however, it was on the shore of what is now Osaka Bay, not far south of the ancient port of Naniwa. Sumiyoshi dates back to the time of Jingū Kōgō, who (at least in legend) conquered Korea and gave birth to the roughly fifth-century emperor Ōjin. Its enduring association is with the sea. Heian poetry, including several examples in *The Tale of Genji*, praises the pines along the beach there and the white breakers glimpsed through their branches. Five reigning emperors, from Tenmu (r. 673-686) to Daigo (r. 897-930), went on pilgrimage to Sumiyoshi, as did such other notable figures as Fujiwara no Senshi (962-1002), the mother of Emperor Ichijō (r. 986-1011), in 1000; Fujiwara no Michinaga (966-1027) and his wife in 1003; and Fujiwara no Shōshi (988-1074), Ichijō's empress and Murasaki Shikibu's patron, in 1031.[7] Analysis of surviving evidence suggests that Murasaki Shikibu's family may have had a particular connection with Sumiyoshi,[8] but there is no need to emphasize this possibility. More important is the ancient link between Sumiyoshi and the Akashi so prominent in the tale.

A first glimpse of Akashi

Akashi first appears in "Wakamurasaki." At the risk of covering already familiar ground, it will be worth discussing consecutively, from the present perspective, this passage and the later ones on Genji's experience there and at Suma.

In "Wakamurasaki" Genji visits a healer at a temple in the mountains north of the capital. Never having left the city before, he marvels at everything he sees along the way. Soon he and his

---

[7] For Senshi and Shōshi: Tanaka Suguru, *Sumiyoshi Taisha shi* 3:38, citing *Midō Kanpaku ki*, *Shōyūki*, and other sources. For Michinaga: Koyama, *Genji monogatari: kyūtei gyōji no tenkai*, 195, citing *Kachō yosei*.
[8] Sakamoto Kazuko, "'Urazutai' kō."

companions are gazing out over more picturesque vistas than he has ever seen. His companions, who rank below him and so travel more, tell him about still greater wonders in distant regions, and one chimes in to praise the more accessible coast at Akashi in the province of Harima. "Not that any single feature of it is so extraordinary," he says, "but the view over the sea there is somehow more peaceful than elsewhere."[9]

The young men have just mentioned Mt. Fuji and "another peak," perhaps Mt. Asama: two great volcanoes that Genji will never see. With Akashi the conversation returns to a spot less remote, but still barely within the same class of beautiful, far-off places that Genji is unlikely ever to visit in person. Akashi (now a city in Hyōgo Prefecture) is situated on the coast of the Inland Sea, seven or eight kilometers west of Suma (now a seaside park within the city of Kobe), which Genji chose in time as his place of exile. His choice rests on literary precedent (that of the historical Ariwara no Yukihira), but it probably has to do also with Suma's location. Suma and Akashi were then in different provinces, despite the short distance between them. Suma was near the western edge of Settsu, while Akashi was just across the border in Harima. Settsu was one of the Kinai ("Inner") provinces immediately surrounding the capital and therefore nominally under direct imperial rule, while Harima was one of the Kigai ("Outer") provinces, beyond the emperor's direct domain.[10] For this reason Akashi was not properly accessible to Genji, an emperor's son. A regulation issued in 853 prohibited even an imperial grandson from leaving the Kinai.[11] Genji may have found Suma painfully unfamiliar, but Akashi was legally alien to him.

If the view from Akashi "is somehow more peaceful than elsewhere," that may be because it includes the mountainous northern tip of Awaji, a large island only three or four kilometers away across the Inland Sea. A passage in "Akashi" describes "the island of Awaji looming in the

---

[9] TTG, 84; GM 1:202.

[10] Fujii Sadakazu first pointed out the significance of this Kinai/Kigai distinction in "Uta no zasetsu," 71.

[11] Kawazoe, *Genji monogatari hyōgen shi: yu to ōken no isō*, 358; quoting material cited by Takahashi Kazuo in "Genji monogatari: Suma no maki ni tsuite."

distance" under a bright moon while, for Genji, "an ineffable yearning seem[s] to fill all the world."[12] Set as it was on the mainland side of the strait, Akashi also marked the point at which the homeward-bound traveler, sailing in from the west, first glimpsed far ahead the hills of Yamato, and the traveler outward bound from the port of Naniwa (now Osaka) finally lost sight of those same hills.[13] Like Suma it was a post station on the coast road toward the west, but the number of post horses cited for each in *Engi shiki* (927) suggests that Akashi was by far the larger of the two.[14] Sure enough, in "Suma" Genji imagines Suma as isolated and only barely inhabited, hence just the kind of place he has in mind, while on arriving at Akashi he finds "the coast there...indeed exceptional, its only flaw being the presence of so many people."[15] Fortunately, the magnificence of his reception makes up for the lack of melancholy solitude.

After praising Akashi, Genji's retainer Yoshikiyo (the speaker in "Wakamurasaki") describes the unusual gentleman who has established himself there. He is not only a minister's son, but also, as the reader discovers later, a cousin of Genji's mother.[16] Eccentric and unsociable, he resigned a high post in the palace guards and personally requested appointment as governor of Harima. This extraordinary step meant a steep drop in rank. "He became a bit of a laughingstock in his province even so," Yoshikiyo says, "and being too embarrassed to return to the City, he shaved his head instead."[17] Thus the gentleman became a *nyūdō* ("novice"), a monk who has taken simple religious vows and continues to live at home.

So far the Akashi Novice sounds like something of a crank, but there is more to him than that. First, he is fabulously rich. As Yoshikiyo tells it, "He may never have made a name for himself in the City, but the sheer scale of the tract he has claimed for himself makes it obvious that he has arranged things...so as to spend the rest of his life in

---

12 TTG, 262-263; GM 2:239.

13 *Man'yōshū* 255, 256; cited by Matsuda, *Genji monogatari no chimei eizō*, 84.

14 Matsuda, *Genji monogatari no chimei eizō*, 82.

15 TTG, 261; GM 2:233.

16 Genji's maternal grandfather is his uncle.

17 TTG, 85; GM 1: 203.

luxury."[18] In "Akashi," Genji is amazed to find that the opulence of this eccentric's establishment rivals anything in the capital. The narrative makes no serious attempt to explain how an incompetent laughing-stock managed to come by all this. The Akashi Novice's mysterious wealth is simply an attribute of his.

The second striking thing about him is his affinity with the sea. Yoshikiyo reports with perplexity that, instead of retiring to a shelter-ed spot in the hills, the Akashi Novice "put himself right on the sea."[19] Yoshikiyo goes on to rationalize this choice, but the impression of strangeness remains, especially when he describes the old man's habitual injunction to his daughter. Yoshikiyo reports him as saying:

> "It is all very well for me to have sunk this low, but she is all I have, and I have [no ordinary marriage] in mind for her. 'If you outlive me,' he tells her, 'if my hopes for you fail and the future I want for you is not to be, then you are to drown yourself in the sea.'"[20]

One of Genji's companions remarks with a laugh, "She must be a rare treasure then, if her father means the Dragon King of the Sea to have her as his queen!" Intrigued, Genji reflects, "I wonder what it means that his ambitions for her reach all the way to the bottom of the sea."

Just as the Akashi Novice's wealth defies comprehension, his daughter's personal quality defies again and again, when at last Genji comes to know her, every conception of what is proper to the daughter of a provincial governor. Her music, near the end of "Akashi," moves Genji to compare her with Fujitsubo, his late father's empress, and with age he seems to find her vast dignity, boundless forbearance, and perfect judgment increasingly baffling. In "Wakana Two," twenty-eight years after first hearing about her, he says of her while reflecting on the women he has known, "I looked down at first on [her] as being

---

[18] TTG, 85; GM 1: 203. According to a regulation dated 895, former provincial governors of the fifth rank and above were forbidden to remain in their former province or to leave the Kinai (Kawazoe, *Genji monogatari hyōgen shi: yu to ōken no isō*, 358). This further confirms the Novice's anomalous character.
[19] TTG, 85; GM 1:203.
[20] TTG, 85; GM 1:204.

unworthy of me, and I assumed that she was a passing amusement, but her heart is an abyss beyond sounding *[nao kokoro no soko miezu]*. She has immeasurable depth" *[kiwa naku fukaki tokoro aru hito ni nan]*.[21] His words echo the deep-sea imagery of "Wakamurasaki" to describe a low-ranking woman whose qualities, taken together, all but transcend the human.

The storm at Suma

About six years after the scene in "Wakamurasaki," political and personal difficulties force Genji into self-imposed exile at Suma. There, a companion reminds him one day, "My lord, this is the day for someone with troubles like yours to seek purification."[22] He refers to a purification performed by a yin-yang master *(onmyōji)* beside the sea. It is unclear which of Genji's troubles the companion has in mind, but at any rate, Genji agrees to go. There on the shore he is engulfed by the great storm that eventually brings about his move to Akashi.

The plot importance of Genji's move is obvious. He would not otherwise meet the Novice's daughter, whose daughter by him is to become empress. However, the significance of the storm is less clear. It strikes suddenly, after Genji protests in a poem (quoted in "The Disaster of the Third Princess") his innocence before all the gods. The narrative never explains what he means, how the gods might take his words, or why they provoke the storm. For that reason the storm's significance has long been debated. The earlier essay acknowledges various views but argues among other things that Genji really is innocent in the gods' eyes. The different material presented below suggests the same conclusion.

Dawn is near, after the first night of the storm.

> When Genji, too, briefly dropped off to sleep, a being he did not recognize came to him, saying, "You have been summoned to the palace. Why do you not come?" He woke

---

21 TTG, 646; GM 4:210.
22 TTG, 252; GM 2:217.

up and understood that the Dragon King of the sea, a great
lover of beauty, must have his eye on him.[23]

Genji's understanding matches widely known legend and folklore. The
dragon king, continuous in a Buddhist world with the sea god
(*watatsumi*, "ocean," written with the characters "sea" and "god")
mentioned in *Kojiki* and *Nihon shoki*, represents the most generalized
conception of the deity of the sea. He inhabits an undersea palace, and
when agitated he causes storms. The *Kakaishō* author listed another
Nihon shoki example immediately after citing the more directly
relevant Hikohohodemi story: that of the hero Yamato Takeru. When
Yamato Takeru's ship was assailed by a violent storm, a concubine of
his threw herself into the sea to save him, and the storm ceased.[24]

Taketori monogatari (9th c.) provides another example. Kaguya-
hime, the heroine, sends a suitor off to slay "the dragon" and steal the
priceless jewel from its head. When a storm threatens the suitor's ship,
the helmsman attributes it to the enraged dragon and urges the suitor
to pray to "the deity" *(kami)*. The suitor therefore addresses the
"helmsman god" *(kajitori no on-kami)* and promises to desist; whereupon the thunder stops and a stiff wind finally drives the ship ashore
at Akashi.[25] The dragon and the helmsman god seem to be continuous
with each other, and this helmsman, himself a generalized sort of
divinity, merges easily in turn with the Sumiyoshi deity, as a passage
from *Tosa nikki* (ca. 935) suggests.[26]

In *Tosa nikki* the author and his party, returning to the capital from
Shikoku, are off the Sumiyoshi coast when a storm arises. The
helmsman suggests that the Sumiyoshi deity wants something. When
minor offerings fail, the author's party throws the most precious
object aboard, a bronze mirror, into the sea. The storm ceases
immediately, as it did when Yamato Takeru's concubine offered her

---

[23] TTG, 253; GM 2:219. The mysterious being can be likened to Shiotsuchi no Oji, who
facilitated Hikohohodemi's journey to the sea god's palace.

[24] Aston, *Nihongi*, 206; Sakamoto Tarō, *Nihon shoki* 1:304.

[25] Horiuchi and Akiyama, *Taketori monogatari, Ise monogatari*, 36-39.

[26] Tanaka (*Sumiyoshi Taisha shi* 2:56) identified the helmsman deity with Sumiyoshi
on this basis.

beauty to the sea.[27] Such concupiscence is typical of the dragon king, who in other stories, too, creates a storm in order to get a treasure that he covets. In Genji's case, that treasure is Genji himself. In other words, the *Genji* narrative suggests that the dragon king (the sea god, Sumiyoshi) created the storm in order to acquire him. Since he would not have done so if Genji had been flawed, he must have considered him innocent of any significant crime.

Although "the same being [keeps] haunting [Genji's] dreams,"[28] he ignores the dragon king's summons, and the storm rages on. How, indeed, could he respond? The *Kakaishō* author remarked that the dragon king wants Genji for his daughter;[29] but Genji, being only human, cannot travel like Hikohohodemi to the sea god's palace. Instead he can accept the Akashi Novice's hospitality and marry his daughter. The fabulously wealthy Novice, in his seaside domain across the Kinai-Kigai border, acts on this accessible earth as the dragon king of the sea. Where Genji is concerned, he therefore also shares in the power and will of Sumiyoshi.

Genji recognizes the continuity of nature and will between the dragon king and Sumiyoshi, for when the storm redoubles in fury he prays to Sumiyoshi,[30] as the suitor in *Taketori* prays to the divine helmsman, to help him. However it is his father who disposes him at last to heed the call of the deep by putting it in terms of plausible action. As the storm subsides and dawn approaches, the late emperor appears to Genji in a dream. "What are you doing in this terrible place?" he admonishes him. "Hasten to sail away from this coast, as the God of Sumiyoshi would have you do."[31] He explains that, finding his favorite son's plight unbearable, "I dove into the sea, emerged on the strand, and despite my fatigue am now hurrying to the palace to have a word with His Majesty [Suzaku] on the matter." Being in league with the dragon king and Sumiyoshi, he actually went to consult with them in the depths of the sea.

---

[27] Suzuki Chitarō, *Tosa nikki*, 51-52; Miner, *Japanese Poetic Diaries*, 83.

[28] TTG, 257; GM 2:223.

[29] Tamagami, *Shimeishō, Kakaishō*, 320.

[30] TTG, 258; GM 2:226.

[31] TTG, 259; GM 2:229.

Soon, still well before dawn, the Novice's boat arrives from Akashi. Genji remembers his dream and wonders that the man should have set sail so quickly through such tumultuous seas. And the Novice, too, has dreamed. Early in the same month, a "strange being" commanded him to prepare a boat for the journey to Suma, and on the supernaturally appointed day he therefore set off, propelled by an "eerie wind." Genji considers the Novice's invitation to Akashi, recalls his father's admonition, and accepts. On the way there, "The same wind blew, and the boat fairly flew....One could only marvel at the will of the wind." The boat reaches Akashi at daybreak, and at the sight of his guest the Novice "felt age dissolve and the years stretch out before him; he bowed at once to the God of Sumiyoshi, wreathed in smiles. The light of sun and moon seemed to him now to lie in his hand."[32]

The Novice's prayers to Sumiyoshi

Sumiyoshi has at last given the Novice the son-in-law he desires, and with him the hope that his granddaughter will one day be empress. Such is the burden of the prayers that, as the reader learns later in the same chapter, he has been addressing to Sumiyoshi for eighteen years, daily at home and, more solemnly, in twice-yearly pilgrimages to the deity's shrine. In "Akashi," however, his feeling of superhuman triumph is tempered by his awe of Genji.

His trans-human quality stands out clearly only much later, in "Wakana One," when his ambition is all but realized. His grand-daughter, now married to the heir apparent, has just given birth (at the age of thirteen) to a son destined to become emperor in his turn. She will be empress. At the news, the Novice writes his daughter a letter to tell her, among other things, the dream that began his quest:

> "My dear, one night in the second month of the year when you were born, I had a dream. My right hand held up Mt. Sumeru, and to the mountain's right and left the sun and moon shed their brightness on the world. I myself stood below, in the shadows under the mountain, and their light

---

[32] TTG, 261; GM 2:234.

did not reach me. I then set the mountain afloat on a vast ocean, boarded a little boat, and rowed away towards the west. That was my dream...Then you were conceived.[33]

His joy, when Genji steps out of the boat at Akashi, acknowledges this sacred dream, which thereafter governed his life. It must have come from Sumiyoshi, who adopted the Novice as an instrument of his will and so lifted him above the ordinary. The Novice also tells his daughter to reflect that she is a *henge* (a direct manifestation of a divine being), the same word that the bamboo cutter in *Taketori* used for the moon-princess Kaguya-hime; and he instructs her to make a pilgrimage of thanks to Sumiyoshi. With his letter he sends a box containing the texts of all the vows he made to the deity at his shrine. They astonish Genji. "How had a mere mountain ascetic managed even to conceive of such things?" he wonders, thinking of the Novice "with growing awe."[34]

It was the Novice himself who requested his posting to Harima, as Genji learned when he first heard of Akashi. Harima, and Akashi in particular, had close ties with Sumiyoshi. According to *Sumiyoshi Taisha jindaiki*, Jingū Kōgō was traveling eastward from Kyushu when she enshrined the Sumiyoshi deity on Mt. Fujishiro in Kii. The deity then declared a wish to reside in Harima. Accordingly, a length of *fuji* (wisteria) vine was cast into the sea, and the deity announced that he would live where it came ashore. That turned out to be Fujie, four kilometers west of the mouth of the Akashi River. The land between there and the river, known then as Nasuki-no-hama, was to be sacred ground *(shinchi)* and the property of the Sumiyoshi Shrine.[35] Another stretch of coast belonging to the shrine was further west, in the vicinity of Kakogawa.[36] In the Harima interior, Jingū Kōgō gave the shrine roughly a thousand square kilometers of timber forest *(somayama),* and vestiges of Sumiyoshi prominence survived in this area even into modern times.[37] Also according to *Jindaiki*, the tomb of

33 TTG, 611; GM 4:114.
34 TTG, 632; GM 4:168.
35 *Sumiyoshi Taisha jindaiki*, in Miyata, *Nihon shomin seikatsu shiryō shūsei*, vol. 26, 39-40.
36 *Sumiyoshi Taisha jindaiki*, 40.
37 *Sumiyoshi Taisha jindaiki*, 36; Tanaka, *Sumiyoshi Taisha shi* 2:301.

Jingū Kōgō's husband, Emperor Chūai, was built at Akashi with stone brought by boat from the island of Awaji.[38]

Sumiyoshi Taisha jindaiki, which claims the date 731, is a history of the Sumiyoshi Shrine. Its content parallels the corresponding *Nihon shoki* passages to a degree, but it includes much else as well. Tanaka Suguru, who studied the extant text in detail, concluded that it is founded on a retouched copy made for Emperor Kanmu's pilgrimage to Sumiyoshi in 789, while Ueda Masaaki assigned it to some time after 875.[39] All authorities agree that it is earlier than Murasaki Shikibu's time. Could she have known it? Few people saw it because it was a shrine treasure. Fukasawa Michio speculated that her uncle, Fujiwara no Tameyori, secured her permission to read it while he was governor of Settsu between 992 and 995.[40] If the Akashi Novice's personal choice of Harima involved (in the author's mind) the more precise intention to settle on the sacred ground of Nasuki-no-hama, this touch could have come only from *Jindaiki;*[41] however, that, too, is only speculation.

The Sumiyoshi Shrine and Jingū Kōgō

"Sumiyoshi" (also "Suminoe") is first of all a place name. *The Tale of Genji* and many other documents sum up the sacred presence there in such expressions as *Sumiyoshi no kami*, which translates most easily as "the Sumiyoshi deity." However, this presence is really composite. The Sumiyoshi Shrine at Naniwa had, and still has, four major sanctuaries. The first three enshrine Sokotsutsu-no-o, Nakatsutsu-no-o, and Uwatsutsu-no-o, the male deities of the bottom, middle depths, and surface of the sea. The fourth, according to *Jindaiki* as well as to shrine literature today, enshrines Jingū Kōgō. However, according to the canonical *Engi shiki*, two other important Sumiyoshi shrines, in Kyushu and in western Honshu, lacked this fourth sanctuary (as they

---

38 *Sumiyoshi Taisha jindaiki*, 30.

39 Tanaka, *Sumiyoshi Taisha shi* 2:248-249; Ueda, "Kaijin no genzō," 8.

40 Fukasawa, *Genji monogatari no shinsō sekai*, 17-19.

41 The surviving *Harima fudoki* fragment tells of Jingū Kōgō enshrining on Mt. Fujishiro not Sumiyoshi, but a child of the deity Niotsuhime (Akimoto, *Fudoki*, 483).

still do) and so honor only the triple deity of the sea.[42] Moreover, after Murasaki Shikibu's time the Sumiyoshi priest Tsumori Kunimoto (1026-1102), an active and successful poet, redefined the fourth sanctuary as the canonical poetess Sotōri-hime,[43] under the name Tamatsushima Myōjin. Thereafter Sumiyoshi was regarded as a great patron of poetry. Thus the close link at Sumiyoshi between the triple sea deity and Jingū Kōgō was not, strictly speaking, inevitable. It represents the perspective of *Kojiki*, *Nihon shoki* and *Jindaiki*. Murasaki Shikibu could have known no other.

According to *Kojiki* and *Nihon shoki*, the three Tsutsu deities were born when Izanagi escaped from the underworld and purified himself in the sea at a place in Kyushu called Tachibana no Odo.[44] Both sources identify them as the triple deity of Suminoe and the ancestor of the Azumi,[45] a major seafaring *(ama)* clan based in northern Kyushu. The Azumi supplied the priests of an important Sumiyoshi shrine there, but they also spread far along both coasts of Honshu.[46]

The Sumiyoshi deity (Sokotsutsu-no-o, Nakatsutsu-no-o, Uwatsutsu-no-o) first came to the attention of the Yamato court thanks to a dramatic oracle delivered to Emperor Chūai through Chūai's empress, Jingū Kōgō. The oracle announced a land of riches across the sea (Korea), one given to the emperor for his taking. However, Chūai refused to believe it. Enraged, the power addressing

---

[42] Ueda, "Kaijin no genzō," 6-7.

[43] The Japanese preface to the *Kokinshū* mentions Sotōri-hime, whose best-known poem appears in the collection as no. 1110. *Nihon shoki* tells her story at length (Sakamoto Tarō, *Nihon shoki* 1:440-444; Aston, *Nihongi*, 318-321; Cranston, *A Waka Anthology, Volume One*, 85-87). She also appears in the *Man'yōshū*.

[44] *Kojiki* and *Nihon shoki* describe Tachibana no Odo as being in "Himuka." If this "Himuka," written with characters later pronounced "Hyūga," corresponds to the later province of that name, then Tachibana no Odo was in modern Miyazaki-ken. However, Miyazaki-ken, in eastern Kyushu, is an unlikely setting for a story otherwise clearly situated in northern Kyushu, above all in the old province of Chikuzen (Fukuoka-ken). Therefore the weight of scholarly opinion redefines the meaning of "Himuka" and locates Tachibana no Odo in Fukuoka-ken (personal communication from John Bentley, May 2007).

[45] Kurano and Takeda, *Kojiki*, 71; Philippi, *Kojiki*, 69-70; Sakamoto Tarō, *Nihon shoki* 1:94-95; Aston, *Nihongi*, 27.

[46] Ueda, "Kaijin no genzō," 7.

him declared that he would therefore not rule that land; no, the son that his empress was to bear would rule it instead. In *Nihon shoki*, Chūai sickened and died nearly five months later, but in *Kojiki* and *Jindaiki* he died on the spot. As for the son, *Kojiki* and *Nihon shoki* allow the reader to assume that the empress was already pregnant and that the child was Chūai's. However, Mishina Shōei gathered from both accounts that the possessing deity (at this point still unidentified) had impregnated the empress and that the child was his.[47] *Jindaiki* makes this reading explicit. The deity utters his reproach, and "That night the emperor sickened and died. Thereupon secret commerce occurred *[hisokagoto ari]* between the empress and the great deity." An ancient gloss now included in the text states, "This means that they engaged in the intimate intercourse of husband and wife."[48] Soon, in a further possession, the possessing powers identified themselves. *Jindaiki* mentions the triple Tsutsu deity (Sumiyoshi); *Kojiki* adds Amaterasu; and *Nihon shoki*, which names all four, adds others as well.[49] Jingū Kōgō's story, and especially her presence in the fourth Sumiyoshi sanctuary at Naniwa, suggests that Sumiyoshi is paramount among these. Jingū Kōgō had indeed become the wife of Sumiyoshi, as she continued to be in *Usa Hachimangū takusenshū*, a fundamental document of the medieval Hachiman cult.[50]

Mishina Shōei characterized this union as a sacred marriage between a deity and a divine woman of the sea, like the one between Hikohohodemi and Toyotama-hime, the sea god's daughter. Toyotama-hime gave birth on the shore to Ugayafukiaezu-no-mikoto, the father of Jinmu, the founder of the imperial line; and it is also on the shore that Jingū Kōgō bore the future Emperor Ōjin, whose enormous tomb mound *(kofun)* at Konda, near Osaka, is the largest in Japan. Mishina described her story and her son's as one of the *kunitsukuri* ("realm-making") that celebrates a new era.[51] This associ-

---

[47] Mishina, "Ōjin Tennō to Jingū Kōgō," 70.

[48] *Sumiyoshi Taisha jindaiki*, 27.

[49] The *Nihon shoki* account recalls the attempts made in the "Aoi" chapter of *Genji* to identify the power tormenting Aoi.

[50] Mishina, "Ōjin Tennō to Jingū Kōgō," 74.

[51] Mishina, "Ōjin Tennō to Jingū Kōgō," 68.

ation of renewal with the birth and reign of Ōjin recalls the renewal brought about by Genji's triumphant return to the capital from Akashi and his shadow-reign through Reizei, his son.[52]

Kojiki (although not *Nihon shoki*) states that Jingū Kōgō's distant ancestor was Ame-no-hihoko ("Celestial Sun Spear"), a legendary prince from the Korean kingdom of Silla, who arrived in Japan bearing treasures associated with mastery of wind and sea. Ame-no-hihoko's descendants settled in Chikuzen province (northern Kyushu), where Jingū Kōgō's career began. Thus she came ultimately from the same land across the sea that the possessing deity invited her earthly husband, Chūai, to take, and that she then set out to conquer herself.

While she prepared her campaign, the triple Tsutsu deity promised in another oracle to protect her person and to assure her success in war. Indeed, she carried her conquest through thanks above all to supernatural control of the tide, which overwhelmed the Silla army. Therefore Jingū Kōgō first enshrined her protector not in Japan, but in Silla.[53] After returning to Japan and bearing her son, she founded the deity's first shrine in Japan at "Anato no Yamada-mura." This is the Sumiyoshi Shrine in Shimonoseki. Then she sailed eastward on a path that would lead her and her son, via Naniwa and Ōmi province, to Tsuruga on the Japan Sea, where the Kehi Shrine honors Ame-no-hihoko's sword. In other words, she followed the route that her ancestor had taken long before.[54]

---

[52] Fukasawa Michio *(Genji monogatari no shinsō sekai,* 12) suggested a connection between Ōjin and Genji when he argued that the *Jindaiki* account of the sacred marriage between Sumiyoshi and Jingū Kōgō inspired the *Genji* author to imagine the affair between Fujitsubo and Genji—an affair that she then made the "core" *(jiku)* of her "tale of kingship" *(ōken monogatari).* Although not especially persuasive, the idea is no less so than the one favored by those scholars who believe, because of visible lexical influence in telltale spots, that the affair between Genji and Fujitsubo is derived from *Ise monogatari,* especially the "imperial huntsman" episode (no. 69). The thematic inspiration possibly provided by *Ise monogatari* goes no further than an instance of transgressive lovemaking between the hero and a priestess-princess. No consequences ensue.

[53] Philippi, *Kojiki,* 263, Kurano and Takeda, Kojiki, 232; *Sumiyoshi Taisha jindaiki,* 30.

[54] Mishina, "Ōjin Tennō to Jingū Kōgō," 122-123.

On the way, the triple Tsutsu deity declared his desire to reside at "Ōtsu no Nunakura no Nagao," so that he might watch the ships passing back and forth.[55] *Jindaiki* and *Settsu fudoki* confirm that this spot was in Suminoe (Sumiyoshi) county of Settsu province. It belonged to Tamomi no Sukune, whom Toyoshima Hidenori likened to the Akashi Novice.[56] Jingū Kōgō wished at first to become the deity's priestess, but the deity refused to accept her service, appointing instead Tamomi no Sukune and his descendants in perpetuity.[57] According to *Jindaiki*, she then declared her wish to reside together with the deity; hence the fourth sanctuary of the shrine. Tamomi's descendants constituted the Tsumori clan, whose members appear repeatedly in the records not only as priests of the Sumiyoshi Shrine, but also as envoys to the continent.[58] As priests, too, they participated in overseas voyages, being entrusted with shipboard rites to ensure safe ocean passage.[59] In this way the Sumiyoshi deity continued to support relations with the continent. Tsumori power seems to have followed the westward spread of Yamato sovereignty and so to have absorbed the sea deity of the Azumi clan of northern Kyushu.[60]

When the deity refused Jingū Kōgō's offer of service, he promised to guard the emperor, the imperial realm, and the people. Later, he repeated his undertaking to defend the emperor and the realm as pervasively as "mists rising in the morning and in the evening."[61] Jingū Kōgō's fidelity to Sumiyoshi, her triumphs, and her long reign had won this pledge of divine protection. The word "reign" is used here advisedly. From the standpoint of later, accepted history Jingū Kōgō was never more than a regent for her son, but *Jindaiki* is not alone in referring to her repeatedly as *tennō* (emperor). Other examples occur in the *fudoki* and elsewhere.[62] Such early documents, especially *Jindaiki*,

---

[55] Aston, *Nihongi*, 237-238, Sakamoto Tarō, *Nihon shoki* 1:344.

[56] Toyoshima, "Suma, Akashi no maki ni okeru shinkō to bungaku no kisō," 172.

[57] *Sumiyoshi Taisha jindaiki*, 31.

[58] Ueda, "Kaijin no genzō," 9.

[59] Shinkawa, "Umi no tami," 149.

[60] Ueda, "Kaijin no genzō," 10.

[61] *Sumiyoshi Taisha jindaiki*, 34.

[62] Mishina, "Ōjin Tennō to Jingū Kōgō," 76.

therefore evoke a figure, historical for Murasaki Shikibu if not for modern scholars, who so dominated her time that she commanded the title *tennō*, even though no enthronement rite had ever conferred it on her.[63] They therefore provide a model of imperial ambiguity—that of someone both in and out of the imperial line—that recalls Genji as well.

Genji as a "king from outside"

Two stories of imperial birth on the shore have been cited above: those of Jinmu and Ōjin. The sea and its powers are prominent in both, but there is also a difference between the two. Scholars of Japanese mythology associate the birth of Jinmu with a "southern line" of myth, in which a divinity from the upper world visits the sea god's palace and marries his daughter. In contrast, the story of Ōjin belongs to a "northern line" associated with Ame-no-hihoko and Silla. This line, unlike the southern one, includes the shamanic element represented by Ōjin's mother and especially prominent, well into historical times, at the great Hachiman Shrine at Usa, in northern Kyushu. According to Mishina Shōei, these two lines merged in the Hachiman cult, which came to regard Ōjin as Jinmu reborn.[64] Both seem to underlie Genji's experience.

Genji's triumphal return to the capital is accomplished by a hierarchical coalition of sea powers whose particular interests give a distinct character to each, but who are nonetheless continuous with one another. (1) The most junior, because the most active and messenger-like, is the spirit of Genji's father. The Kiritsubo Emperor wants to spare his favorite son the anguish of further exile and restore him to his rightful place in the world, and to this end he collaborates with the Akashi Novice and Sumiyoshi. (2) The second, intermediate in rank, is the dragon king (sea god), in the visible person of the Novice. The Novice is desperate to marry his daughter to a great lord from the heights that he himself once abandoned, in order to restore the

---

63 The character used in *Nihon shoki* to report her death *(hō/kuzureru)* shows that the compilers considered her to have reigned as *tennō* (personal communication from John Bentley, June 2007).
64 Mishina, "Ōjin Tennō to Jingū Kōgō," 100.

fortunes of his house, and for that he has long prayed to Sumiyoshi. Where Genji is concerned, he, too, is an instrument of Sumiyoshi. (3) The third is the Sumiyoshi deity, whose nature includes that not only of the three depths of the ocean, Jingū Kōgō's allies, but also of Jingū Kōgō herself. In spirit Jingū Kōgō therefore participates directly in restoring Genji to glory, just as, in life, she worked to assure the glory (judging from the size of the Konda tomb) of Ōjin's reign. Sumiyoshi's efforts on behalf of Genji therefore suggest, behind Genji, the latent image of Ōjin, whose anomalous position in the imperial lineage needs no emphasis.

Sumiyoshi's role is similarly anomalous. Izumiya Yasuo described the Ame-no-hihoko myth, hence that of Jingū Kōgō, as unrelated to the religion *(shinkō)* of the Yamato court; while the *Genji* scholar Hirota Osamu, noting the peripheral role Sumiyoshi plays in *Kojiki* or *Nihon shoki* (focused as these are on the orthodox imperial line) called him an "alien deity" *(ikyō no kami)*.[65] Such views highlight the meaning of Genji's passage from Suma to Akashi. Genji comes under Sumiyoshi's protection (the great storm having been a device to this end) by crossing from the "inner" Kinai region, under direct imperial sway, into the "outer" Kigai, the Akashi Novice's domain; and since the Novice's figurative value is that of the dragon king, the Kinai-Kigai border functions as the boundary between land and sea. Therefore it is from the sea, figuratively speaking, that Genji returns to the capital (the land, the imperial realm). This movement, too, associates him with the image of Ōjin, whom Mishina Shōei and Izumiya Yasuo described as embodying the motif of the sun-child born of the sea.[66] More generally speaking, Genji returns to reclaim his inherent "kingship" *(ōken)* as what some have called a "king from outside" *(gairaiō)*.[67]

---

[65] Izumiya, "Richū zenki no shinwateki seikaku," 14; Hirota, "Monogatari ron to shite no ōken ron to Kiritsubo no mikado," 50.

[66] Mishina, "Ōjin Tennō to Jingū Kōgō," 86; Izumiya, "Richū zenki no shinwateki seikaku," 14.

[67] Toyoshima, "Suma, Akashi no maki ni okeru shinkō to bungaku no kisō," 179.

The Yasoshima matsuri

If Genji can be thought to achieve "kingship," however veiled, the narrative should hint, however discreetly, at accession to it. In practice, this means looking for the shadow of a Daijōsai, the imperial accession rite. In recent decades scholars have done so. In 1989, Abe Yoshitomi argued that every major step of the Daijōsai is obliquely encoded in a series of events that take place in "Momiji no ga," "Sakaki," "Suma," and "Akashi."[68] Major examples are Genji's transgressive (according to Abe) affair with the aging Dame of Staff, his transgression with Oborozukiyo, and the great storm, which functions as a ritual purification. However, others have preferred to pursue the possibility offered by the Yasoshima matsuri.

Ichijō Kanera first raised this possibility in his *Genji* commentary *Kachō yosei* (1472). Genji returns to the capital at the end of "Akashi." In the next chapter ("Miotsukushi") he makes a formal pilgrimage to the Sumiyoshi Shrine, accompanied by the whole court, "to give thanks for many answered prayers,"[69] and on his way back "he under[goes] the most solemn purification" at Naniwa.[70] Kanera linked this purification to the Yasoshima matsuri, an imperial purification rite once performed in the year following a Daijōsai.

In 1989 Mitani Kuniaki published an influential development of Kanera's remark. More recently, Kawazoe Fusae developed both his thesis and Abe's to argue that Genji's exile to Suma, his passage to Akashi, and his subsequent return to the capital constitute a shadow-Daijōsai, which is then followed, as indeed it once was in history, by a (shadow) Yasoshima matsuri.[71]

The Yasoshima matsuri (literally, "ritual of the eighty [i.e. many] islands") appears twenty-two times in historical records, as well as in a good many *waka* poems. It probably originated in the fifth century,

---

[68] Abe Yoshitomi, "Genji monogatari no Suzaku-in o kangaeru."
[69] TTG, 289; GM 2:302.
[70] TTG, 291; GM 2:306.
[71] Mitani Kuniaki, "Miotsukushi no maki ni okeru eiga to tsumi no ishiki," 235-248; Abe Yoshitomi, "Genji monogatari no Suzaku-in o kangaeru"; Kawazoe, *Genji monogatari hyōgen shi: yu to ōken no isō*.

and it died out soon after the beginning of the Kamakura period (1185-1333).[72] The rite took place at Naniwa, in an area dominated by the Sumiyoshi Shrine, and all speculative lists of the deities invoked include Sumiyoshi.[73] Its name suggests that it involved several now-vanished islands near the mouth of the Yodo River, but by the mid-Heian period only the one called Tamino seems to have mattered. *Jindaiki* mentions the "deity of Tamino island" as a "child deity of Sumiyoshi.[74] The shrine there, Tamino-shima Jinja, was built in 869.[75] In "Miotsukushi," an exchange of poems between Genji and the lady from Akashi suggests that both, separately, underwent purification on Tamino. A poem by the Sumiyoshi priest Tsumori Tsunekuni, written on the occasion of the Yasoshima matsuri of 1191, also celebrates the purification there.[76]

Between 699 and 771, five emperors went to Naniwa in the year after their Daijōsai; presumably the Yasoshima matsuri was performed on these occasions.[77] However, Kanmu (r. 781-806), who moved the capital to Heian-kyō, instituted another purification ritual at the more convenient Karasaki, near Ōtsu, at the southern end of Lake Biwa. No emperor ever went again in person to Naniwa.[78] Instead, the ritual manual *Gōke shidai* (late 11th c.) describes how, in the year after a Daijōsai, a *naishi* (female court official), properly the emperor's nurse, carried a box containing one of the emperor's robes to Naniwa. A master of the *wagon*, the "Japanese koto," went with her. An altar was then erected on the shore, probably on Tamino. To the sound of the *wagon*, the *naishi* opened the box and, facing the sea, shook the robe. This was the heart of the rite.[79]

---

[72] Okada Shōji, "Nara jidai no Naniwa gyōkō to Yasoshima matsuri," 60.

[73] Tanaka, *Sumiyoshi Taisha shi* 2:383.

[74] *Sumiyoshi Taisha jindaiki*, 23.

[75] Koyama, *Genji monogatari: kyūtei gyōji no tenkai*, 204.

[76] *Shin gosenwakashū* 1604; cited by Tanaka, *Sumiyoshi Taisha shi* 2:404.

[77] Okada Shōji, "Nara jidai no Naniwa gyōkō to Yasoshima matsuri," 59-60.

[78] Okada Shōji, "Nara jidai no Naniwa gyōkō to Yasoshima matsuri," 63-64.

[79] Okada Shōji, "Nara jidai no Naniwa gyōkō to Yasoshima matsuri," 60. Tanaka Suguru discussed the rite at much greater length in *Sumiyoshi Taisha shi* 2:376-420.

The first Yasoshima matsuri mentioned explicitly in the records is that of Emperor Montoku (r. 850-858) in 850. Many later emperors had it performed as well, although not all. Those of interest in connection with *The Tale of Genji* include Daigo, Suzaku (r. 930-946), Murakami (r. 946-967), Reizei (r. 967-969), and Sanjō (r. 1011-1016). The last was Go-Horikawa (r. 1221-1232).[80] Murasaki Shikibu set the early part of her tale precisely during the time during which the Heian-period Yasoshima matsuri was done most faithfully.

However, whether or not the Genji of "Miotsukushi" has just been through a shadow-Daijōsai, he is not on the face of it an emperor, and for that reason he cannot be imagined going through a Yasoshima matsuri proper.[81] In any case, he visits Naniwa in person, unlike any Heian emperor. Some have therefore suggested that his purification at Naniwa consisted in practice of a rite known as Nanase no harae (literally, "purification on the seven shoals," but perhaps, more simply, "sevenfold purification"). This rite would therefore have had, in Genji's case, the value of a shadow-Yasoshima matsuri. [82] Indeed, some authoritative versions of the text (for example SNKBT 2:115) mention *nanase*, although others (for example SNKBZ 2:306) have instead *nado* ("and so on"). The Tyler translation, which relied on the latter, reads, "At Naniwa he underwent the most solemn purification." Adding the *nanase* might yield, "At Naniwa he underwent the most solemn seven-fold purification." The Nanase no harae therefore sounds possible. However, Yoshikai Naoto showed that, although this purifi-cation *could* be done at Naniwa (as at Karasaki and in Heian-kyō itself, on the banks of the Kamo River), it could not have been, even there, a reduced version of the Yasoshima matsuri because it was not a shrine rite at all, conducted by Shinto priests. Instead it was an Onmyōdō rite,

---

80 Tanaka, *Sumiyoshi Taisha shi* 2:376-377.

81 *Engi shiki* mentions that the Yasoshima matsuri could be done also for the heir apparent or the empress *(chūgū)*, but scholars seem not to have made an issue of this wider scope for the rite. See Okada Shōji, "Nara jidai no Naniwa gyōkō to Yasoshima matsuri," 64.

82 For example, Mitani Kuniaki in "Miotsukushi no maki ni okeru eiga to tsumi no ishiki," 240.

conducted by yin-yang practitioners,[83] and was therefore akin to the Onmyōdō purification rite that precedes the great storm in "Suma." Yoshikai found no evidence to support the proposition that Genji's purification at Naniwa was a Nanase no harae.[84]

Two other items have been cited to argue that Genji's purification at Naniwa acts out a sort of latent kingship. One is the location of the ceremony, the island of Tamino. The Yasoshima matsuri hypothesis requires that access to Tamino should have been restricted to a very great lord seeking purification at that level. However, no evidence to that effect exists. Since the lady from Akashi goes there for the same purpose, anyone of some standing could apparently do so. The second has to do with the Yasoshima envoy's departure. *Gōke shidai* states that when the *naishi* envoy started back toward the capital, the singing girls of Eguchi (at the mouth of the Yodo River) gathered to her train, from which they received largesse. Similarly, when Genji started home, "Singing girls crowded to his procession, and all the young gallants with him, even senior nobles, seemed to look favorably on them."[85] However, this does not mean that the singing girls *(asobi)* treated Genji's train as an imperial envoy's. Documents of the time show that they sought to derive whatever benefit they could from the passage of every wealthy lord or lady.[86]

The Yasoshima matsuri hypothesis therefore dissolves, and with it the hope of finding veiled evidence of a Daijōsai. However, Kawazoe Fusae advanced an intricate argument to support another line of reasoning. She suggested that Genji's night in the "kitchen" after lightning had struck his part of the Suma house, and his vision of his father there, correspond to the practice of the Daijōsai, during which the new emperor eats and sleeps with the ancestral spirits;[87] and that the province of Harima had a special place in the development of the dual Yuki-no-kuni, Suki-no-kuni structure of the Daijōsai.[88] In order to

---

[83] Yoshikai, "'Nanase no harae' no shiteki tenkai," 445.

[84] Yoshikai, "'Nanase no harae' no shiteki tenkai," 460.

[85] TTG, 292; GM 2:307.

[86] Goodwin, *Selling Songs and Smiles*, 11-27.

[87] Kawazoe, *Genji monogatari hyōgen shi*, 353.

[88] Kawazoe, 359-363.

connect Genji's experience to the agricultural, celestial sun-deity cult underlying the historical Daijōsai, she found herself obliged to argue that the Akashi Novice's Sumiyoshi is a deity not only of the sea, but also of rice. She therefore characterized the lady from Akashi as a "water woman" *(mizu no onna)*, meaning a "paddy woman" *(ta no onna)*, a woman associated with the fresh water that nourishes the crops. In this way she argued that Genji's marriage to the Novice's daughter shadows the Daijōsai marriage between the new emperor and the fructifying source of plenty for his realm.[89] In reality, however, nothing associates this lady with any water but that of the sea.

Genji's sovereignty

A distinction made by Abe Yoshitomi and others helps to clarify the situation. Abe distinguished two possible modes of sovereignty. He called the first *kōken*, the "emperorship" characteristic of the Japanese sovereign in particular, and that assumed by attempts to link Genji's experience to the Daijōsai. The second, *ōken*, then designates a more generalized conception of "kingship" or sovereignty. After presenting his detailed argument for an encrypted Daijōsai, Abe acknowledged that Genji's rise nonetheless lifts him above "emperorship," to a "kingship" achieved at "the level of *physis*."[90] He defined *physis* (a Greek word) as "the essence of nature, or the absolute energy hidden within the earth."[91] Thus, despite his search for a Daijōsai between the lines of the narrative, Abe recognized Genji as a hero whose greater glory comes from depths beyond local title, custom, ritual, or precedent: a hero whose singular destiny is his alone. Abe's *physis* resembles the deep, propelling force exerted in Genji's favor by the powers of the sea.

These powers are as visibly at work in the events associated with the storm and its aftermath as they are in the Hikohohodemi myth. Genji, whose domain is the capital (the mountains), stumbles (the loss of the fishhook) when he is caught in bed with Oborozukiyo. This

---

[89] Kawazoe, 364-365.
[90] Abe Yoshitomi, "Genji monogatari no Suzaku-in o kangaeru," 11.
[91] Abe Yoshitomi, 1.

enrages those who back his elder brother and gives them an excuse to get rid of him (Honosusori's anger). He therefore retreats to the shore at Suma, feeling deeply wronged. From there Sumiyoshi (Shiotsuchi no Oji)[92] leads him to the Akashi Novice's (sea god's) residence. Genji marries the Novice's daughter (Toyotama-hime), who is pregnant when he returns to the capital and triumphs over Suzaku and his faction. She then bears him, beside the sea, a child who will engender an emperor. This child is a daughter, not a son as in the myth; but no Heian hero, not even Genji, could have fathered a dynastic founder. Since a commoner could overtly merge his lineage with that of the emperors only through a daughter, a son could have neither lifted Genji higher nor answered the Novice's prayers to Sumiyoshi. The change from son to daughter therefore transposes the myth into a Heian setting. As for the Novice's daughter, she ranks too far below Genji either to claim or to receive open acknowledgment as his daughter's mother. It is Murasaki (Tamayori-hime) who will rear the little girl for the high station to which Sumiyoshi destines her, while she herself fades into the background of Genji's life.

Genji's exile thus follows the pattern of the myth. Study of this myth from the perspective of the imperial accession rite shows that this rite originally involved a sacred marriage between a celestial deity and a woman of the nether world, thanks to which the celestial deity (the new emperor) assumed the quality of an earthly sovereign; and that the marriage between Hikohohodemi and the sea god's daughter is a model of this rite. There are many parallels (lexical items, accessories, actions) between the Daijōsai and sea god's welcome to Hikohohodemi.[93] Echoes of the Daijōsai seem therefore to be present in the narrative after all, but the implied "enthronement" has nothing to do with Heian "emperorship" proper. Genji never seeks to overthrow his brother, as the Kokiden Consort apparently suspects him of doing. Instead, the issue for the author seems to be the hero's acquisition of

---

[92] In the myth it is Shiotsuchi no Oji who urges and arranges Hikohohodemi's passage to the undersea palace. Thus he combines the roles played by Genji's father and the Sumiyoshi deity in the tale. He appears in *Jindaiki* (34), too, as a direct agent of Sumiyoshi.

[93] Kawakami, "Toyotama-hime shinwa no ichikōsatsu," 103-106.

supreme personal prestige outside the framework of the imperial succession—a prestige that will not survive him. As noted in earlier essays, Genji regrets in "Wakana Two" having been unable to found through Reizei (who has no son) a continuing line of emperors, but the author surely never meant him to do. His supremacy is for one generation only, and it lies outside established forms. Hikohohodemi's triumph over his elder brother, in a world of essential patterns far removed from particular Heian practice, therefore offered the author a model that required her only to change the hero's child into a girl. Her hero shines once and then is gone.

Further evidence strengthens the connection between the myth and a generalized acquisition of sovereignty, and connects its sea god to Sumiyoshi. Toyotama-hime and her father, together, are the marine deity of the Azumi clan.[94] They are therefore another way of describing the triple sea deity born of Izanagi's purification after his escape from the underworld—the deity who spoke through Jingū Kōgō in the original oracle and who then became Sumiyoshi. The fourth *Nihon shoki* variant of the story even has Hikohohodemi setting out for the undersea palace from Tachibana no Odo, where Izanagi purified himself.[95]

Because the Azumi provided the food offerings for the Daijōsai, Miyake described Hikohohodemi's marriage to Toyotama-hime as, among other things, an affirmation of the clan's proud service to the imperial house.[96] The Akashi Novice's role parallels theirs, as Genji's parallels Hikohohodemi's. Miyake further suggested that the story of Hikohohodemi, culminating in the birth of Emperor Jinmu, was added to that of the imperial lineage between the mid-seventh and the early eighth centuries, thanks to the power of the Azumi clan.[97]

In contrast Honosusori, the elder brother, is the ancestor of the Hayato, a Kyushu people whose long resistance to Yamato domination ended for good in 721. The dance of the Hayato *(Hayato-mai)* was

---

[94] Matsumae, "Toyotama-hime shinwa no shinkōteki kiban to hebi nyōbō tan," 90-91; Miyake, "Umi no sachi yama no sachi shinwa no keisei ni tsuite," 7-10.
[95] Miyake, "Umi no sachi yama no sachi shinwa no keisei ni tsuite," 7.
[96] Miyake, 9.
[97] Miyake, 13.

presented at the palace annually, in token of Hayato fealty, and in this spirit the Hayato, too, took part in the Daijōsai.[98] According to *Shoku Nihongi* (797) and *Fusō ryakki* (ca. 1100), the court prayed for victory over the Hayato at the great Hachiman shrine at Usa, and the final campaign against them was led by the Hachiman priestess Karashima no Masa. Masa, the "staff" *(mi-tsue)*, or vessel, of the deity therefore played the same role as Jingū Kōgō in the Silla campaign.[99]

Genji and Suzaku

Haruo Shirane identified Honosuseri with Suzaku in the tale, but in practice this correspondence has not received much attention. The *Kakaishō* author implied it, but he did not mention it. Many pages of the preceding essays have been devoted to the relationship between the two brothers and to the proposition that it is complex, meaningful, and even dramatic. However, most readers take the narrator at her literal word and believe the brothers to be close, with only warm feelings for each other. Suzaku viewed in this way may be weak, but he is also kind, tolerant, upright, and without personal bitterness toward Genji. He has even been described as simply Genji's "inevitable shadow." [100] Nonetheless, the defeated Honosuseri—if he were a character anything like as developed as Suzaku—could hardly help resenting his brother's victory deeply. *The Tale of Genji* read in this light acquires a new depth that in no way displaces its more obvious brilliance. Nearly three decades ago Mitoma Kōsuke reached a comparable although less developed conclusion. Citing the Hikohohodemi myth, among other examples from early literature, he classified the story of Genji and Suzaku, through Part One of the tale, as an example of what he called the *basshi seikō tan* ("younger brother outdoes elder") pattern.[101] In Part Two, however, the *Genji* author carried the story of the brothers far beyond anything suggested either by the myth itself, or by its historical association with Sumiyoshi and

---

[98] Miyake, "Umi no sachi yama no sachi shinwa no keisei ni tsuite," 2, 5.

[99] Mishina, "Ōjin Tennō to Jingū Kōgō," 77-79.

[100] Yamakami, "Suzaku-in," 252.

[101] Mitoma, *Genji monogatari no minzokugakuteki kenkyū*, 342-344.

the Azumi. Hikohohodemi and his line triumphed forever over the Hayato, but the story that begins in Part Two takes a different course.

It is in Part Two ("Wakana Two") that Genji makes his second and last pilgrimage to Sumiyoshi, The occasion is grand, and the narrative gives it generous space, but it raises few questions, and perhaps for that reason it is relatively little discussed. It seems to close a phase of Genji's life. The main reason for the pilgrimage is the Akashi Novice's insistence that his daughter should go to Sumiyoshi and thank the deity for answering his prayers. Genji takes the occasion to renew his own thanks as well.

> It was the middle of the tenth month; the kudzu vines clambering along the sacred fence had turned, and the reddened leaves beneath the pines announced not only in sound the waning of autumn. The familiar Eastern Dances, so much more appealing than the solemn pieces from Koma or Cathay, merged with wind and wave; the music of the flutes soared on the breeze through the tall pines, conveying a shiver of awe not to be felt elsewhere; the rhythm, marked on strings rather than on drums, was less majestic than gracefully stirring; and the place lent its own magic to the whole...Dawn broke slowly, and the frost lay thicker still. While the cressets burned low, *kagura* musicians too drunk by now to know what they were singing gave themselves to merrymaking, oblivious to the spectacle they made, yet still waving their *sakaki* wands and crying "Ten thousand years! Ten thousand years!" until one imagined endless years of happy fortune.[102]

The scene recalls the close of Zeami's famous *Takasago*, when the Sumiyoshi deity, in the form of a beautiful young lord, dances to the music and chorus of his people;[103] but in the tale the scene is poignant as well. The shadows are falling over Genji and Murasaki, whom "ten thousand years" do not await, and over Suzaku as well. Sumiyoshi has

---

[102] TTG, 633-635; GM 4:171-175.

[103] In painting the Sumiyoshi deity's canonical form is that of an old man, one perhaps resembling Shiotsuchi no Oji. This vision of him in *Takasago* is unique.

had his way, but all he has done now merges into the greater current of karma and time.

Conclusion

According to medieval legend,[104] Murasaki Shikibu's initial conception of the tale sprang from personal distress over the exile of Minamoto no Takaakira (914-982) to Kyushu in 969. She therefore wrote the "Suma" and "Akashi" chapters first, in a creative rush, and added the others one by one only later on. Takaakira's exile may not really have inspired her that directly, since she was not even born until the early 970s. However, the pathos of exile was so familiar to her from Chinese literature that allusions to the exile of the great Tang poet Bo Juyi (772-846) pervade "Suma." Beside Takaakira, she also knew several other examples, including Ariwara no Yukihira (818-893), who preceded her hero at Suma; Fujiwara no Korechika (974-1010), a contemporary of hers; and above all the great statesman and scholar Sugawara no Michizane (845-903), whose unmerited exile to Kyushu, where he died, had enormous repercussions. The "Suma" narrative alludes to it poignantly.

If the sorrows of exile aroused Murasaki Shikibu's personal and imaginative sympathy, and if she wished to bring *her* hero back from them to unheard-of honor, then the will of the Sumiyoshi deity furthered her purpose, and the associated Hikohohodemi myth gave her the pattern of her story. Her genius transmuted it into something wholly new.

---

[104] Told, for example, in the introduction to *Kakaishō*: Tamagami, *Shimeishō, Kakaishō*, 186.

PITY POOR KAORU

"The Possibility of Ukifune" suggested that Part Three differs significantly from the two earlier parts of the tale. "Pity Poor Kaoru" will pursue the question of difference further. It will briefly discuss the way Kaoru has been received and contrast the handling of the theme of "surrogates" in Genji's case and his. The greater part of it will then argue that the treatment of Kaoru and his troubles is intended above all to elicit the reader's pity for him, without regard to the other characters involved, and that it employs visible artifice to this end.

An essay on Kaoru by Paul Schalow[1] might almost concern an analogous figure in a different book. It illustrates the gulf that can separate divergent perspectives on the same work. Schalow placed in strict parallel the "foundational relationship between Genji's parents...from which radiates the central dynamic of multiple substitutions in the tale," and the "new hero and...new foundational relationship for the tale beginning in "Hashihime."[2] This is the relationship between Kaoru and the Eighth Prince, for whom, according to Schalow, Kaoru conceives a "heroic passion."[3] Schalow wrote, "When the Eighth Prince dies...his death reverberates throughout the remainder of the tale in the form of another pattern of multiple substitutions."[4] Therefore, "At their core the Uji chapters depict Kaoru's attempts to keep alive the memory of his friendship with the Eighth Prince by pursuing a displaced intimacy with the Prince's three daughters."[5]

"Pity Poor Kaoru," on its side, will deny that any "central dynamic of multiple substitutions" exists in Parts One and Two of the tale, and argue that in this regard Part Three differs strikingly from what

[1] "The Uji Chapters: Maidens of the Bridge," in Schalow, *A Poetics of Courtly Male Friendship in Heian Japan*.
[2] Schalow, *A Poetics of Courtly Male Friendship*, 163.
[3] Schalow, 167.
[4] Schalow, 163.
[5] Schalow, 164.

precedes it. In agreement with the tale itself on the subject, it will take the series of substitutions in Part Three to begin with the bond between Kaoru and Ōigimi, the Eighth Prince's oldest daughter, and from this standpoint it will discuss several passages that do not appear in Schalow's work: those that attribute to Kaoru urgent desire for a member of the opposite sex. Where Schalow wrote of "the chaste nature of Kaoru's fascination with Ukifune," this essay takes it as understood that Kaoru makes love with Ukifune during their first night together, and then presumably whenever he visits her at Uji. Above all, "Pity Poor Kaoru" will approach Kaoru's feelings and motives from a different direction. Rather than probe his psychology, it will question (in concert with several contemporary Japanese scholars) the idea that Kaoru has any coherent psychology at all.

When so many writers have discussed Kaoru in psychological terms, although with many inevitable differences of emphasis, the idea that he has no psychology may sound startling and gratuitously critical of the chapters that feature him. However, this essay does not question the brilliance of the Uji chapters, which even without Parts One and Two would still be the masterpiece of Heian fiction. Instead, "Pity Poor Kaoru" represents an initial and certainly imperfect attempt to come to grips with a significant aspect of the complex differences of tone, range of interest, narrative method, and so on that characterize this part of the work. One theme in *Genji* scholarship has to do with interpreting motifs and passages throughout the tale in such a way as to integrate Part Three more convincingly with what precedes it. Schalow's parallel between Genji and Kaoru (each with his "foundational relationship" and his series of "multiple substitutions") illustrates that trend.

It is natural that many scholars should prefer to grasp the work in this manner and so affirm the integrity of the whole. In practice, however, there are many reasons to find Part Three unusual. While the repetition of the pattern discerned by Schalow gives the tale an apparent consistency, the radical difference in content between the two foundation relationships, and between each of these relationships and its ensuing substitute series, only underscores how dissimilar Part Three really is. In the immediate postwar period this part was seen as the culmination of the tale, but current readings shun evaluation.[6] Some, especially Mitani Kuniaki's influential "Genji monogatari daisanbu no hōhō" (1982),[7] make it difficult to understand how Part Three could be by the same author, although authorship is not an issue that scholars raise. The relationship of Part Three to the rest of the tale seems therefore to remain tacitly unsettled. Under these circumstances there is reason also to identify, for the sake of argument, what makes this part so unlike the rest and to attempt to define the difference. This analysis of the figure of Kaoru attempts to do so.

From Genji to Kaoru

Readers have always seen a difference between Genji and Kaoru. Later Heian fiction writers did not imitate Genji, however greatly they may have admired him. Their heroes resemble Kaoru, in whom the author of *Sarashina nikki* saw her ideal.[8] By the end of the Heian period Genji's behavior with women had apparently become an issue, since the woman author of *Mumyōzōshi* (ca. 1200) wrote of him, "There are many things about him that one might wish otherwise."[9] In contrast she wrote of Kaoru, "There is nothing about him that one would wish to be different."[10] Her criticism of Genji recalls the attitude adopted by the monk Chōken (1125-1203), who condemned the tale on moral grounds in his *Genji ippon kyō*. In contrast, she defended Kaoru against any sign of similar disapproval. To someone who objected that Kaoru is not always to be trusted in intimate situations she replied, "That is not his fault. Women are unfortunately much too susceptible."[11] She also cited as model women characters *(konomoshiki hito)* in the tale the undoubtedly chaste but also impossibly unattractive

---

[6] Despite perceptions of difference and vagaries of personal taste, no one seems ever to have suggested seriously that Part Three is inferior. A passage on this issue by Charo d'Etcheverry *(Love After* The Tale of Genji, 3-4) leaves an erroneous impression.

[7] Mitani Kuniaki, "Genji monogatari daisanbu no hōhō."

[8] Mitani Kuniaki, "Torawareta shisō," 283.

[9] Higuchi and Kuboki, *Mumyōzōshi*, 198.

[10] Higuchi and Kuboki, 202.

[11] Higuchi and Kuboki, 202-203.

Suetsumuhana and Hanachirusato. [12] If the original patrons and audience of the tale had felt this way about Genji, Murasaki Shikibu might never have left such a hero to posterity.

From the *Mumyōzōshi* author's perspective, one apparently common in her time,[13] it is Kaoru's *kokoro* ("heart") that makes him so admirable: the thoughtfulness, tact, and steadfastness of feeling on which the narrator insists. Still, Genji, too, was known to be thoughtful and loyal. Perhaps the decisive difference has to do with Kaoru's announced reluctance to make love to a woman without her consent, as well as with his unfailing tact (according to the narrator) under intimate circumstances. No such reluctance deterred Genji. Kaoru's attitude can be seen as the heart of what Mitani Kuniaki, in the title of his essay on the subject, called the "Kaoru illusion" *(Kaoru gensō).*

Surrogates and idols

An important difference between the two heroes, and between the parts of *The Tale of Genji* that feature each, emerges from an analysis of the theme of erotic surrogacy, or substitution. Sometimes in the tale a man's affection shifts from one woman to another when the first passes beyond his reach, and the second woman then becomes to him a replacement, or surrogate, for the first. As Schalow pointed out, this motif appears at the very beginning of the tale.

Genji loses his mother while he is still too young to remember her. His father, the reigning emperor, eventually marries Fujitsubo because she looks so like Genji's mother, and this resemblance fascinates Genji when he learns of it. Fujitsubo is sixteen when she comes to the palace, and Genji eleven. Puberty therefore separates them, but only provisionally. Nonetheless, as noted in "The Disaster of the Third Princess," Genji's father encourages close contact between the two. He says to Fujitsubo,

> For some reason it seems right to me that he should take you
> for his mother. Do not think him uncivil. Just be kind to him.

---

[12] Higuchi and Kuboki, 193.
[13] Mitani Kuniaki, "Torawareta shisō," 287.

His face and eyes are so like hers that your own resemblance
to her makes it look quite natural.[14]

Soon the young Genji "lost no chance offered by the least flower or
autumn leaf to let her know in his childish way how much he liked
her."[15] At his tender age he is already courting her, and eventually he
will make love with her: first out of the reader's sight, then visibly in
"Wakamurasaki," when he is eighteen and Fujitsubo twenty-three. The
image of his mother, merging into that of his father's empress, gives
his love for Fujitsubo the authority almost of destiny and a compelling
power that ennobles his desperate transgression.

Fujitsubo is beyond the adult Genji's reach, except for rare, furtive
moments that cause her intense distress; hence his excitement when
he comes across a girl of about ten who resembles her
("Wakamurasaki"). He instantly and explicitly understands why the
girl so attracts him, and the attraction is confirmed when he discovers
that she is Fujitsubo's niece. Thus he defines for the reader the motif of
erotic substitution associated with the tale.

Norma Field made this motif a "central part of her study" of *The
Tale of Genji*,[16] and her particular emphasis on it has encouraged
writers on the tale in English to take its validity for granted. It has
been cited repeatedly to assert that all the women with whom Genji
enters into love relationships are in one way or another, directly or
indirectly, surrogates for Fujitsubo and, through her, for Genji's
mother. However, nothing explicit in the narrative supports this
reading, which is not current in Japanese scholarship.[17] On the contrary,
the narrative distinguishes the link (for Genji) between Fujitsubo and
Murasaki from that between Fujitsubo and any other woman by giving
it, twice, a particular name: *murasaki no yukari*. The narrative does not
explicitly extend this "*murasaki* tie" either backwards from Fujitsubo

---

[14] TTG, 15; GM 1:44.

[15] TTG, 15; GM 1:44.

[16] Okada, *Figures of Resistance*, 357, n. 31. Field described Utsusemi, Yūgao, and
Suetsumuhana as "substitutes" and Oborozukiyo as a "surrogate" for Fujitsubo *(The
Splendor of Longing*, 31).

[17] Takahashi Tōru did not even mention it in a long chapter (entitled "'Yukari' to
'katashiro': Genji monogatari no tōji hō") of his *Genji monogatari no shigaku*.

to Genji's mother, or forward from Fujitsubo and Murasaki to the Third Princess. In practice, however, scholars accept that to varying degrees the *murasaki no yukari*, which according to the letter of the text involves only Fujitsubo and Murasaki, links all four.

With respect to Fujitsubo and the *murasaki no yukari* proper, the young, naive Genji of the earliest chapters might well believe that, if only he had Fujitsubo, he would never again look at another woman. However, he would probably not remain exclusively faithful to her if he did. As it is, nothing connects her to his other affairs, for which the narrative suggests other sources of inspiration. For example, the vistas opened for him by the "rainy night conversation" ("Hahakigi") prompt his adventure with Utsusemi and his pursuit of Suetsumuhana, which itself parodies a passage of that same conversation and is also driven by rivalry with his friend Tō no Chūjō. The narrative never links Yūgao, Rokujō, or Oborozukiyo to Genji's preoccupation with Fujitsubo. Having established the motif of the erotic surrogate, it therefore strictly limits its range and presents a gallery of other affairs unrelated to it. The motif of erotic substitution outside the extended *murasaki no yukari* series appears only once, briefly, in Part One. In "Hotaru" Genji pleads with Tamakazura because to him (intoxicated as he already is with desire) she looks so like her mother, Yūgao. However, nothing further happens.

This is the extent of the "surrogate" motif in Part One and (counting the Third Princess) Part Two. In Part Three, the word for what sounds in English like the same motif changes from *yukari* to *katashiro*. The narrative in the Uji chapters describes Ukifune three times (from Kaoru's perspective) as a *katashiro* for Ōigimi.

Yukari and *katashiro* are not synonyms.[18] Shirane translated the first as "link" and the second as "doll, substitute."[19] The first therefore designates an association between persons, and the second a more or

---

[18] Takahashi Tōru *(Genji monogatari no shigaku*, 268) discussed the conflation of the two and concluded that it is not entirely wrong, but he nonetheless stressed that *yukari* and *katashiro* are not the same.
[19] Shirane, *The Bridge of Dreams*, 155.

less impersonal, or depersonalized, object. [20] *Katashiro* is all but synonymous with *hitogata* and *nademono*, both of which also describe Ukifune in relation to Ōigimi, seen from Kaoru's point of view. All three refer to a human effigy (of paper or some other material) that is first rubbed *(nade-)* against the body in order to transfer impurities into it, then sent floating away down a stream or out to sea. Among these three terms, only *hitogata* occurs, once, before Part Three. In Genji's next-to-last poem in "Suma" it refers directly to such an effigy.[21]

The Uji chapters therefore give the surrogate motive a new, sharper outline, and a character at once more tangible and less personal. After Ōigimi's death, Kaoru becomes infatuated instead with her younger sister Nakanokimi, who suddenly looks and sounds to him just like her. When his dangerously indiscreet attentions threaten her marriage to the jealous Niou, she deflects them by telling him about Ukifune, a younger half-sister unknown to the reader, to Kaoru, and, until recently, even to herself. The way she steers Kaoru toward the abruptly invented Ukifune betrays the kind of plot manipulation inevitable in any fiction but never so obvious in Parts One and Two. Kaoru then spies on Ukifune, sees that she resembles Ōigimi, and pursues her instead. In the next-to-last chapter ("Tenarai") the author extends the surrogate motif even further. Kannon's miraculous intervention brings Ukifune to the nun of Ono as a surrogate for the nun's late daughter, and the nun urges Ukifune on her late daughter's widower as a surrogate for his wife.

The more this motif recurs in Part Three, the more depersonalized the surrogate herself becomes. Kaoru professes the highest respect for Ōigimi, but after her death he assimilates the living Nakanokimi to his

---

[20] Earl Miner recognized this tendency toward depersonalization when he wrote "To [Kaoru], Ukifune is not very much more than a *katami*, a surrogate, an inferior substitution for something in the past...But it is...questionable to treat a person as a *katami* for another person, since such treatment depersonalizes" ("The Heroine," 67). Miner gave *katami* ("memento"), a word that does not actually appear in the text in this connection, the force of *katashiro* as discussed here.

[21] Takahashi, *Genji monogatari no shigaku*, 283. TTG, 252; GM 2:217. Shirane discussed *katashiro* and *hitokata*, and ideas concerning their thematic implications, in *The Bridge of Dreams*, 155-156, and 242, n. 10. These implications go beyond anything that *yukari* could suggest.

remembered image of her. Ukifune then appears when Kaoru laments to Nakanokimi that he longs to "make a doll *[hitogata]* in [Ōigimi's] likeness...and pursue my devotions before [it].[22] Thus Ukifune enters the story as a doll memento of someone else.

Genji's evolving relationship with Murasaki, his *murasaki no yukari* link with Fujitsubo, takes the opposite course. In Part One, he delights in her intrinsic quality and repeatedly loses sight of how closely she resembles Fujitsubo. Rediscovering this resemblance turns him not toward idolatrous worship of a memory but toward growing recognition of Murasaki's own worth. Fujitsubo dies in "Usugumo." Near the end of the next chapter, "Asagao," Genji and Murasaki are looking out over their moonlit, snow-covered garden.

> Leaning forward a little that way to look out, [Murasaki] was lovelier than any woman in the world. The sweep of her hair, her face, suddenly brought back to him most wonderfully the figure of the lady he had loved, and his heart, which had been somewhat divided, turned again to her [Murasaki] alone.[23]

Genji's heart has been "divided" not by the memory of Fujitsubo, but by his failed courtship of Princess Asagao. When Murasaki's pose recalls "the lady he had loved" (Fujitsubo), he understands that Murasaki, in her own person, gives him all he had ever wanted from Fujitsubo, and he renounces his thoughts of Asagao. That night Fujitsubo comes to him in a dream, angry and accusing, and he awakens in anguish. The meaning of this dream is debated, but at any rate, Fujitsubo disappears at this point from the narrative. Thereafter she belongs to the past, and however cruelly Genji may fail in Part Two to understand Murasaki, he treats her fully as herself, not as a stand-in for someone else. In contrast, Kaoru ends up worshiping an idol.

For Ukifune, the process of objectification continues as the end of the book approaches. Unlike Ōigimi and Nakanokimi, who are both princesses, she is the child of an illicit affair. Because her father refused to recognize her, she grew up in the household of a provincial governor and so ranks far below her half-sisters. Kaoru accordingly

---

[22] TTG, 954; GM 5:448.
[23] TTG, 374; GM 2:494. This passage is quoted also in "Genji and Murasaki."

treats her as a mistress and visits her when he has time. Despite his preoccupation with her, she remains nothing to him in herself. Then she disappears, to end up at Ono, where the Ono nun's former son-in-law pursues her like a stalker, without even knowing who she is. After she becomes a nun, a glimpse of her at her devotions only spurs him on, and he decides that he will have her.[24] She has become a mere sex object.

In "Kagerō," after Ukifune's disappearance, Kaoru similarly depersonalizes his wife. The First Princess preoccupies him, and he has recently managed to spy on her unseen. He saw her seated among her women (who include his mistress, the gentlewoman Kozaishō), wearing only transparent silk gauze in the summer heat and holding a piece of ice. The sight so stirred him that he now seeks to replicate it at home by dressing his wife (also a princess) in similar gauze, which she never normally wears, and having her, too, hold a bit of ice. Thus he turns her into a doll of the First Princess. Unfortunately, his wife has never interested him, and to his chagrin this simulacrum of an erotic vision purloined elsewhere still leaves him unmoved.

Kaoru's behavior in this scene can be understood not unreasonably to demean both his wife and himself, although the scene also offers the possibility of cruel humor. Mitani Kuniaki remarked that in a world as pervaded as the Uji chapters by "liminality" or "ambiguity," any scene may turn at any moment, intentionally or not, into farce,[25] a breath of which may be felt here. However, the gauze and ice hint at the chief effect probably intended. Taken together, these material props constitute a device that figures in the three erotic scenes discussed below. It distracts the reader's attention from the unhappiness of the woman in order to focus it solely on Kaoru's feelings. Nothing the woman herself says or does damps Kaoru's ardor; the prop does that. In three of the four cases (as here), and perhaps in all of them, it means something particular to him alone. Once the narrator focuses the reader's attention on this object, through Kaoru's present or remi-

---

[24] TTG, 1104; GM 6:352.
[25] Mitani Kuniaki, "Genji monogatari daisanbu no hōhō," 92.

niscing gaze, the woman in the scene no longer matters. Kaoru is alone with his disappointment, and the reader is free to pity him.

Pity poor Kaoru

All the characters in Parts One and Two appear to have the narrator's respect and, usually, her sympathy. She does not mock or belittle even the villainous Kokiden Consort of Genji's early years; and if the Akashi Novice's ways are sometimes amusing, the intensity of his ambition for a daughter so vital to Genji's future, and the divine sanction this ambition enjoys, restore his dignity. Despite the comedy around her, Suetsumuhana retains her stature as a princess and as a human being. Even the randy Dame of Staff has wit and accomplishment that narrow her absurdity to that single obsession and otherwise suggest personal distinction. In amorous relationships the narrator never demeans Genji, even if at times she deplores his behavior, and her women, such as the vividly complex Utsusemi, are convincingly alive. The Uji chapters are not like this.

Contrasting passages from "Yomogiu" and "Agemaki" illustrate the difference. In "Yomogiu," Suetsumuhana's aunt presses her destitute niece to accompany her to Kyushu as a governess for her children. Suetsumuhana replies mainly with silence, but her ancient, starving women beg her to say yes, as does her foster sister Jijū. However, Suetsumuhana will not compromise her dignity as a princess or abandon the property left her by her father, and she blindly trusts Genji to honor his word and rescue her in the end. No, she finally says aloud, "I just want to fade away as I am."[26] Her guiding interests differ completely from her women's, but neither she, nor the narrator on her behalf, blames them for feeling as they do. No wonder they long to leave a house that is collapsing around them. Jijū, who has no sensible choice but to go, still understands that her mistress should prefer to stay, and Suetsumuhana, heartbroken by Jijū's departure, refrains from reproaching her. Instead, she hunts through her meager possessions for a suitable parting gift.

---

[26] TTG, 306; GM 2:340.

Perhaps the similar situation in "Agemaki" parodies the earlier one. Ōigimi, also a princess, likes Kaoru, but out of loyalty to what she believes were her late father wishes she refuses to marry him and move to the capital. If she goes on this way she will risk Suetsumuhana's fate. Her old governess (Ben, now a nun) replies at length with sentiments just as reasonable as the women's protests to Suetsumuhana. No one with Ōigimi's best interests at heart (as the world commonly and sensibly understands such interests) could possibly speak otherwise. To Ōigimi, however, her words are "repellant and offensive." To silence Ben she lies face down on the floor. Naturally the other women of the household, too, hope that she will accept her distinguished suitor, just as they hope that Nakanokimi will marry Niou. However, the narrator dismisses them repeatedly as ignorant, selfish, officious, base-minded nuisances. There seems to be no communication at all between the sisters and their women; nor, on this issue, is there any between the sisters themselves, or between Ōigimi and Kaoru.

Others have noted this failure or refusal of communication between the characters in the Uji chapters. Amanda Stinchecum wrote in her study of "Ukifune":

> While in Woolf's novel [To the Lighthouse] we see the continuity of thought and feeling between one character and another, in "Ukifune" the uniformity of diction reveals disjunctions in thought, misunderstandings, and, even in dialogue, a lack of receptiveness, a turning away from each other."[27]

"Continuity of thought and feeling between one character and another" is as present especially in Part One of *The Tale of Genji* as it is in *The Lighthouse*, and as absent from the Uji chapters in general as it is from "Ukifune" in particular. The effect of this shift in narrative character can be compared loosely to a contrast noted by the narrator in Marcel Proust's *À la recherche du temps perdu*.

---

[27] Stinchecum, "Who Tells the Tale? 'Ukifune': A Study in Narrative Voice," 388.

Having seen a young woman encouraging her female lover to desecrate an image of her (the young woman's) father, the narrator observes:

> It is behind the footlights of a Paris theatre and not under the homely lamp of an actual country house that one expects to see a girl encouraging a friend to spit upon the portrait of a father who has lived and died for her alone; and when we find in real life a desire for melodramatic effect, it is generally sadism that is responsible for it.[28]

"A Paris theatre" translates *théâtres de boulevard*, places of popular entertainment that favor the lurid or melodramatic.[29] The comparison suggested here involves neither sadism nor any notion that the Uji chapters actually are melodrama. Rather, it appeals to a general feature of *mélodrame* as understood in French: stress on calculatedly pathetic effect.[30] The shift in question is therefore one from apparent naturalness to visible artifice, or from convincingly natural emotion to affective states dramatically unfamiliar enough to strain comprehension. It also recalls the Chief Equerry's distinction, in "Hahakigi," between paintings of "commonplace mountains and streams, the everyday shapes of houses, all looking just as one knows them to be," and of "things like Mount Hōrai, raging leviathans amid stormy seas...or the faces of invisible demons."[31] The former corresponds to Proust's "under the homely lamp of an actual country house," and the latter to his "girl encouraging a friend to spit upon the portrait of a father who has lived and died for her alone."

Ōigimi's feelings about marriage to Kaoru illustrate the latter. Despite refusing to marry him, she still feels such possibilities of spiritual communion with him that she wants to have her younger sister turn away *her* suitor, Niou, and marry Kaoru instead. "I feel as

---

[28] Proust, *Remembrance of Things Past* 1:178-179; and *À la recherche du temps perdu* 1:161.

[29] Specifically, the drama typical of the popular theaters along the Boulevard du Temple, before Haussmann's redesign of Paris in 1862 destroyed them.

[30] Stress on pathetic effect is central to such generally available definitions of *mélodrame* as that given in *Dictionnaire historique de la langue française*.

[31] TTG, 27; GM 1:69-70.

though I should then be with both," she explains to Ben, "and our two hearts, hers and mine, would be one in her."[32] She means to unite herself with Kaoru after all, but through her sister. As Norma Field put it: "An extraordinary vision, this: shrouded and thus invisible in her sister's body, Ōigimi will be able to see (possess) Kaoru's and conclude a marriage of true minds."[33] Although heartrending in its desperate ingenuity, Ōigimi's imagined solution to her dilemma is also as impenetrable in practice as the rage and hatred of Proust's young woman. Suggesting as it does a degree of artifice, it therefore reveals, on the underside of the author's expertly woven brocade, the threads of intention that lead to Kaoru's agonizingly chaste night with Nakanokimi and then maneuver Ōigimi, Nakanokimi, and Kaoru through it.

Discussions of Ōigimi, as of Kaoru and other characters in the Uji chapters, generally approach her from a psychological perspective, thus treating her as an autonomous agent whose refusal to marry Kaoru and subsequent death from self-starvation can be explained from what the narrator reveals, more or less transparently, about her. However it is also possible to view what she says, does, or feels, as well as what she knows about the attitudes and intentions of others, from the standpoint of plot construction. Being relatively isolated from one another, the characters in the Uji chapters are available to be manipulated for the purpose of achieving a desired effect. The analysis of Kaoru will pursue this theme of disassociation not only between characters, but also between elements of individual personality.

Ōigimi's father makes it clear to Kaoru that he hopes Kaoru will look after his daughters after he is gone ("Hashihime"). In Part Two ("Wakana One"), Retired Emperor Suzaku similarly asks Genji to look after his favorite daughter, the Third Princess. He means that Genji should marry her, as Genji does. Kaoru apparently understands Ōigimi's father to mean the same thing, especially since he contemplates taking possession of both. He and the reader are therefore entitled to believe that if he marries Ōigimi, he will do so

32 TTG, 880; GM 5:248
33 Field, *The Splendor of Longing*, 242-243.

with her father's posthumous approval. As Ben's lengthy reply to Ōigimi shows, the whole household believes that Ōigimi's father desired this marriage, having heard him say "often enough that, should [Kaoru] be so inclined, he would very gladly see [Ōigimi] that well settled."[34]

However, Ōigimi knows nothing of this. She believes that her father merely warned his daughters against taking any rash step in the direction of marriage, lest they court shame and misfortune, and she is unaware that he ever favored her accepting Kaoru. To her, the notion of marriage is therefore dangerous and unauthorized.[35] She accepts that her father counted on Kaoru to look after them materially, but she recognizes no connection between material support and marriage. This makes her unique in the tale. The purpose of her misapprehension therefore seems to be an impasse designed for pathetic effect.

Personal feeling on either side furthers the impasse. Each feels a community of spirit with the other, encouraged by the high-minded sentiments that Kaoru professes both to Ōigimi and to himself. However, Kaoru also desires her sexually, while for her sexual relations (marriage) are out of the question. On this level, neither has the slightest comprehension of the other. To secure the impasse, and to drive Ōigimi to mortal despair, the author must insure that Kaoru never achieves with Ōigimi what Genji's son Yūgiri does with Princess Ochiba ("Yūgiri").

Princess Ochiba, the widow of Yūgiri's friend Kashiwagi, resists Yūgiri when he pursues her. She has no parental authorization to accept him, and she also knows that Kashiwagi found her unattractive. This, together with her age, convinces her that she is in any case too unsightly to remarry. However, Yūgiri perseveres. His first attempt to make love with her ends badly when she escapes through a door he

---

[34] TTG, 880; GM 5:249

[35] The issue of parental authorization is discussed in Tyler, "Marriage, Rank and Rape." Many other explanations have been offered. See Bargen, *A Woman's Weapon*, 194-205; Field, *The Splendor of Longing*, 235-250; and Shirane, *The Bridge of Dreams*, 141-144. *Kekkon kyohi* (rejection of marriage) is a theme in Japanese scholarship on the tale; see Takada, *Genji monogatari no bungakushi*, 164-189, especially 173-180.

cannot open, and his prolonged presence in the house, at night, nonetheless convinces outsiders that he has succeeded. The shock kills her mother, weakened as she already is by illness. Eventually, he more or less corners her in a room where she cowers with a robe over her head, sweeps the robe aside, and accomplishes his purpose at last. The act constitutes the marriage he desired, and it saves her. She would have been lost otherwise.

The same outcome would serve Ōigimi equally well. Kaoru would not fail her. The mechanism that moves her toward death therefore sums up the purposeful desolation of these chapters as fully as her death itself. Critical to this mechanism is Kaoru's sexual tact, discretion, or diffidence. The shining Genji was so daring and resourceful in love, and in sexual relations so quick to act, that the *Mumyōzōshi* author objected to him. Kaoru's compunction can seem admirable in comparison. Some readers may also feel an affinity with him because of his slips and failures in the intimate situations that are so important to us all and that do not always go smoothly.

The *Mumyōzōshi* author was probably thinking especially of Kaoru's "hope that in time [Ōigimi, who has just frustrated his advances] would yield to him on her own."[36] She presumably accepted the narrator's repeated assurances that Kaoru is kind, steadfast, thoughtful, tactful, and deeply pious. However, it is possible to ask whether Kaoru really is what he seems, and even whether a coherent Kaoru exists at all. If none does, then Kaoru's reason for not taking the decisive initiative with Ōigimi comes into question. The author then fosters the "Kaoru illusion" by focusing the reader's whole sympathy on him, as on a beloved child at odds with the world, and weaves her narrative so as to make him suffer repeatedly as the innocent victim of fate, birth, ill luck, or misunderstanding. To achieve this pathetic effect she leaves visible threads of intention on the underside of her weave.

Mitani Kuniaki stated in his "Genji monogatari daisanbu no hōhō" that Part Three (especially the Uji chapters) throws the "myth of unity" of character into question and that Kaoru's character, in particular, is "dispersed" and without central meaning. "Speech, interior monologue,

---

[36] TTG, 875; GM 5:235.

the unconscious, and so on," he wrote, "lose their unity, disperse, and enter into 'dialogue' with one another."[37] More recently, Kanda Tatsumi noted similarly that Kaoru knows nothing about himself because his self is "hollowed out" (a expression borrowed from Mitani) and lacks any foundation. As a result, Kanda wrote, the narrator is obliged at times to supply, in her own comments, a psychology of which Kaoru himself knows nothing.[38] This Kaoru is therefore not psychologically conceived. He dissolves as a character if the reader ceases to commiserate with him. His apparent psychological complexity can then be described as an illusion created by the many ways devised by the author to renew the reader's sympathy for him. Seen in this light he has iconographic attributes rather than psychological traits. These include, among other things, seriousness, piety, dilatoriness, and subjection to desire. They are not psychologically integrated.

This lack of integration extends to Kaoru's love life. Many readers must have wondered why he never successfully consummates a relationship either with Ōigimi or with her younger sister. His failure, which seems at first to resemble Genji's with Princess Asagao, could almost be seen as an elaboration on it. Asagao and Ōigimi both like the gentleman well enough but resolutely reject his advances. Both distrust men (Asagao distrusts Genji especially), and both come to suspect their gentlewomen of conniving against them. Kaoru claims to be waiting for Ōigimi's assent, while Genji, who is "biding his time" until "his devoted attentions...soften [Asagao] toward him," "seems never to have considered forcibly breaking her resistance."[39] This uncharacteristic discretion makes him resemble Kaoru after all. However, the two diverge on a critical point. Although Genji likes Asagao, he is not in love with her. He has been courting her for other reasons, and desire is not one of them.

Kaoru, however, desires Ōigimi, if the narrator is to be believed. Nevertheless, he holds back when he has his one great chance with her,

---

[37] Mitani Kuniaki, "Genji monogatari daisanbu no hōhō," 94.

[38] Kanda, "'Kaoru' no bunretsu o genzen saseru tasō na kotoba," 115.

[39] TTG, 380, GM 3:20.

and again with her sister. The narrator insists that he does so because he is so much nicer, kinder, and so on than anyone else, but these protestations are not entirely convincing. Perhaps he has low libido, for example, or some other condition that discourages him unusually easily. The homoerotic feeling for the Uji sisters' father mentioned by Doris Bargen[40] and strongly implied by Paul Schalow suggests that possibility. However, even though this reading makes sense with respect to that single relationship, nothing elsewhere in the narrative encourages extending it further.

Mitani Kuniaki suggested another way to solve the problem of Kaoru's diffidence. He argued that Kaoru's admiration for the Eighth Prince led him to elaborate for himself a "superego" identified with the Eighth Prince's purely spiritual nature and to attribute the same nature to his daughters, who were to him extensions of their father. Since no physical desire for Ōigimi or Nakanokimi could then be legitimate, Kaoru's "superego" intervened to quell it whenever it arose. Mitani's theory does not acknowledge the narrative's explanations, discussed below, for Kaoru's failure to act. It also requires a psychology more coherent than the one Mitani himself attributed to Kaoru when he reasserted in this article the disparate nature of Kaoru's character. He wrote that Kaoru's conversation, unvoiced thoughts, behavior, unconscious, and physical person all diverge in different directions.[41] No such character could have either psychology or autonomy. He could not function at all unless his creator manipulated his disparate parts so as to make them work together toward particular ends.

According to the narrator, Kaoru's desire for Ōigimi and then Nakanokimi is compelling, and he certainly seems capable of possessing Ukifune as soon as she comes into his hands ("Azumaya").[42]

---

[40] Bargen, "The Search for Things Past in the *Genji monogatari*," 192.

[41] Mitani Kuniaki, "Torawareta shisō," 296.

[42] The text says nothing explicit about what goes on during the first night that Kaoru spends with Ukifune. However, in order to claim full possession of her, as he certainly does, he would have to have intercourse with her; and what the narrator says about his desire for Ōigimi and Nakanokimi suggests that he is capable of doing so. He may not excite or satisfy Ukifune as Niou does, but he seems to be her lover.

His relationship with the gentlewoman Kozaishō ("Kagerō," ch. 52) appears to be straightforward. Perhaps his last-minute discretion with Ōigimi and Nakanokimi indeed proves that he is as kind as the narrator claims and, in the service of his tact, as fully the master of his ardor. But perhaps it does not.

The first two scenes of all-but-intimacy between Kaoru and Ōigimi or Nakanokimi occur in "Agemaki," and the third in "Yadorigi." Each dramatizes the discrepancy between Kaoru's pious intentions and the behavior to which desire drives him. Each also offers, to a greater or lesser degree, the same possibility of mocking comedy as the scene in which Kaoru dresses his wife up in silk gauze and has her hold a piece of ice. That phantom element of comedy is detectable as well in a fourth scene ("Agemaki") in which, despite Kaoru's entreaties, Ōigimi keeps a locked door between herself and Kaoru, despite Kaoru's entreaties, even as Niou, inside the house, makes love to Nakanokimi. The circumstances throughout are intricately manipulated.

Kaoru and Ōigimi

The first scene[43] starts with Kaoru longing merely (or so he believes) to spend the night in quiet conversation with Ōigimi. *Monogatari su* ("chat"), like the more common *katarau*, is a cover expression for lovemaking, but the narrator has him take it literally. However, Ōigimi detects in his manner a "vague irritation" *(monouramigachi naru on-keshiki)* that may portend something else. She is reluctant to receive him, but he has always been so kind that she does so nonetheless, after taking care to protect herself and keep the place well lit. He complains, then makes himself at home and soon starts thinking "how silly it [is] of him, with no more than a screen and a blind between them, to remain so slow to act on his ardent desire."

This callous "silly" *(okogamashiku)* counters the thoughtfulness for which Kaoru is known and extends a pattern, initiated by the complaints mentioned, that pervades these scenes: a layered alternation of tact and petulance, generosity and self-pitying anger.

---

[43] TTG, 874-877, GM 5:232-239.

Such mood shifts occur in living people, too, but in Kaoru's case the alternation continues as though the narrator highlighted now one iconographic attribute, now another; or as though Kaoru were a puppet in a split costume, red and blue, and the puppeteer displayed now one side, now the other. As Suzuki Hideo observed, Kaoru's self-justifications "sound reasonable but make no sense."[44] Throughout the Uji chapters Kaoru vacillates in the same way between pious sentiment and helpless subjection to erotic longings. Noting this phenomenon, Mitani observed that it is useless to search the Uji chapters for any deepening of theme or characterization. Kaoru remains the same from beginning to end. Mitani called this a manifestation of the "absence" that characterizes Part Three.[45]

When Ōigimi moves to retire, Kaoru reproves her, sweeps aside the screen between them, enters the room, and seizes her skirts. Furious, she accuses him of appalling behavior. He bitterly protests injured innocence, but nothing in Parts One and Two supports him: violation of a woman's privacy and claims of innocent intentions are mutually contradictory. He has already crossed the line, and in a moment he will go further: "By the intriguingly dim lamplight he swept her streaming hair aside and looked at her face." If there is anywhere in *The Tale of Genji* a genuine example of what Richard Bowring called "visual rape,"[46] this is it. A kind, tactful Kaoru genuinely intent on respecting her wishes could not possibly do such a thing. The effect on her self-esteem is devastating, as the narrative shows later on, but he goes on nonetheless to congratulate himself for not having done what any "lustful man" would have done in his place. His sentiments call on the reader to admire his restraint, but his actions make them unintelligible. While he tries to soothe her feelings, she silently laments that he has now seen, "caught in the lamplight," the grey she wears in mourning for her late father. This thought, too, is pure misery.

The room contains also her father's altar, with its conventional offerings of star anise *(shikimi)* and burning incense. Decorously from

[44] Suzuki Hideo, "Kaoru ni okeru dōshin to shūshin," 536.
[45] Mitani Kuniaki, "Genji monogatari daisanbu no hōhō," 90.
[46] Bowring, *Murasaki Shikibu: The Tale of Genji*, 13.

his standpoint, perhaps, but suggestively from the reader's, Kaoru places a curtain between them and the altar, and then lies down beside her. Has the moment come after all? No, this time the incense and the scent of star anise trouble him, to whom (the narrator reminds us) the Buddha means so much. "Especially now when she is still in mourning," he says to himself, "struggling to regain his composure, any thoughtless concession to my impatience would be an offense against what I aspired to first [a life of Buddhist renunciation]." In other words, his alleged respect for Ōigimi's wishes, and her obvious distress, restrain him less than the Buddhist fragrances wafting about him and the grey of her robes, both of which recall his own pious aspirations, and both of which he should have foreseen from the start. Despite the pathos in this collision between Eros and piety, the piety may also look naïve and selfish. The night ends with a picture of the pair looking out together at a poignant dawn sky.

For Kaoru it is the incense smoke and those grey robes, rather than respect for Ōigimi, that live on in mind as the reason he went no further. However, they do not deter him from trying once more. The next scene begins, "[Kaoru], too eager to await the ninth month when [Ōigimi] would no longer wear the mourning he had felt obliged to respect, now came again."[47]

Kaoru and Nakanokimi (1)

Ben's remonstrances to Ōigimi and Ōigimi's plan to steer Kaoru toward Nakanokimi prepare this scene. Never mind Ōigimi's mourning; Kaoru cannot wait. If he were psychologically conceived, his resolve to act decisively this time would be obvious, even before Ōigimi refuses to receive him and he says to Ben, "Then tonight you must find me a way to steal in to where she is sleeping." However, precedent in these chapters suggests something unexpected, something that purports to demonstrate Kaoru's good will and invites commiseration with him.

---

[47] TTG, 878-883; GM 5:243-256.

Kaoru enters the room and finds there a single recumbent figure. She is not Ōigimi. The two sisters always sleep together, and the vigilant Ōigimi, who hears him coming, slips away without a word while her sister sleeps on. The scene seems to parody the one in which Utsusemi slips away just before Genji's arrival, leaving him the sleeping Nokiba no Ogi ("Utsusemi"). That episode is unmistakable, engaging comedy. This scene, too, offers a ghost of comedy, but with a mocking flavor. While Utsusemi escapes with her self-respect intact into another part of the house, Ōigimi has nowhere to go beyond that same room and so is reduced to hiding between a screen and the wall. In anguish she watches Nakanokimi wake up, horrified, while Kaoru lies down beside her. Infuriated by Ōigimi's treachery and reluctant at the same time to leave Nakanokimi to anyone else, Kaoru nonetheless refrains from possessing her because he still wants to assure himself possession of Ōigimi *first*. The "Utsusemi" scene is charmingly simple in comparison with this labyrinth of scheming and calculated desire.

"On this resolve he spent the night, as before [with Ōigimi], in sweet and amusing conversation" (*okashiku natsukashiki sama ni kataraite akashi-tamaitsu*). It is a disarming picture, except that under the surface Nakanokimi is still miserable, Kaoru is still furious, and Ōigimi spends the entire night cowering ignominiously behind the screen. There is nothing wrong with taking this scene as the author apparently meant it to be taken, but there is also no denying, on reflection, that the elements in it cast unpleasant shadows. Meanwhile, the women of the household cackle to each other like a flock of hens (the narrator's touch) about what they mistakenly think is going on. The next morning, Ben is "dumbfounded and filled with pity" when Kaoru gives her an account of the night. He says he wants to die and assures her that he would, if only the memory of the sisters' loving father did not make him reluctant to abandon them even now. To drive home his hurt and self-pity, the narrative gives him a particularly cruel dig at the hapless Ōigimi. "I gather that [Niou] is unashamedly pursuing [Nakanokimi]," he says, "and I suppose [Ōigimi] feels that she might as well reach as high as she can."

The end of Ōigimi's story

The drama continues in the same spirit[48] when Kaoru, who has repeatedly considered appropriating both sisters, decides instead to bring his friend Niou (understood to be the next heir apparent) into the game. His silent calculations on the issue, and his banter with Niou, are confusing not only in themselves, but also in the light of what the reader already knows about him, Niou, and Ōigimi. The maneuvers, delusions, and deceptions that follow belong indeed on the stage of a *théâtre de boulevard*. The only figure to emerge satisfied from it all is Niou: secretly introduced into the Uji house by Ben, at Kaoru's order, he enjoys a gratifying night with Nakanokimi. By the time he and Kaoru leave again, Nakanokimi is no longer on speaking terms with her sister, Ōigimi is beside herself with outrage at Kaoru's behavior, and Kaoru, wounded and pleading, has spent the night locked out of the house.

All this ends with Ōigimi making up her mind to die.[49] However, she still loves Kaoru. "I cannot possibly keep him away," she reflects, "now that he is close beside me and knows everything about me, but even so, what seems to be strong affection would fade on both sides with familiarity and end in misery and grief." Kaoru "knows everything about" her because he has seen and touched her face. To Ōigimi they are therefore as nearly married as, once, Kaoru nearly succeeded in marrying her. The author has brought her theme of tragically failed love almost to its conclusion. There remains only for Ōigimi to die of self-starvation with Kaoru beside her and for Kaoru, beautiful and endlessly affecting in his grief, to mourn.

Kaoru and Nakanokimi (2)

Kaoru goes on to a transitional involvement with Nakanokimi and subsequent preoccupation with Ukifune. His intimate scene with

---

[48] TTG, 884-887, GM 5:261-268.
[49] TTG, 907-909, GM 5:323-330.

Nakanokimi[50] follows the pattern of the one with Ōigimi. Once, he assured both Ōigimi and himself that he could not possibly shift his affections to Nakanokimi, whom the narrative presented as quite distinct from her sister. After Ōigimi's death, however, he notices that Nakanokimi looks and sounds just like her, so that he remains on the same path as before. In other respects, too, he remains the same. The rashness, the self-pitying reproaches, the cutting accusations reappear in his scene with Nakanokimi, layered between talk of his tact and his good intentions; and so, too, does the phantom of mocking humor. A hip band that Nakanokimi wears because she is pregnant plays this time the role of Ōigimi's mourning grey.

The major difference between the two scenes is the folly of the second. Decisiveness with Ōigimi might have saved her life, but success with Nakanokimi could destroy hers. Niou, to whom Nakanokimi is now married, is already suspicious of her relationship with Kaoru. Despite her unhappiness over Niou's recent marriage also to a daughter of Yūgiri, she is better off than she would have been had she remained at Uji. Kaoru's paroxysm of desire risks wrecking what she has, and it is so intense that he forgets Niou completely. "Think what this will look like to other people!" she cries out in protest at the liberties he is taking; to which he retorts, "Why should anyone mind? ...Just remember that other time! Your sister approved, after all!" The thoughtful Kaoru has taken leave of his senses. This time he goes further than he did with Ōigimi, since he actually gets his hands under Nakanokimi's clothes. As the narrator observes, "The scene was not of the kind one may dwell on at length." That is how he discovers the hip band that she has on; whereupon "the rare tact that was always his, even long ago, restrained him even now from acting on his desire." "Yes," he reflects after leaving, "what kept me back was mainly feeling sorry for her over that hip band she was so embarrassed about."

Straightforward consideration for the woman again fails to move Kaoru. Instead the reader's attention is deflected, as before, away from the woman's feelings and toward an object that arouses Kaoru's delicate tact and consequent disappointment. The mourning grey and

---

[50] TTG, 946-948, GM 423-430.

the hip band,[51] not the woman's resistance, are what frustrate Kaoru's desire and so arouse the reader's sympathy for him—a sympathy all the greater is this second scene because his desire is even more recklessly consuming. "He could not imagine not having her," the narrator says, but he still asks himself, "How can I possibly have my desire without causing a scandal?" There is no answer to his question, and his hopeless longing cries out as ever for pity.

The journey to Uji

No passage in the Uji chapters illustrates the cultivation of pathos more vividly than Kaoru's journey to Uji with Ukifune.[52] To judge from a recent conference presentation by Mitamura Masako, many readers admire this passage particularly.[53] However, its main features also support the argument of this essay.

After taking possession of Ukifune, Kaoru sets out with her the next morning for Uji. The two occupy the front of the carriage, while the gentlewoman Jijū and the nun Ben ride in the back. The passage has been abbreviated as much as possible.

> Now that Jijū could see [Kaoru] a little she forgot every demand of decent manners and gave in to rapt and longing wonder.
>
> [Ukifune] lay face down, dazed by the shock. "The rocky places are very difficult," he said and took her in his arms. The silk gauze long dress hung to divide the carriage glowed in the light of the newly risen sun, and the nun felt excruciatingly out of place. Ah, she reflected sadly, it is [Ōigimi] I should have seen like this with [him]!...Her face puckered up, and...she

---

[51] Kaoru, who should not have discovered the hip band in the first place, does not think when he finds it, "Good God, she's pregnant with Niou's child! I simply can't go on with this!" Instead, the narrator's focus on Nakanokimi's embarrassment when he finds it excludes Niou (his friend, her husband) from consideration and reduces the situation solely to Kaoru-and-Nakanokimi. Kaoru can then be movingly tactful about an embarrassment that is very minor in comparison with all that he has ignored.

[52] TTG, 1002-1003, GM 6:94-96.

[53] Mitamura, "Genji monogatari no 'kuruma' no kūkan."

wept...Jijū thought her perfectly horrid. Why, she thought, she doesn't belong here anyway at the happy start of a marriage! What business does she have blubbering away like that?

[Ukifune] was his now...but under such skies his sense of loss only mounted, and the further they went into the hills, the more thickly the mists seemed to rise around him. Their sleeves as he leaned on an armrest, lost in thought, trailed away out of the carriage, one on the other, wet with the mists of the river. The scarlet of the gown looked wrong against the petal blue of the dress cloak: he noticed it at the top of a steep slope and drew both in.

> *"Now that she is mine,*
> *to keep fresh that memory,*
> *how the morning dew*
> *settles in fast-fallings drops*
> *on these sadly moistened sleeves!"*

he murmured...At this the nun only drenched her sleeves the more...[Her] stifled sniffling started [Kaoru] quietly blowing his nose as well.

Concern for [Ukifune's] feelings...prompted him to observe, "It makes me sad...to think how often I have taken this path over the years. Do sit up a little...You are so silent!" He made her sit, and the way she looked shyly out, her face prettily hidden behind her fan, struck him as remarkably similar [to Ōigimi], except that she seemed all too worryingly meek and mild. His lost love had had a childlike quality too, but also what depth of reflection! His sorrow, which still had nowhere to go, seemed capable of filling the vast, empty heavens.

Jijū's rapturous glimpses of Kaoru's beauty introduce the scene. The silk curtain glows theatrically in the light of the rising sun, and before it Kaoru takes Ukifune tenderly in his arms to protect her from bumps and jolts. Ben's lament for Ōigimi moves the audience to appreciate Kaoru's own mood. Then Ben weeps, and Jijū, swept away by romantic fancies, thinks her "perfectly horrid" for blighting the moment with her ill-omened tears. The narrative's mocking attitude toward the old nun in "Tenarai"[54] suggests that, by inviting her audience to share Jijū's indignation, the author seeks again to emphasize the depth of Kaoru's melancholy.

All goes well as long as the audience sympathizes fully with Kaoru. However, it is important that the audience's sympathy should not wander to include others caught up in his misfortunes. If the young woman in his arms is not Ōigimi, that is because he failed ever to possess Ōigimi. The one with him now, Ukifune, means less to him in her own person than Jijū imagines. He has no intention of establishing with her a relationship that anyone who matters could possibly mistake for a marriage; that is why he is taking her to distant Uji in the first place. No doubt he has been desperate to get her, having among other things suborned a nun to serve this profane purpose, but to him she is still only a stand-in for her late half-sister. Ukifune hardly figures in his thoughts, except as the "doll" of which he once spoke to Nakanokimi. None of this is very nice, but the point of the scene is elsewhere. Poor Kaoru is suffering the torments of a noble, ill-fated love, and "his sorrow...seem[s] capable of filling the vast, empty heavens."

Inflated sentiments may collapse suddenly. While melancholy mists rise around him, Kaoru notes a discordant tint in the sleeves that spill outside the carriage. The moment recalls the effect of the ice held by Kaoru's wife, of the incense smoke and Ōigimi's mourning grey, and of Nakanokimi's hip band. Ukifune's scarlet over his light blue yield a grey-mauve that reminds him of mourning,[55] and in a gesture of vain struggle against the mood that has already overwhelmed him he draws the sleeves in. There is no more artfully precious touch in the whole tale. Then Kaoru murmurs his dewy poem; Ben begins crying again, to Jijū's disgust; and her sniffling starts Kaoru himself blowing his nose. The scene threatens to tip over into self-parody.

---

54 TTG, 1092-1093, GM 6:319-321.
55 The published Tyler translation (1002) fails to make it clear that one of the sleeves appears to be his and one hers.

Eros and piety

Kaoru's misfortunes in love spring from one comprehensive misfortune: that he loves, yearns, desires at all. Even before he loses Ōigimi, his longing for her represents a loss of his earlier, pure aspiration to a life of Buddhist piety and practice. One gathers in "Niou Miya" that this aspiration grew in him because he suspected some irregularity in his birth and so felt out of place in the world. Too fastidious to accept the kind of teachers more readily available to him, he at last found what he sought in the Eighth Prince at Uji: a refined gentleman whom disappointment with the world had likewise turned, years before, to Buddhist devotion. It is only after a few years of visiting the Eighth Prince, to study and discuss the Buddha's teaching, that Kaoru first hears the sisters making music together and sees them through a gap in the fence. Then his troubles begin.

Thereafter Kaoru remains caught between his original hope to lead a life of renunciation and all the sorrowful distractions of repeatedly failed love. Many writers on Part Three have noted the prominence of religious aspiration in these chapters and have seen depth in his spiritual conflict. Konishi Jin'ichi, for example, discerned a pair of themes for each part of the tale (reality and clear insight; karma and predetermined suffering; piety and spiritual blindness); wrote that each pair embraces all the preceding ones; and thus read Part Three as summing up in Kaoru's basic dilemma (no doubt prolonged by Ukifune's) the fundamental concerns of the entire work. [56] His evaluation of Part Three as a supreme masterpiece therefore corresponds to that of Takeda Munetoshi, quoted in the Introduction. Mitani Kuniaki summed up the theme of Part Three, first announced at the start of the Uji chapters, in the question, "Can a layman lead a truly Buddhist life?" *(zoku hijiri to wa kanō ka),*[57] or, more generally, "Can one really be in the world but not of it?"

---

[56] Konishi, *A History of Japanese Literature,* Volume Two, 333.

[57] Mitani Kuniaki, "Genji monogatari daisanbu no hōhō," 87. *Zoku hijiri* ("a holy man in lay life") is an expression used in the text to describe the Eighth Prince.

The question may be profound, but not every treatment of it is necessarily deep. The one in the Uji chapters might go further if Kaoru were truly a character. As it is, the main functions of his piety are to arouse the reader's sympathy for admirable sentiments so unusual in a young man, especially one as attractive as he, and to act as a foil for his hapless ventures into the realm of desire. His professed indifference to worldly concerns so absorbing to others, and his nostalgia for a purely spiritual life, invite one to feel sorry for him when cruel passion and circumstance entangle him nonetheless in profane suffering.

If the author's treatment of the theme Mitani proposed were convincing psychologically, this where that psychology might begin to show, but it never does. Nothing changes. Just as generous Kaoru and angrily self-pitying Kaoru alternate in intimate scenes without ever actually meeting, pious Kaoru and love-struck Kaoru blink on and off in alternating colors. There is no struggle, no evolution, only an endlessly renewed invitation to feel sorry for him.

Even Kaoru's discovery of the truth about his birth goes nowhere. "Niou Miya," the first chapter of Part Three, describes him as deeply anxious about this matter, which

> was always on his mind...What *did* happen? he often
> wondered. Why was I born to such constant anxiety? If only
> I was enlightened like Prince Zengyō, when he asked himself
> the same sort of thing!

> *What can it all mean,*
> *and whom have I to question?*
> *What is my secret,*
> *when I myself do not know*
> *whence I come or where I go?*

But there was no one to give him an answer.[58]
Then he learns the truth ("Hashihime"), and the chapter ends with him expecting to "reflect on [it] in every way."[59] However, he does not. Citing this blank as evidence of the repetition, as distinguished from

---

[58] TTG, 787; GM 5:23-24.
[59] TTG, 846; GM 5:166.

development, characteristic of the Uji chapters, Mitani mentioned the only visible consequence of Kaoru's discovery. It appears in "Shiigamoto," just after the Eighth Prince's death. Having talked again to Ben, who told him the whole story and gave him the letters exchanged by his mother and his real father, Kaoru assumes that since old women are always such gossips, she must at least have told the tale to her bashful mistresses, even if she had not simply blurted it out to everyone, and this was no doubt so galling and embarrassing that he considered it reason enough to make sure that neither sister went to anyone else.[60] What really concerns him is therefore to make sure that no one else finds out. Ensuring both sisters' silence could constitute for him reason enough to keep both for himself.

This sharp focus on self-interest, to the exclusion of all other considerations, is not implausible. Such thoughts flit through anyone's mind. After learning the truth of his birth, a psychologically conceived Kaoru would begin an internal debate of which this would probably be an element. Naturally he would fear the consequences if everyone were to learn whose son he really is, but he would also recoil from knowingly disavowing his true father and living a conscious lie before the world. Such thoughts would occur to anyone in his position, in any time or place, and certainly in Heian Japan.[61]

Two similar situations figure in Part One of the tale. Upon learning that his true father is Genji ("Usugumo"), the Reizei emperor trembles at the thought that he has never honored Genji enough and seeks to remedy that lapse immediately. In the second, Tamakazura and Genji have always known that Tamakazura's father is Tō no Chūjō, but when Genji brings her to live on his Rokujō estate ("Tamakazura") he presents her to the world as his own daughter—in other words, as a Minamoto, like himself. However, she is really a Fujiwara. Genji knows that the truth will come out in the end, and this certainty affects his

---

[60] TTG, 860; Kaoru describes his feelings to Ben in these terms.
[61] Mitani Kuniaki ("Genji monogatari daisanbu no hōhō," 96) cited the fact that discovering the secret of his birth has no influence on Kaoru, psychological or otherwise, as further evidence that Kaoru is not psychologically conceived.

planning for her future. There will come a time when she *must* be able openly to honor the Fujiwara ancestral shrine ("Miyuki").[62]

Kaoru's discovery means the same change from Minamoto to Fujiwara, since his real father was Tō no Chūjō's son. However, Kaoru never gives the matter a thought, nor does inner debate ever take place. Instead, the narrator drops the matter so completely that one suspects her, too, of having forgotten about it. Reflecting on some remarks made about Kaoru by Genji's daughter (the Akashi Empress), the narrator says in "Kagerō," "It was true that she and [Kaoru] were brother and sister *[on-harakara naredo],* but she was still somewhat in awe of him..."[63] The problem has vanished, and Kaoru is now Genji's son. Kaoru's natural fragrance, so prominent in the opening chapters of Part Three, eventually vanishes, too. First mentioned in "Niou Miya," it is Kaoru's somewhat rarified counterpart to Genji's light, and it marks him, too, as exceptional. Insisting on his beauty, grace, and dignity, "Takekawa" describes him as favored by all, just as Genji had been at that age. The fragrance appears in passing as late as "Azumaya," when some gentlewomen associate it with his reputation for piety.[64] However, when Niou impersonates Kaoru ("Ukifune") in order to make love to Ukifune, no one in the house, not even Ukifune herself, notices that the gentleman who claims to be Kaoru and imitates Kaoru's voice lacks the scent that always used to give Kaoru's presence away.

Kaoru's birth, his scent: these ancillary matters seem to have dropped out once the author had him fully established as a pathetic hero caught between renunciation and desire, kindness and cruel circumstance. Mitani Kuniaki is not alone in having pointed out that his plight never changes. Suzuki Hideo, too, wrote that the method adopted throughout is to keep Kaoru in equilibrium between attachment to the profane world and emancipation from it, adding that

---

[62] TTG, 502; GM 3:295-296.

[63] TTG, 1066; GM 6:

[64] TTG, 998; GM 6:54-55. Regarding the way the women associate Kaoru's fragrance with that of the Medicine King in the *Lotus Sutra,* Hyōdō Hiromi remarked that this makes the tale told in the Uji chapters a very "cynical" one (Hyōdō, "Monogatari no katarite to sei," 87).

this method explains many obvious manipulations of the plot.[65] But what does it achieve?

The secret of Kaoru's birth and his scent both hark back to Genji. As the Uji chapters progress, however, this entanglement with Genji's memory becomes less and less meaningful. Busy with his own troubles and, in the background, rising steadily in the world, Kaoru comes to stand on his own. By the time he and the Akashi Empress are simply "brother and sister," he has become less a successor to Genji than, in "Ukifune" and beyond, a major figure in a brilliantly melodramatic novel featuring suspense, intrigue, agonizing love, death, supernatural intervention, mystery, and so on. Sometimes even Kaoru's soft appeal drops away, as when he orders a sort of thug boss to post guards around the house at Uji ("Ukifune"). However, his preoccupation with renunciation on the one hand, and the call of desire on the other, continue unresolved to the end of the book, apparently so that noble, unwavering aspiration should to the end render his profane sorrows as poignant as they can possibly be.

In the end the story threatens to burst the bounds of this invariant method. By "Yume no ukihashi," the last chapter, Kaoru's profane desires seem to have mastered him. As once in "Ukifune" he had the nun Ben act as a procuress for him, he now appeals to Yokawa no Sōzu, the greatest healer of his time, to deliver Ukifune again into his hands. "It would be a sin for me to play any such part in bringing you to her," Yokawa no Sōzu replies, even though by this time the Ukifune affair has seriously compromised him as well. But Kaoru claims innocence.

> [Kaoru] smiled. "I am mortified that my request should seem to you to carry the danger of sin. I myself hardly understand how I can have lived this long as a layman...I take care never to do what the Buddha forbids, to the extent that I understand these things, and at heart I am no less than a holy man myself. How could I possibly place myself at risk of sin in so trivial a matter?..."

---

[65] Suzuki Hideo, "Uji no monogatari no shudai," 367. Suzuki further suggested (375) that Ōigimi's death itself is required in order to preserve this balance.

His Reverence nodded his assent. "Your intentions are
most praiseworthy," he said...[66]

Overwhelmed by Kaoru's rank and (despite Kaoru's protestations) by
the evident urgency of his desire, Yokawa no Sōzu has no choice but at
least to seem to believe him. However, it is difficult to take seriously—
indeed, to accept as meaning anything at all—the idea that even now
Kaoru should represent himself as "at heart...no less than a holy man."

Conclusion

This experiment in grasping the figure of Kaoru from the perspective
of literary artifice rather than psychology has highlighted several
distinct differences between Part Three of the tale and the two parts
that precede it. It has argued that Part Three develops the motif of
surrogacy beyond anything seen earlier and gives it a new character
that tends to depersonalize the surrogate. It has discussed the
characters' isolation from one other and suggested a connection
between this isolation and plot manipulation by the author. It has also
detected in the Uji chapters a recurring flavor of mocking humor. In
Kaoru's case it has analyzed the isolation even of separate aspects of
the same character and treated it as a technique designed to achieve
ever-renewed pathetic effects. Finally, it has similarly interpreted
Kaoru's vacillation between religious aspiration and erotic desire less
as a searching treatment of this theme than as a device to heighten his
sentimental appeal, and it has noted that this vacillation continues
unchanged all the way to the end of the book.

In contrast, Parts One and Two follow the trajectory of a hero's life
shaped from within and without not only by the background passage
of the years, but also by such integrated issues as pride, ambition,
desire, and ever-changing public as well as private circumstance.
Unlike Genji, Kaoru never engages visibly in any political or
interpersonal struggle, even with his rival Niou, and his position at
court (to which he repeatedly professes indifference) is never
threatened. As presented to the reader he has no ambition; he merely

---

[66] TTG, 1115; GM 6:256

floats upward. Good intentions or not, his pride shows more in petulance than in magnificence. Knowing that the Eighth Prince's two recognized daughters far outrank unrecognized Ukifune, he treats Ukifune accordingly. Even from Ōigimi, however, he has neither political nor material advantage to gain. She has no relationship to his society, hence no practical standing in it and no wealth.[67] His interest in her lacks all the grosser elements that give substance to Genji's affairs. In this way his private troubles are utterly sequestered from his public world, and with them the author beads the thread of a life that simply runs on passively with time.

This reading of Kaoru by no means achieves a comprehensive grasp of its elusive subject, and it claims to convey only one possible perspective among many. There are more intriguing things about Part Three than any single study could conceivably acknowledge. A few emerged in "The Possibility of Ukifune," and "Pity Poor Kaoru" has brought out a few more. However the character of Part Three, and the relationship between the separate parts of the tale, will always remain elusive.

---

[67] Haraoka, *Genji monogatari no jinbutsu to hyōgen: sono ryōgiteki tenkai*, 449.

TWO POST-*GENJI* TALES ON *THE TALE OF GENJI*

Two roughly late-twelfth century works represent a transition in the reception of *The Tale of Genji*. The first, *Genji shaku* by Sesonji Koreyuki (d. 1175), begins the long line of scholarly commentaries that are still being written today.[1] The second, *Mumyōzōshi* (ca. 1200, attributed to Shunzei's Daughter), can perhaps be said to round off the preceding era, when Genji was simply a monogatari (tale) among others, enjoyed above all by women. In contrast with Koreyuki's textual glosses, *Mumyōzōshi* gives passionate reader responses to characters and incidents in several monogatari, including *Genji*. The discovery of something like it from much earlier in the preceding two hundred years would be very welcome.

Fortunately, some evidence of earlier reader reception survives after all, not in critical works, but in post-*Genji* tales themselves. Showing as they do demonstrable *Genji* influence, these tales presumably suggest at times, in one way or another, what the author made of *Genji*, or how she understood this or that part of it. This essay will discuss examples from *Sagoromo monogatari* (ca. 1070-1080, by Rokujō no Saiin Senji, who served the Kamo Priestess Princess Baishi)[2] and *Hamamatsu Chūnagon monogatari* (ca. 1060, attributed to the author of *Sarashina nikki)*. Chief among them are the meaning of the chapter title "Yume no ukihashi"; the question of what happens to Ukifune between "Ukifune" and "Tenarai"; and the significance of Genji's affair with Fujitsubo. Discussion of these topics, especially the second, will hark back at times to material presented in the preceding essays, although this time with a different purpose.

---

[1] *Hikaru Genji ichibu uta* (1453), by the nun Yūrin (fl. ca. 1450), and the work of Kaoku Gyokuei (1526-after 1602) constitute the only significant writing on *Genji* by women between *Mumyōzōshi* and modern times. Thanks are due Gaye Rowley for this information.

[2] On the author of *Sagoromo monogatari* and her context, see D'Etcheverry, "Rethinking Late Heian," 42-69; and *Love After* The Tale of Genji, 39-57.

Two introductory examples

A passage from *Hamamatsu* illustrates simply how a post-*Genji* monogatari can shed light on the way a particular Genji passage might have been understood by its original audience. It concerns the trials inflicted on Genji's mother by her jealous rivals ("Kiritsubo"). Their nature remains vague, despite talk of the possibility of a "nasty surprise awaiting her along the crossbridges and bridgeways, one that horribly fouled the skirts of [her] gentlewomen..."[3] Her distress is easy to imagine, but one may still wonder whether her rivals did anything more pointed to cause her death.

The stories about curses included in *Konjaku monogatari shū* suggest an answer with which the *Hamamatsu* author apparently concurred. At the beginning of the surviving portion of her work, the first chapter of which is missing, she transposed the plight of Genji's mother to the Chinese court, complete with an unmistakable counterpart of the hostile minister of the right. In *Hamamatsu* this minister "places all sorts of curses" on Kara no Kisaki, the counterpart of Genji's mother, and many of the Chinese emperor's women do the same.[4] *Midō Kanpaku ki*, the diary of Fujiwara no Michinaga (1027), likewise mentions attempts to lay curses, once probably on himself, and once probably on a lady of the court.[5] In the end, Kara no Kisaki, like Genji's mother, leaves the palace for good, although she does not die—her home, unlike that of Genji's mother, being a very long way from the Chinese emperor's palace and therefore much safer. Her experience and the testimony of Michinaga provide nearly contemporary confirmation of a reasonable conjecture about what remains unstated in the *Genji* narrative. It also highlights the contrasting approach taken by Murasaki Shikibu, who, by means of silence and understatement, turned a little world as jealous and vindictive as any other, as her original audience well knew, into a model of elegance for the ages.

---

[3] TTG, 4; GM 1:20.

[4] Ikeda Toshio, *Hamamatsu Chūnagon monogatari*, 44.

[5] Hérail, *Notes journalières de Fujiwara no Michinaga* 2:581 (Chōwa 1.4.10 [1012]) and 3:121 (Chōwa 4.7.2 [1015]).

A second, more diffuse issue concerns the nature of the hero in *Sagoromo* and *Hamamatsu*. The authors, who had the models of Genji and Kaoru to choose from, seem to have been more at home with Kaoru. Presumably their audiences were, too. The chapters of *The Tale of Genji* that cover Genji's life are impressive, but it is the Uji chapters that announce the fiction of later Heian times and beyond.[6] Although Genji makes a memorable hero, he seems to have had no successor.

The *Sagoromo* and *Hamamatsu* authors did not make their heroes perfect. Sagoromo no Taishō and Hamamatsu no Chūnagon, especially the former, are not above betraying husbands and fathers, or ruining women's lives. Like Kaoru, however, they both enjoy brilliant worldly success in the background, while displaying in the foreground a dreamily melancholy, otherworldly side. Sagoromo's fantasies of entering religion so resemble Kaoru's that he has been described as "a second Kaoru,"[7] while in *Hamamatsu*, Buddhism as a sort of fantasy world is replaced by China, and by repeated oracles and dream communications. The closing section of *Hamamatsu* even features an extended variation on the rivalry between Kaoru and Niou over Ukifune. Just as the reader of the Uji chapters is constantly invited to sympathize with Kaoru's sorrows, whatever they may be, so in *Sagoromo* and *Hamamatsu* the hero's sorrowful feelings alone matter, regardless of what he may have done to arouse them. The beautiful hero enjoys full indulgence. The narrator's treatment of him little resembles the shifting, sometimes critical, and always personally engaged attitude toward Genji evident in his story.

Yume no ukihashi: the bridge of dreams

The final chapter of *The Tale of Genji* is entitled "Yume no Ukihashi." A good deal has been written about this intriguing expression over the centuries, and in any case it is no wonder that some should have taken the title of the closing chapter to be particularly significant. The range of interpretation has been wide. The reading suggested by *Hamamatsu*

---

6 Shioda, "Monogatari no yukue (1)," 329.
7 Gotō, "Mō hitori no Kaoru," 68-89.

Chūnagon monogatari therefore stands at the beginning of a long thread in *Genji* reception.

Yume no Ukihashi in *Hamamatsu*. At a certain point in *Hamamatsu*, the author has her hero "remember her [a love now inaccessible to him] sadly, feeling just like *yume no ukihashi*."[8] This occurrence of the expression seems not to be widely recognized as an allusion to the *Genji* chapter title, but three parallel *Hamamatsu* passages suggest that it is one.[9]

This mention of *yume no ukihashi* is one of four *Hamamatsu* passages that sum up a scene or mood with a brief allusion on the pattern, "[It was] just like X." In two, "X" is a now-lost monogatari. The first goes, "It was just like a picture from the monogatari entitled *Karakuni*"; the second simply caps a description with the words, "as in *Ōi no monogatari*"; and the third says, (3) "no doubt just like *Ono no shigure no yado*."[10] "Ono no shigure no yado" may or may not be the title of a lost monogatari, but the expression clearly refers to a specific story. The fourth is the passage in question here.

It has long been recognized that the *Genji* author must have invented the expression *yume no ukihashi* for the purpose of naming her last chapter, which made it famous. It does not appear in earlier literature. For this reason alone the *Hamamatsu* mention of *yume no ukihashi* probably refers to the *Genji* chapter, and the pattern of allusion just described confirms the idea. In *Hamamatsu* the expression clearly alludes to a monogatari or monogatari-like story familiar to every reader in the author's time, and that story can only have been the *Genji* chapter. The *Hamamatsu* author's allusion shows that, to her, the chapter title described the painfully precarious bond between Kaoru and Ukifune, as experienced especially by Kaoru.

However, contemporary scholarship refrains from taking the *Hamamatsu* passage that way, at least in any formal context. The

---

[8] Ikeda, *Hamamatsu*, 250.

[9] The present *Genji* chapter titles existed by the late twelfth century, but no evidence indicates when they originated or, in particular, whether the author applied them to the chapters herself. The discussion below assumes only that the tale's final chapter had acquired its current title by the time *Hamamatsu* was written.

[10] Ikeda, *Hamamatsu*, 32, 324, 354.

relevant headnotes in the NKBT and SNKBZ editions of *Hamamatsu Chūnagon monogatari* treat *yume no ukihashi* as a common noun meaning a perilous passage traversed in dreams (NKBT) or simply a precarious link, for example between lovers (SNKBZ). [11] Neither mentions the *Genji* chapter title.

This position is consistent with recent, conservatively presented *Genji* scholarship. No recent edition of *Genji monogatari* (SNKS 1985, SNKBT 1997, SNKBZ 1998) suggests such a reading of the chapter title, nor does the *Genji* manual *Jōyō Genji monogatari yōran* (1995).[12] All four note that the expression *yume no ukihashi* is absent from the chapter itself but that *yume* occurs several times; and all mention, hesitantly, a possible connection between the chapter title and a poem originally cited by Fujiwara no Teika in his *Okuiri* (early 13th c.), in connection with a passage in "Usugumo." Two *(Yōran, SNKBT)* tentatively suggest an allusion to Ukifune's nightmarish life of rootless wandering *(sasurai)*. That is all.

The poem first mentioned in *Okuiri* (one regularly acknowledged by later commentaries) goes, *Yo no naka wa/ yume no watari no/ ukihashi ka/ uchiwataritsutsu/ mono o koso omoe*: "Is this world of ours a floating bridge crossed in dreams, that crossing it should call up such sorrows?"[13] The "Usugumo" passage reads:

> The [Akashi] lady at Ōi led a life at once quiet and distinguished. Her house was unusual, but as for herself, Genji admired whenever he saw her the looks and the mature dignity of demeanor that placed her very little below the greatest in the land. If only it were possible to pass her off as simply another provincial governor's daughter, people would be glad enough to remember that this was not the first time such a thing had happened. Her father's fame as an egregious crank was a problem, but he had quite enough to him to make him

---

[11] Endō and Matsuo, *Hamamatsu Chūnagon monogatari*, 300, n. 4; Ikeda, *Hamamatsu*, 250, n. 3. However, the Kuge Haruyasu edition of the text (125, n. 13) recognizes the allusion to the *Genji* chapter title and notes its reference to Kaoru and Ukifune.

[12] Nakano, *Jōyō Genji monogatari yōran*.

[13] TTG, 352, n. 11. The published translation, corrected here, has "tossing" instead of "floating."

acceptable. Genji did not at all want to rush home again, since this visit had no doubt been too short for him as well. "Is it a floating bridge crossed in dreams?" he sighed...[14]

Genji's "Is it a floating bridge crossed in dreams?" (*yume no watari no ukihashi ka*, the words glossed by Teika) refers to the complexities that keep him from visiting Ōi more often. The note in the translation therefore explains that *yume* (Genji's and the poem's) alludes to erotic liaisons, and the poem's *yo no naka,* too, to matters of love. Nothing about this explanation is controversial, but its theme has vanished from the four discussions of the chapter title "Yume no Ukihashi" just cited, despite their acknowledgment of the poem. Instead, two of them mention Ukifune's sufferings, while the other two suggest nothing at all.

Yume no ukihashi in the *Genji* commentaries. Thus material from either end of the *Genji* millennium suggests an early association between *yume no ukihashi* and Kaoru's longing for Ukifune, and a late reluctance to accept that association. Generally speaking, the pre-modern commentaries encourage this reluctance.

Most of the content of these four recent treatments of the chapter title can be found in the commentaries. *Shimeishō* (late 13th c.), *Kakaishō* (ca. 1365), and others note as an anomaly the absence of the expression *yume no ukihashi* from the chapter text itself; observe that *yume* occurs five times in the chapter; and suggest a tentative connection between the chapter title and the poem Teika cited. *Ichiyōshō* (1494) and four sixteenth-century commentaries link the title to Ukifune's painfully rootless life. However, all these works emphasize other matters. As the *Kakaishō* author observed, "[The title's meaning] has always been uncertain *[korai fushin nari].*"[15]

The dominant trend is clear already in *Shimeishō*. A questioner who wants to know the meaning of *ukihashi* remarks that "most people" *(yo no hito)* take it as referring to Ukifune's refusal even to open Kaoru's letter. As evidence, the questioner mentions the words *fumi minu* ("did not read the letter"), which the chapter text only implies. This *fumi*

---

[14] TTG, 352; GM 2:440.

[15] Tamagami, *Shimeishō, Kakaishō,* 600.

minu plays on an implied negative verb *fumi-minu* ("did not tread [the bridge of dreams]").[16] Thus, according to the *Shimeishō* questioner, "most people" take *ukihashi* as alluding to the broken communication between Kaoru and Ukifune. This reading is compatible with the *Hamamatsu* author's.

However, the *Shimeishō* author disagreed. "This monogatari," he wrote, "reveals impermanence and demonstrates that all living beings come to naught. Therefore this chapter, unlike the others, is founded upon *yūgen* and is intended also to establish a link with enlightenment [*bodai no en*]." He therefore saw in this chapter a grander, graver theme than the failure of the bond between two lovers. Not that he excluded eros, since he also cited the *ame no ukihashi* ("floating bridge of heaven") story from *Nihon shoki* and wrote, "The distinction between male and female, the separation of man from woman, began with [*ame no*] *ukihashi*. How, then, could the heart of one with a taste for gallantry and a fondness for love not cross this *ukihashi*?" However, he placed greater emphasis on *yume*, which he took in a mainly religious or philosophical sense. Having quoted the *Nehan-gyō* and other sutras on the theme "Life, death, and impermanence are all a dream," he concluded: "Present reality is a dream, good and evil are a dream...Therefore, the final chapter was probably named "Yume no ukihashi" because this title brought together both the *ukihashi* of this sullied world [*edo*] and the dream of the dharma-nature [*hosshō no yume*]."[17]

Seen from this perspective, *ukihashi* no longer represents the bipolar tension of perilous desire between lovers but becomes instead one term of a greater tension on the same pattern: that between "this sullied world" (of samsara) and *hosshō no yume:* the dream of, or the dream that is, pure, timeless truth. Some *Genji* scholars still hold that the chapter title refers to a bridge between earth and heaven, this world and the next, and so on.

---

[16] Tamagami, 178. This tortuous explanation of *ukihashi* is spelled out explicitly in *Genji monogatari teiyō* (1432).

[17] Tamagami, *Shimeishō, Kakaishō*, 178-179.

Kakaishō (followed by others) develops this more expansive sort of reading, one tending to favor *yume* at the expense of *ukihashi*, by suggesting that "Yume no Ukihashi" is at the same time an alternate title for the whole tale.[18] This approach of course does not eliminate the erotic dimension of the "dream," especially considering the tale's general reputation as an erotic work. However, this erotic dimension receives less and less explicit acknowledgment. *Genji kokagami*, a digest from about the same period as *Kakaishō* and perhaps, like *Kakaishō*, a product of the circle surrounding Nijō Yoshimoto (1320-1388), illustrates this trend. It explains that the title refers to Genji's rise to dream-like glory and to the "single painful moment" *(tada hitofushi no on-nageki*, probably Murasaki's death) of his life that at last, before he dies, awakens him to the truth. It also suggests that the final chapter is entitled "Yume no Ukihashi" because it is meant to convey impermanence.[19] This sort of reading suggests Chuang-tzu's dream of the butterfly, or the story of the pillow of Kantan, and indeed several commentaries mention them.

In *Kachō yosei* (ca. 1470), Ichijō Kanera (1402-1481) referred the reader to the long *Kakaishō* entry on the closing chapter title, but he suggested on his own that it adds pathos *(aware)* to the situation evoked at the end of "Tenarai" and refers particularly to Kaoru's longing for Ukifune.[20] This reading agrees with the *Hamamatsu* author's. However, Fujiwara Masaari, the editor of *Ichiyōshō* (ca. 1494), soon disagreed. "The source of this tale has nothing to do with talk of love," he wrote. "It reveals the swift passing of all things and teaches that the mighty must fall."[21] Regarding the term *ukihashi* itself, he wrote that it has no special meaning apart from the broad notion of the passage from birth to death. *Rōkashō* (1510), edited by Sanjōnishi Sanetaka (1455-1537), affirms similarly that the meaning of the chapter title is carried by *yume*, and that *ukihashi* has no meaning of its own; so does the *Mōshinshō* (1575) of Kujō Tanemichi (1507-1594).[22]

---

[18] Tamagami, 601.

[19] Takeda Kō, *Genji kokagami*, 411.

[20] Ii, *Kachō yosei*, 347.

[21] Izume, *Ichiyōshō*, 498.

[22] Ii, *Rōkashō*, 328; Nomura Seiichi, ed., *Mōshinshō* 2:333-334.

The more ambitious later commentaries, such as *Sairyūshō* (1510-1513), *Mingō nisso* (1598), or *Kogetsushō* (1673) tend to reproduce the entries from earlier ones without adding anything new, thus juxtaposing divergent ideas without visibly favoring any. However *Tama no ogushi* (1796), the influential *Genji* commentary by Motoori Norinaga (1730-1801), is different. Norinaga took a new approach to the subject of "Yume no ukihashi," as he did to others. "As the old commentaries say," he wrote, "the title of this chapter applies to the entire tale. However, it would be wrong to call it a title for the whole. The content of the tale is convincingly real, but all of it is invented.... Everything in it is as though seen in a dream." Norinaga condemned the earlier commentators for citing Buddhist and Chinese writings to argue that the chapter title means life is a dream. "That is wrong," he declared. "It only means that everything written in this tale is a dream."[23] His focus on the author is of interest, but more relevant here is the absence of any reference to love or erotic tension, whether particular (Kaoru and Ukifune) or generalized (the "floating bridge of heaven"). The *yume* of the chapter title has obliterated the *ukihashi*. Norinaga's interpretation has the same cool respectability as the four contemporary discussions of the title cited above.

Closing reflections on *yume no ukihashi*. Still, two of those discussions mention the miseries of Ukifune, the most pressing of which have to do with love. They confirm a tendency in the commentaries, noted by Masuda Katsumi in 1991, to read the chapter title from her standpoint. Masuda argued that the chapter is really told more from Kaoru's.[24] Indeed, Mori Asao had already stated in 1988 that the *Genji* chapter title refers to the precarious bond between Kaoru and Ukifune, and especially to the severing of that bond as the chapter ends. Komachiya Teruhiko, writing in 1992, agreed: the issue is the breaking of the bond—the *ukihashi*—between Ukifune and Kaoru. "Ukifune [now a nun] goes off into a world beyond Kaoru's comprehension, leaving him behind, alone, in the profane world."[25]

---

[23] Ōno, *Motoori Norinaga zenshū* 4:521.

[24] Masuda, "Genji monogatari kara mananda koto," 367.

[25] Mori Asao, "Yume no ukihashi," in *Kodai waka to shukusai*, Yūseidō, 1988: passage discussed without page reference in Komachiya, "Yume no watari no ukihashi," 214.

Thus Komachiya recognized the *ukihashi* between Kaoru and Ukifune after all but, echoing *Shimeishō*, assimilated it to the unbridgeable gulf between the sacred and the profane.

In *Hamamatsu Chūnagon monogatari*, however, the hero remains in touch by letter with the lady for whom he longs, and although circumstances keep them apart, nothing suggests that she would not meet him if she could. Whether or not they are, in practice, parted forever, the bond between them is not broken. A gap therefore still separates the *Hamamatsu* author's reading of the *Genji* chapter title from that adopted by Mori Asao or Komachiya Kazuhiko, who hold the break to be final.

The analysis of Ukifune's story in "The Possibility of Ukifune" suggests that the *Hamamatsu* author was right. The events, situations, and relationships described in "Tenarai" and "Yume no ukihashi" make it difficult to believe either that Kaoru will never see Ukifune again, somewhere past the end of the book, or that Ukifune is in any position to reject him indefinitely.

Motoori Norinaga wrote in *Tama no ogushi*, "The closing chapter [of *Genji*] functions as a conclusion, but really it is as though the dreamer had awakened before the dream was anywhere near complete."[26] Written speculation about events beyond the end of the tale began with *Yamaji no tsuyu*, an apocryphal *Genji* chapter now attributed to Kenreimon'in Ukyō no Daibu (1157?-1233?). In *Yamaji no tsuyu* Kaoru does see Ukifune again, and at the end of it the situation remains unresolved. *Yamaji no tsuyu* therefore comments on "Yume no ukihashi" as meaningfully as the work of a medieval or modern scholar. It also seconds the *Hamamatsu* passage. No one will ever know what the title "Yume no ukihashi" "really" means, but the *Hamamatsu* allusion to it belongs to the history of *Genji* reception. Considering that the author lived 95% closer to Murasaki Shikibu's time than we do and inhabited the same world, perhaps it even deserves an extra unit or two of weight.

---

[26] Ōno, *Motoori Norinaga zenshū* 4:521.

Ukifune and Asukai

At the end of the "Ukifune" chapter of *Genji*, Ukifune decides to drown herself. In the first chapter of *Sagoromo monogatari*, Asukai no Himegimi does the same. Both then disappear. The *Sagoromo* author so obviously adopted so many *Genji* motifs that the *Genji* influence in this case is beyond question. What happened to Asukai therefore begins a curious thread in the history of *Genji* reception. Ukifune will be discussed first.

Ukifune's disappearance. Nearly everyone familiar with *Genji* in any form (including received folklore) assumes that, between "Ukifune" and "Kagerō," Ukifune throws herself into the Uji River to drown but is then swept away by the current, washed ashore downstream, and saved by Yokawa no Sōzu. Relatively few people, most of them academic specialists, doubt that Ukifune genuinely attempts *jusui*: suicide by drowning. "The Possibility of Ukifune" has covered this topic already, but a brief recapitulation will be useful.

In reality, Ukifune never even approaches the water. Yokawa no Sōzu finds her not on the riverbank, but under a great tree in a silent wood, behind a residence known as the Uji Villa. The text of "Tenarai" provides enough evidence to show how she got there. It allows only one answer: after stepping out onto the veranda of her house with the intention of going down to the river, Ukifune was possessed by a spirit that transported her supernaturally to the place where she was found.

Being unable to choose between two lovers, Kaoru and Niou, Ukifune decides to drown herself in the river that flows past her house. The ending of "Ukifune" convinces the reader that she is about to act, and at the start of the next chapter, "Kagerō," she is indeed gone; the entire household is hunting for her. Only some way into "Tenarai," the chapter after that, does the author provide a consecutive account of the event in the form of Ukifune's silent reminiscences. Although quoted already in "The Possibility of Ukifune," the passage deserves renewed attention here.

> They were all asleep, and I opened the double doors and went out. There was a strong wind blowing, and I could hear the river's roar. Out there all alone I was frightened, too

frightened to think clearly about what had happened or what was to come next, and when I stepped down onto the veranda I became confused about where I was going; I only knew that going back in would not help and that all I wanted was to disappear bravely from life. Come and eat me, demons or whatever things are out there, do not leave me to be found foolishly cowering here! I was saying that, sitting rooted to the spot, when a very beautiful man approached me and said, 'Come with me to where I live!' and it seemed to me that he took me in his arms. I assumed he was the gentleman they addressed as 'Your Highness', but after that my mind must have wandered, until he put me down in a place I did not know. Then he vanished. When it was over I realized that I had not done what I had meant to do, and I cried and cried.[27]

Motoori Norinaga praised this way of conveying what happened to Ukifune as "a most entertaining manner of writing" *(ito omoshiroki kakizama),*[28] In practice, however, so many readers miss, ignore, or dismiss the passage, at least in modern times, that one can perhaps fairly say that it no longer works.

Asukai's disappearance. The Asukai no Himegimi of *Sagoromo monogatari* is a Yūgao-like waif (many writers, starting with Hagiwara Hiromichi in 1854, have noted the parallel) of decent birth but without future prospects. Sagoromo, the hero, discovers her and makes love to her, but he never allows her to find out who he is. In time she becomes pregnant. Meanwhile Michinari, one of his retainers, learns about her as well. Never suspecting her relationship with his lord, he decides when he is posted to Kyushu to abduct her and take her there with him on the ship. Asukai's nurse, who scorns the frivolous ways of noble youths like Asukai's still-anonymous lover, supports this plan so effectively that the outraged and astonished Asukai is soon bundled aboard.[29] Rejecting Michinari's blandishments, she resolves to throw herself into the sea.[30]

---

[27] TTG, 1083-1084; GM 6:296-297.

[28] Ōno, *Motoori Norinaga zenshū* 4:516.

[29] Charo D'Etcheverry discussed this subject in "Out of the Mouths of Nurses," 58-87.

[30] Komachiya and Gotō, *Sagoromo monogatari* 1:143.

Surviving manuscripts of *Sagoromo monogatari* differ significantly among themselves, as do the published texts. This essay will refer to four: those edited by Mitani Eiichi and Sekine Keiko (NKBT), Suzuki Kazuo (SNKS), Komachiya Teruhiko and Gotō Shōko (SNKBT), and Yoshida Kōichi (Koten Bunko). With respect to the closing passage of the first chapter, the one that matters here, the SNKS and Koten Bunko texts are equivalent. The SNKBT text adds a sentence, and to this sentence the NKBT text adds a paragraph.

Asukai's moment comes as the ship approaches Mushiake no Seto, a narrow passage between the island of Nagashima and the Bizen coast of the Inland Sea. The passengers are asleep. Tormented by memories of Sagoromo, Asukai wants to write a farewell poem on a fan that he once gave her, but tears blind her, her hand trembles, and she has difficulty doing so. Before she can finish, she hears someone nearby *(hito no kehai no sureba).* She therefore

> (SNKS 1:122-123, Koten Bunko 1:137) gazed at the sea before hastening to throw herself in. She was terrified, they say.
>
> (SNKBZ 1:152-153) gazed down into the sea before hastening to throw herself in. Even this much terrified her, however, and she lay face down, trembling, they say.
>
> (NKBT 114-115) gazed down into the sea before hastening to throw herself in. Even this much terrified her, however, and while she trembled, someone held her back. "I knew it!" she thought, aghast and feeling as though she were dying. She said not a word while the person picked her up and carried her aboard another ship. "What is going on?" she wondered in blank horror, with her clothing pulled over her head. Meanwhile, she gathered that day was about to break. She was thinking in bitter disappointment, "I seem not to have managed to do it," when the person approached her and said, "Do not be afraid. I had been looking for you for years, wondering where you went and how you were, when I heard that you were on your way to Kyushu and took the same route in the hope of meeting you...What is it that decided you on so desperate a deed?" She could not forget having heard

that thin, weeping voice when she was little: it was her elder brother's.

Asukai's brother then tells her that he lost an eye as a boy and became a monk. She feels reassured. They go together to the Capital, and he takes her to the house of an aunt, now a nun. When the nun asks Asukai to tell her story, Asukai speaks of having wanted to die anyway, and of having then been taken aboard an *ukifune* ("drifting boat"), which made her detest life even more. "I feel safer now that I have met you," she says. "If you would be so kind, please make me a nun." The nun agrees to do so after Asukai's baby is born. Asukai's brother agrees, urging her to remain until then where she is, quiet and unnoticed. He then leaves, saying that he has various pilgrimages to make.

Each of these versions corresponds roughly to a step in the account quoted from "Tenarai." The SNKS and Koten Bunko texts leave Asukai at the stage of Ukifune's fright when Ukifune actually goes outside and hears the noise of the river; the SNKBZ text leaves her, like Ukifune, overcome by fear; and the NKBT text then has her carried away like Ukifune by a mysterious man. The NKBT text even incorporates the word *ukifune* and has Asukai ask to be made a nun, as Ukifune eventually did.

Asukai's disappearance devastates the hero, who early in the second chapter receives an oral report from the abductor's (Michinari's) younger brother. The content is the same in all four texts: "Some very strange news has reached me. Michinari's wife threw herself into the sea. Everything the lady's nurse told me, weeping, suggests that the lady in question is the very one who has disappeared." (SNKS 1:129; Koten Bunko 1:141; SNKBZ 1:158-159; NKBT 120) His report leaves Sagoromo in the same position as Kaoru, once Kaoru learns in "Kagerō" of the disappearance and presumed drowning of Ukifune.

However, each different first chapter ending leaves the reader in a different place. The SNKS/Koten Bunko ending corresponds roughly to the close of "Ukifune": the reader knows that Asukai plans to drown herself and cannot yet assume that either the presence of someone nearby *(hito no kehai)*, or fear itself, guarantee failure. The SNKBZ reader knows that fear has mastered her (as Ukifune recalls it doing in "Tenarai") and so can reasonably take her failure for granted. However, only the NKBT text actually tells what happens next. Presumably the NKBT narrative is meant to explain a surprise present in all four versions: Sagoromo's discovery, late in the second chapter, that Asukai is alive and in her brother's care.[31] (She dies before he can see her again.) However, what "really happens" to Asukai, as to Ukifune, remains in the end unfathomable unless one simply accepts in Ukifune's case that a spirit carried her off bodily, and in Asukai's that her brother appeared from nowhere, at sea in the middle of the night, to do the same. Regarding Ukifune, readers and scholars in recent times, reluctant to accept supernatural intervention, have tended to replace what the text says with something more intelligible. Confusingly enough, the silent assumption, or the reluctance to deny, that Ukifune somehow threw herself in after all has been encouraged since at least the fifteenth century by ambiguous use of the term *jusui* and related expressions. Modern insistence on finding source materials for the *jusui* motif in Heian times may also have played its part.

Ukifune's *jusui* in the commentaries. The earliest of the major commentaries, *Shimeishō* and *Kakaishō*, say nothing to suggest that the content of Ukifune's experience is anything other than self-evident. Later works *(Genji kokagami, Kachō yosei, Mōshinshō, Bansui ichiro, Mingō nisso, Kogetsushō)* note that she was carried off either by someone she thought was *miya* ("the prince"), or, more explicitly, by a spirit she believed to be Prince Niou. These two readings amount to the same thing. They refer to Ukifune's memories—memories that Motoori Norinaga apparently accepted, since he praised the way the author let the reader know what had happened to her. Meanwhile, *Genji kokagami* and *Hikaru Genji ichibu uta* (seconded by the Noh play

---

[31] Suzuki Kazuo, *Sagoromo monogatari* 1:152-154; Yoshida, *Sagoromo monogatari* 1:294-296; Komachiya and Gotō, *Sagoromo monogatari* 1:301-302; Mitani and Sekine, *Sagoromo monogatari*, 212-213.

Kodama Ukifune)[32] say that Ukifune was carried off by a *kodama* ("tree spirit"), and in 1854 Hagiwara Hiromichi agreed.[33] Finally, several medieval commentaries or digests identify the place where Ukifune was found as the site of the Byōdō-in, thus tacitly accepting the inevitable conclusion that the spirit carried her bodily *across* the river.[34]

The first hint of what looks like ambiguity on the subject occurs in the mid-Muromachi *Genji ōkagami*, which begins its account of "Kagerō" as follows: "Everyone is distraught that Ukifune should have thrown herself [into the river], but they are wrong. She meant to do so, but once she opened the door and went outside..."[35] The text then summarizes Ukifune's later memories. Nonetheless, the "Tenarai" section says: "[At the Uji Villa the nuns] gathered her up and put her in the carriage. The time when Ukifune threw herself in *[mi o nagetarishi toki]* was the end of the third month."[36] Taken out of context, this passage suggests that the writer believed Ukifune literally threw herself into the river. However, he clearly did not. Perhaps he meant the expression *mi o nagu* (equivalent to *jusui su*, "drown oneself") to acknowledge intention over failed execution. More probably, however, he simply found no more economical way to refer to an otherwise untidily enigmatic event—an event the real content of which no one in his time seemed to doubt.

Kachō yosei and *Sairyūshō*, followed respectively by *Mōshinshō* and *Rōkashō*, do much the same thing. In *Kachō yosei*, the first gloss on "Kagerō" reminds the reader of Ukifune's obvious plan to take her own life and goes on, "It would have been pointless to write about her actually throwing herself in, since no one [among the household at Uji]

32 Takeda Kō, *Genji kokagami,* 409; Imai Gen'e, *Hikaru Genji ichibu uta,* 284, 288. Janet Goff discussed this issue and translated both the *Hikaru Genji ichibu uta* passage and *Kodama Ukifune* in *Noh Drama and* The Tale of Genji, 81-83, 193-197.

33 Caddeau, "Tree Spirits (kodama) and Apparitions (henge)," 2; Hagiwara Hiromichi, "Sōron," 342. As shown in "The Possibility of Ukifune," this idea, equally based on the text, does not contradict what Ukifune remembers.

34 Other commentaries question this identification, but there is no reason to believe they do so because the author rejected the notion of the spirit carrying off Ukifune.

35 Ishida and Kayaba, *Genji ōkagami,* 392.

36 Ishida and Kayaba, *Genji ōkagami,* p. 393.

knows she did it." Further on, however, the writer accepts Ukifune's memories and explicitly acknowledges her recognition that she had failed.

Similarly, *Sairyūshō* glosses the first words of "Kagerō" *(kashiko ni wa)* as meaning "the place [Uji] where Ukifune threw herself in *[mi o nage-tamaishi ato]*," even though later on it acknowledges the same evidence that she did not. In connection with a mention of heavy rain,[37] it likewise states that the rain fell "on the day after Ukifune's *jusui.*" The linked-verse poet Satomura Jōha (1527-1602) used the same sort of language on the subject at about the same time. In his *Sagoromo shitahimo* (1590), a short commentary on *Sagoromo monogatari*, Jōha wrote that the moment when Asukai seems about to throw herself into the water "recalls Ukifune's *jusui* in *Genji.*"[38] Thus Jōha included under the rubric of *jusui* two incidents in which no *jusui* takes place. Modern scholars have done the same.

In the Edo period, Motoori Norinaga and Hagiwara Hiromichi seem to have recognized, either tacitly or explicitly, that Ukifune was abducted.[39] In his *Kogetsushō* (1673), Kitamura Kigin quoted the *Kachō yosei* and *Sairyūshō* glosses on the first words of "Kagerō," but he also glossed Ukifune's vision of the "beautiful man" in "Tenarai" by quoting *Mōshinshō*: "The spirit [that had possessed Ukifune] appeared to her, and she saw it as Niou." Regarding Ukifune's memories of what happened, he wrote nothing at all. Presumably he accepted them. However, if the Confucian thinker Kumazawa Banzan (1619-1691) had been able to carry *Genji gaiden*, his ambitious commentary on the tale, beyond "Fuji no Uraba," he would probably have rejected both the "beautiful man" and the *kodama*." Banzan's approach was resolutely historical and rational. He attributed Yūgao's death not to the phantom woman that Genji saw, but to fear, and he denied that Rokujō's spirit actually left her body to torment Aoi.[40] This quasi-psychological view

---

[37] "Unfortunately a downpour was threatening": TTG, 1079, GM 6:284.

[38] Nihon Tosho Sentâ, *Sagoromo monogatari kochūshaku taisei*, 463.

[39] In his *Genji monogatari taii*, dated 1830, Amano Naokata, too, noted that Ukifune was taken away by "someone she believed to be the prince [*miya*]" and left by him under a tree at the Uji Villa (Amano, *Genji monogatari taii*, 201).

[40] McMullen, *Idealism, Protest, and the* Tale of Genji, 329-330.

of spirit possession foreshadows an influential line of interpretation put forward in recent decades: one that strives to rationalize and psychologize Ukifune's experience.

Ukifune's *jusui* in modern times. Since scholarly books and articles still refer routinely to *Ukifune no jusui*, one might assume that their authors and readers nonetheless know what really happened, as people apparently did in medieval times; and perhaps in most cases nowadays they really do. However, it is not clear that they always have. Much evidence suggests that Ukifune's literal *jusui* has long been taken for granted not only by the reading public at large, but by academics as well. How did this happen?

Meiji scholars and readers, caught up in the spirit of enlightenment and progress, and eager to set *The Tale of Genji* beside the greatest novels of the nineteenth-century West, might easily have rejected the tale's supernatural elements in favor of rationally modern readings. Patrick Caddeau has suggested that they did so, citing as evidence the headnotes in the first modern, popular edition of *Genji:* the five-volume *Nihon bungaku zensho* text published by Hakubunkan in 1890.[41] The notes at the start of "Kagerō" sound tersely confidant that Ukifune genuinely threw herself in. However, they are based ultimately (via *Kogetsushō*) on the corresponding *Kachō yosei* and *Sairyūshō* glosses, so that their intended meaning is not really obvious. The "Kagerō" and "Tenarai" headnotes in a 1927 edition of *Genji* say nothing bearing on the question of what happened to Ukifune.[42]

The source of the confusion therefore remains unclear. Simple convenience may help to explain why articles, chapter titles, and so on still refer to *Ukifune no jusui* as though it really happened.[43] However, given the near-universality of the misreading, it is striking that some should still have written within the last few years that, "Having thrown herself into the river *[jusui shita]*, bearing her burden of sin, Ukifune is

---

[41] Caddeau, "Tree Spirits (kodama) and Apparitions (henge)," 11-15.

[42] Kokumin Tosho Kabushiki Kaisha, *Genji monogatari* 2.

[43] For example, "Ukifune no jusui o megutte," in Ōasa, *Genji monogatari zokuhen no kenkyū*.

saved by Yokawa no Sōzu...";[44] that, "After giving herself to two men, [Ukifune] plumbs the depths of suffering and as a result throws herself into the Uji River *[Ujigawa ni mi o nagete shimau]*";[45] and that, "[Caught between two lovers, Kaoru and Niou, Ukifune] soon threw herself into the Uji River *[Ujigawa ni mi o tō-ji]*, was saved, and became a nun."[46] Perhaps these writers indeed take intention for achievement, but if they do, their view of the matter little resembles Ukifune's; for when Ukifune understood her failure, she wept. They also perpetuate an error.

On this subject, current *Genji* summaries, dictionaries, and manuals are not always helpful. Five representative examples are *Genji monogatari no makimaki* (1987), *Genji monogatari jiten* (1993), *Genji monogatari o yomu tame no kenkyū jiten* (1995), *Genji monogatari yōran* (1995), and *Genji monogatari jiten* (2002). Only the 1993 *Genji monogatari jiten*, edited by Akiyama Ken, clearly recognizes that Ukifune became possessed at all. The article states that she seems to have fainted on the way to the river, that she was possessed by the spirit of a monk, and that "she wandered between dream and reality" until she collapsed behind the Uji Villa.[47] Unlike such texts as *Genji ōkagami*, it says nothing about what Ukifune herself remembers happening. A particularly modern touch is the explanation that Ukifune walked to the Uji Villa. Reason demands something similar, but reason in this case is not good enough. At the time, Ukifune's house was surrounded every night by guards, posted by Kaoru to keep Niou away and severely enjoined by him to be vigilant. They would have noticed her. Moreover, she was found without a mark on her. Her

---

[44] Haraoka, "Keikai no onnagimi: Ukifune," in *Genji monogatari no jinbutsu to hyōgen*, 550.

[45] Setouchi, "Shinsaku nō *Yume no ukihashi* ni tsuite," 9.

[46] Hasegawa Masaharu, *Tosa nikki, Kagerō nikki, Murasaki Shikibu nikki, Sarashina nikki*, 299, n. 20. Thanks are due Patrick Caddeau for this reference. Haruo Shirane, too, wrote of Ukifune "being saved from the turbulent waters of the Uji River" *(The Bridge of Dreams*, 161); and twenty years later, despite the Asukai material quoted above, Charo d'Etcheverry wrote that, "rather than betray the hero, [Asukai] leaps overboard *(Love After* The Tale of Genji, 64). The pull of the *jusui* image is almost irresistible.

[47] Akiyama, *Genji monogatari jiten*, 59-60.

passage to the Uji Villa, like Asukai's passage from a Kyushu-bound ship to her brother's care at Kokawa-dera, simply defies reason. Nothing can be done about this.

The first of the other works just mentioned *(Genji monogatari no makimaki)* treats parallels between Yūgao and Ukifune, then discusses Ukifune's state of mind after she recovers.[48] The second *(Genji monogatari o yomu tame no kenkyū jiten)* discusses *mononoke* in *Genji* without stating that a *mononoke* possessed Ukifune.[49] The third *(Jōyō Genji monogatari yōran)* has Ukifune found "on the bank of the Uji River" *(Ujigawaberi de)*, when she was not.[50] The fourth *(Genji monogatari jiten)*, the most recent, summarizes Ukifune's experience without mentioning either spirit possession or her memory of what happened, and a separate article presents "the prototypes of the suicide by drowning motif" *(jusuitan no genkei)* without acknowledging that Ukifune did not commit *jusui*.[51]

There are more noteworthy aspects to Ukifune's story than can be accommodated in a dictionary or manual entry, but considering the prevalence of the error, such works might at least ensure that those who consult them do not make it. Instead, discussions of Ukifune often ignore the subject completely, if possible; or, if they must address it, they may argue in effect that it is irrelevant. Thus Mitani Kuniaki granted the *mononoke* exorcised by Yokawa no Sōzu no other significance than to reveal the unconscious preoccupations of the Sōzu himself and then of Ukifune when, after the exorcism, she remembers seeing the "beautiful man."[52] In a similar mood, Fujimoto Katsuyoshi denied that the man Ukifune remembers seeing has anything to do with the spirit that speaks to Yokawa no Sōzu (claiming once to have been a monk), because Ukifune does not remember ever having been possessed by a monk.[53] This sort of argument reduces Ukifune's memories to the fantasies of a young woman suffering a nervous

---

[48] *Genji monogatari no makimaki,* 138-141.

[49] *Genji monogatari o yomu tame no kenkyū,* 114-115.

[50] Nakano, *Jōyō Genji monogatari yōran,* 63.

[51] Hayashida, *Genji monogatari jiten,* 67-68 ("Ukifune"), 214 ("Jusuitan").

[52] Mitani Kuniaki, "Genji monogatari daisanbu no hōhō," 100-102.

[53] Fujimoto, *Genji monogatari no 'mononoke',* 95-99.

breakdown and the exorcism to a psychotic episode on the part of Yokawa no Sōzu. Meanwhile, Ōasa Yūji presented Ukifune as a steadfast heroine, firm and rational in her resolve to drown herself, whose last-minute fears and hesitations are all quite normal in terms of the "psychology of suicide"; and he presented the spirit as a mere literary device to achieve the author's aim, which is to save Ukifune by making sure she does not drown.[54] If the conundrum of Ukifune's possession amounts to no more than that, then the author could have arranged more simply to have her throw herself into the river and be washed ashore downstream.

Concluding reflections on the case of Asukai. Asukai no Himegimi's experience at Mushiake no Seto is interesting as the earliest surviving post-*Genji* step toward the anomalous situation just described, unless by any chance *Asakura monogatari* came first. Like *Hamamatsu*, this now-lost tale has been attributed to the author of *Sarashina nikki*. Scholars have reconstructed some notion of it thanks to the many poems from it included in *Shūi hyakuban utaawase* and *Fūyō wakashū*. The heroine's mother is dead, and her father has become a monk and disappeared. Alone in the world, she accepts Sanmi no Chūjō (later, Asakura no Kanpaku) as a lover, but meanwhile she is also courted by Shikibukyō no Miya. Eventually she sets out for Michinoku to find her father, but on the way, at Awazu no Hama, she throws herself into Lake Biwa. *Fūyō wakashū* 1047 is a poem written by Asakura no Kanpaku on a pilgrimage to Ishiyama, "upon hearing that a woman he loved had thrown herself [into the lake] at Awazu no Hama." However, the heroine seems actually to have been saved, possibly by her father. Asakura no Kanpaku takes her in, and she serves the court under the name Kōtaigō no Miya no Dainagon.[55] Things worked out much better for her (if *Asakura* really ended on that note) than for Ukifune or Asukai, but otherwise the similarity is obvious.

The *Genji* author presumably knew the *jusui* motif well, since it was established in literature and art. The *kotobagaki* to *Yoshinobu shū* 389

---

[54] Ōasa, *Genji monogatari zokuhen no kenkyū*, 495-527, 563-564, 570.
[55] Morishita, "Jusuitan no keifu," 113.

(Ōnakatomi Yoshinobu, 921-991) describes a painting of a woman looking down from a high bank while a man watches her from below; the poem suggests she is about to drown herself because her lover has stopped coming. Likewise, the *kotobagaki* to *Dōmyō Ajari shū* 17 (Dōmyō, 974-1020) evokes a painting in which a woman looks down from a high bank before throwing herself in. The poem has her regretting only the reputation that will survive her. Finally, *Yoshinobu shū* 389 concerns a scene similar to the one that begins "Kagerō." The *kotobagaki* describes a picture illustrating *Sumiyoshi monogatari*. Jijū (a gentlewoman) stands at the outlet to a pond named Narabi no Ike. She is looking for her mistress, Himegimi, who has thrown herself into the pond. The poem says, "If only she had told me where she went in, I would go in search of her, even if that meant parting the water-weeds myself to do so."[56]

However, these poems only capture moments in stories that remain otherwise unknown. As prototypes for the *jusui* motif, reference works and scholarly studies repeatedly cite two stories from *Yamato monogatari*. In no. 147, a young woman's two suitors are so equal in all ways that she cannot decide between them. When a test to set one above the other fails, she drowns herself in despair, and both young men drown while trying to save her.[57] In no. 150, an *uneme* (young woman attendant) at the Nara court rejects every suitor and reserves herself for the emperor, who finally summons her. However, he never does so again, and she drowns herself in Sarusawa no Ike.

The similarity between these stories, especially no. 147, and those on the Ukifune *"jusui"* pattern is self-evident, but it goes only so far. The two *Yamato monogatari* heroines really throw themselves into the water and genuinely drown, whereas Ukifune, Asukai, and apparently the *Asakura* heroine do not. In no. 147 the two suitors drown as well, whereas, in *Genji*, Kaoru and Niou live on in good health. Nor does

---

56 All three poems are cited in Morishita, "Jusuitan no keifu," 114. The extant *Sumiyoshi monogatari* is a Kamakura-period work, but the original one dated from the 10th c. Narabi no Ike, near the southern end of the Narabi ga Oka hills in present Ukyō-ku, Kyoto, seems to have disappeared in the 17th c.

57 This is the story of the Maiden Unai, told earlier in the *Man'yōshū* by Takahashi Mushimaro and others, and dramatized in the Noh play *Motomezuka*.

Asukai's predicament convincingly parallel the dilemma affecting Ukifune and the heroine of *Yamato monogatari* 147. No doubt two men claim her attention, but she is not caught emotionally between them; she is a kidnap victim. Obvious though all this is, the academic emphasis on prototypes and sources tends to obscure it, and perhaps even to encourage withholding explicit recognition that, in Ukifune-pattern stories, no *jusui* occurs at all.

While acknowledging a motif from the past, Ukifune's failure to drown herself thus establishes what amounts to a new monogatari device: the unrealized *jusui* that serves to move the heroine to a new life-situation. The *Sagoromo* author's version of it follows that of the *Genji* author faithfully in the sense that she, too, left her reader unable to picture sensibly how her heroine passed, physically, from her old life to her new one. However, the *Sagoromo* author removed from this passage the element of the supernatural. (So, apparently, did the author of *Asakura.*) This change in turn highlights a difference between her tale and *Genji*. Divine visions, visitations, and oracles certainly figure in *Sagoromo*, but not possessions or *mononoke*. The reasons can hardly be the same ones that for most modern scholars cast such a shadow over Ukifune's possession, but the coincidence is intriguing. Considering that medieval readers seem to have accepted Ukifune's possession without question, the *Sagoromo* author's avoidance of it comments interestingly on an enigmatic *Genji* issue.

Asukai's experience dramatically changes her circumstances (as the *Asakura* heroine's apparently does hers), but nothing suggests that it changes Asukai herself. The reader never even sees her again. Psychologically, it is flat. Is Ukifune's? Most writing on her seems to assume that the way she gets from her house to the Uji Villa is immaterial; all that matters is what happens after she gets there. She might just as well have been swept downstream, and nothing is lost if, for the sake of convenience, that notion is allowed to stand. This assumption is debatable. Perhaps the *Sagoromo* author disagreed with it and, to keep things simple, adjusted her use of the motif accordingly.

Sagoromo's enthronement

Early in *Sagoromo monogatari* the hero (a second-generation Minamoto) secretly violates a princess (Onna Ninomiya), as Genji violates Fujitsubo. To save this princess's reputation the empress, her mother, presents the resulting son to the emperor as her own, thus placing herself voluntarily in the same position as Fujitsubo. Then, near the end of the tale, the emperor wishes to abdicate in this young prince's favor. An oracle from Amaterasu Ōmikami at Ise immediately identifies the prince's real father (Sagoromo himself) and requires the emperor to cede *him* the throne instead, on the grounds of proper precedence. The oracle also describes Sagoromo as so gifted and beautiful that his being a commoner has long offended the gods.[58] Thus Sagoromo becomes emperor thanks to beauty and other gifts that resemble Genji's, and thanks above all to his having a secret son by an imperial woman. That the woman is not the empress suggests that the *Sagoromo* author may have found Genji's intercourse with Fujitsubo too strong to adopt undiluted.[59] However, in *Sagoromo monogatari* the emperor assumes after the oracle, and after recognizing Sagoromo's features in the boy, that the boy's mother is indeed his now-deceased empress. Thus he gathers that his empress had intercourse with the hero just as Fujitsubo did with Genji.

The *Mumyōzōshi* author objected violently to Sagoromo's accession. Actually, she disliked all the supernatural manifestations in the tale, but this one was just too much. "More than absolutely anything else," she wrote, "the hero's becoming emperor is utterly revolting and appalling." She then went on to venture the opinion that Genji should not have become honorary retired emperor, either. "However," she wrote, "he, at least, was genuinely an emperor's son..."[60]

Thus the author of *Mumyōzōshi* noted and discussed the parallel between Sagoromo's enthronement and Genji's appointment as honorary retired emperor. This parallel has probably struck many

---

[58] Komachiya and Gotō, *Sagoromo monogatari* 2:343.

[59] Fujitsubo was not yet empress when Reizei was conceived, but she became empress soon after her son's birth.

[60] Higuchi and Kuboki, *Mumyōzōshi*, 223.

readers over the centuries, although the works collected in *Sagoromo monogatari kochūshaku taisei* say nothing about it. Motoori Norinaga acknowledged it, [61] and Mitani Eiichi wrote about it in 1968, speculating that the *Sagoromo* author's initial idea for the plot involved an adulterous affair between the hero and Sen'yōden no Nyōgo (an imperial consort and a minor figure in the existing tale), patterned on Genji's affair with Fujitsubo.[62] Mitani went on to suggest that when Sagoromo's affair with Asukai made this idea unworkable, the author fell back on Onna Ninomiya instead. "In order to have Sagoromo, her hero, succeed to the throne," he wrote, "the author had to devise an adulterous affair between him and an imperial daughter or consort."[63]

Others, too, have acknowledged this *Genji-Sagoromo monogatari* parallel.[64] However the corollary reading, to the effect that the *Genji* author devised Genji's affair with Fujitsubo as a natural step toward having him appointed honorary retired emperor, is missing from *Genji* scholarship.

The parallel shows that the *Sagoromo* author saw in Genji's transgression the engine that drove his rise, and that she therefore adopted a similar device for her own work. Sagoromo may personally resemble Kaoru, but the trajectory of his life shadows the first part of Genji's—faintly, as the dim outer arc of a rainbow repeats the bright, inner one. In "Fuji no Uraba" Genji becomes honorary retired emperor, while near the end of *Sagoromo* the hero becomes the reigning emperor. In each case it is the hero's violation of an imperial woman, and the consequent birth of a son, that make possible his rise to imperial grandeur.

Why should the author of *Sagoromo monogatari* have wished, or even dared, to repeat a pattern of which the *Mumyōzōshi* author disapproved in about 1200, and which later became a scandalous problem for many *Genji* admirers? Kumazawa Banzan (1619-1691)

[61] Ōno, *Motoori Norinaga zenshū* 4:232.
[62] Mitani Eiichi, *Sagoromo monogatari no kenkyū*, 135.
[63] Mitani Eiichi, 137.
[64] Horiguchi, "*Sagoromo monogatari* no kōsō," 250, 272; Inoue, "Sagoromo monogatari no kōzo shiron," 58.

had excruciating difficulty with it,[65] and in 1703 Andō Tameakira wrote of people who, because of it, could not even pick up the book.[66] Inoue Mayumi highlighted the issue in her article on *Sagoromo monogatari*. After explaining the link between the hero's affair with Onna Ninomiya and his eventual enthronement, she suggested that Sagoromo knows he violated a taboo, deceived the emperor, committed lèse-majesté, and so on, and therefore feels that as emperor himself he is an imposter; and it is to these sentiments that she attributed at least a part of his gloom at the end of the book.[67] Sagoromo's self-criticism, as she understood it, is the same criticism long directed at Genji himself. It makes the *Sagoromo* author's adoption of the motif difficult to explain.

It is at least possible, however, to suggest that Genji's affair with Fujitsubo did not offend Murasaki Shikibu's patrons as it did the *Mumyōzōshi* author, let alone a Kumazawa Banzan or the ultra-nationalist readers of the 1930s and early 1940s. If it had, Murasaki Shikibu would have devised something else. Sure enough, Amaterasu's oracle in *Sagoromo* contains no such criticism, either. The deity has not a word of reproach for the hero's uninvited lovemaking with Onna Ninomiya, even though this lovemaking ruins both Onna Ninomiya's life and her mother's. On the contrary, Amaterasu makes it clear that, thanks to the hero's behavior, she (Amaterasu) can at last act on her only concern, which is to do him justice. Amaterasu's championing of Sagoromo resembles the Sumiyoshi deity's championing of Genji. Genji's transgression with Fujitsubo is precisely what enabled Sumiyoshi at last to give him his due.

---

[65] McMullen, *Idealism, Protest, and the* Tale of Genji, 321. Being unable to take Genji's affair with Fujitsubo at face value without condemning the entire work, Banzan interpreted it as the author's signal to the reader not to take the tale's amorous tone seriously. To make sure the reader understood her higher intent, the author invented an incident so gross that no one could fail to get the point; and, just to make sure, she then turned this incident into what Banzan called (in McMullen's translation) "the climax of the novel."

[66] Andō, "Shika shichiron," 220.

[67] Inoue, "Sagoromo monogatari no kōzō shiron," 58.

Written only fifty or sixty years after *Genji monogatari* itself, *Sagoromo monogatari* therefore appears to support a reading of Genji's transgression that has long been almost inconceivable. As already argued in "The Disaster of the Third Princess," Genji's lovemaking with Fujitsubo was no crime in eyes of the gods, but instead an opportunity toward merited glory. It is remarkable that the *Sagoromo* author should have grasped this and exploited it in her own tale of supernatural success, especially since, just a century and a half later, the motif seems no longer to have meant anything to the author of *Mumyōzōshi*, let alone to the many readers who followed her. In adopting this pattern from *Genji monogatari*, the *Sagoromo* author left an exceptionally powerful comment on the whole tale.

Conclusion

The *Sagoromo* and *Hamamatsu* authors did not identify themselves as commentators on *Genji monogatari*, nor have they been recognized as such. However, their work contains passages and motifs that illuminate *Genji* reception in a time before formal *Genji* commentary began—a time when *Genji* was still a monogatari among others and not yet a recognized cultural monument. This essay affords a glimpse of what might be gained from reading post-*Genji* fiction not as simple imitation of *Genji monogatari*, or even sometimes as reaction against it, but as interpretation and commentary in the context of undoubtedly changing reader assumptions and tastes. The material it presents suggests in particular that Genji's affair with Fujitsubo may not have been taken from the start as the self-evident crime seen in it by readers of later times. It also highlights the greater complexity and richness of *Genji*, when compared with later fiction, as well as some of the profound originality that makes this great masterpiece so endlessly fascinating.

FEMININE VEILS OVER VISIONS OF THE MALE

In certain scenes of *The Tale of Genji* one or more viewers, usually male, admire a beautiful man. Sometimes the viewer wishes the man were a woman; sometimes he imagines himself as a woman; in one anomalous case the female watchers compare the man favorably to a woman; and in other instances men are swept away by male beauty mediated by a feminine image. This intriguing motif might therefore be called "feminine veils over visions of the male," or, more concisely, "feminine veils."

What the motif really means remains elusive, but this essay will at least discuss the passages in which it occurs and draw three fairly obvious conclusions. First, male-male homoerotic feeling, hence presumably homo-erotic relationship between adult men, was always possible at the Heian court. Second, the *Genji* author shied away from treating this possibility directly, although in three passages of the tale she alluded plainly enough to such relationships between men and boys.[1] Third, such

feelings, or relationships, might be encouraged by a junior's (perhaps a man's as well as a boy's) need for attentive, effective patronage. The essay will close by situating the theme of "feminine veils" in the context of Heian fiction in general, and of *The Tale of Genji* as a whole. This survey of the subject will highlight a final distinction between the earlier and later parts of the tale.

Men Wish a Man Were a Woman

The first *Genji* passage of this kind easily catches the reader's attention. It occurs during the famous "rainy night conversation" about women in "Hahakigi." Four young men (Genji, his friend Tō no Chūjō, and two

---

[1] These passages occur in "Hahakigi" (TTG, 44), "Kōbai" (TTG, 801), and "Yume no ukihashi" (TTG, 1116). The first is particularly famous.

junior officials) are gathered in Genji's room at the palace. One of the officials has just evoked an imagined treasure of a girl "hidden away in some ruinous, overgrown old house." The narrative continues,

[1] Oh come now, Genji thought, it is rare enough to find anyone like that among the highborn. Over soft, layered white gowns he had on only a dress cloak, unlaced at the neck, and, lying there in the lamplight against a pillar, he looked so beautiful that one could have wished him a woman [onna nite mitatematsuramahoshi].[2]

The appeal of this gracefully staged moment is difficult to define. The verb miru ("see") can range in meaning from "look at" to "be on terms of physical intimacy with," but the basic question remains the same. What are the onlookers actually thinking? The idea of a man contemplating another man with desire is simple enough, but not that of a man wishing the male object of his gaze were a woman. Marcel Proust wrote of having "always been curious about the effects of the transposition of a friend's or loved one's face from the masculine sex into the feminine and vice versa," and at the age of twenty or so he identified "feminine charm" as his favorite quality in a man;[3] but the present case is not quite comparable.

A contrasting passage from the same chapter highlights the issue. Genji is at the house of his father-in-law, where again all eyes are upon him. This time, however, the watchers are young women.

[Genji] amused himself chatting with such particularly worthwhile young gentlewomen as Chūnagon and Nakatsukasa, who were delighted to see him, loosely clothed as he was in the heat. His Excellency then appeared and talked with his son-in-law through a standing curtain, since Genji was not presentable.[4]

Here, too, Genji's casual state of dress gives him a special and entirely understandable allure. Moreover, both the women named are in love

---

2 TTG, 24; GM 1:61.

3 Carter, Marcel Proust: A Life, 141, 643. The youthful Proust's counterpart in a woman to "feminine charm" (des charmes féminins) in a man was "manly virtue and openness in friendship" (des vertus d'homme et la franchise dans la camaraderie).

4 TTG, 35-36; GM 1:91.

with him and probably already have a sexual relationship with him.[5] In contrast with [1], there is nothing mysterious about this naughtily amusing scene.

A second example of the pattern seen in [1] occurs in "Momiji no Ga." Desperate to talk to Fujitsubo, who keeps him at a distance, Genji visits her home. There he meets the somewhat foppish Prince Hyōbu ("His Highness of War"), her brother and Murasaki's father. One may imagine Genji all at once envying Hyōbu's easy access to Fujitsubo; feeling guilty and defiant because of his own illicit relationship with Hyōbu's sister; and being mischievously pleased with himself because, unknown to Hyōbu, he has possession of Hyōbu's daughter, Murasaki.

[2] Elegant and romantically languorous as His Highness [Hyōbu] was, Genji speculated privately about the pleasures of his company if he were a woman *[onna nite min wa okashikarinubeku]* and, having a double reason to feel close to him, engaged him in intent conversation. The Prince, for his part, noted how much more open and easy Genji was than usual, liked his looks a great deal, and, unaware that Genji was his son-in-law, indulged his roving fancy in the pleasure of imagining him, too, as a woman *[onna nite mibaya to iromekitaru ōnkokoro ni wa omōsu].*[6]

The "open and easy" corresponds in mood to Genji's earlier casual dress, and the current of feeling between the two men is palpable. However, it is still not clear what the reader is to make of it.

It is difficult to tell whether Japanese scholars have wondered the same thing, despite their evident interest in [1] and the other numbered passages discussed below. Yoshikai Naoto summarized seventeen articles on the subject published between 1928 and 1991,[7] but none appears to have addressed the matter.[8] Instead, scholars

---

[5] According to passages in "Suetsumuhana" (TTG, 116; GM 1:274) and "Aoi" (TTG, 182; GM 2:59)

[6] TTG, 138; GM 1:318-319.

[7] Yoshikai, *Genji monogatari no shinkōsatsu*, 329-330.

[8] However, Kanda Tatsumi argued that Kaoru and Niou are in a homoerotic relationship *(danshoku kankei)*, even if this relationship is not necessarily carnal (Kanda, *Monogatari bungaku, sono kaitai*, 40).

have focused on the precise linguistic pattern central to both [1] and [2], as well as to [3] and [4] below: *onna nite miru*, "see as a woman." They have therefore touched only peripherally on those passages ([5] and [6]) in which the operative words are simply *onna nite* ("as a woman") or *onna naraba* ("if I were a woman") and excluded those ([10] to [12]) containing none of these three expressions.

Yoshikai showed that the accepted reading of *onna nite miru* has changed over the centuries. The pattern as it occurs in [1], in the form *onna nite mitatematsuramahoshi*, will serve as an example. The *mi-* of the third word means "see"; for the rest, *tatematsura-* conveys respect (the watchers all rank below Genji), while *mahoshi* expresses volition ("want to see"). Each watcher "wants to see [Genji] as a woman." But to whom does *onna nite* ("as a woman") apply? In *Amayo danshō* (1487) the poet and literary authority Sōgi, glossing the expression for the first time in writing, assigned *onna nite* to the watchers: each wishes not that Genji were a woman, but that he himself were a woman watching Genji. Later commentaries, through the monumental *Mingō nisso* (1598), take the same position, although *Kogetsushō* (1673) and *Genji Monogatari tama no ogushi* (1796) remain silent on the issue. In pre-modern times only Ishikawa Masamochi (1750-1830), in his undated *Genchū yoteki*, rejected Sōgi's reading. Hagiwara Hiromichi's important *Genji monogatari hyōshaku* (1854) then reaffirmed Sōgi's position. Not until 1928 did the grammarian Matsuo Sutejirō demonstrate conclusively that Sōgi and his successors were wrong.[9] However, his article had little impact, and opinion remained divided until the immense authority of Tamagami Takuya settled the matter in the 1960s.[10] In short, the demonstrably correct reading of the pattern *onna nite miru* in *Genji* gained full acceptance only in the second half of the twentieth century.

The Sōgi misreading is excusable, since in four passages of the tale ([5] to [8]) a man really does view another man from a woman's perspective. However, it is also curious. It at least confirms that *onna nite miru* has confused readers for a long time.

---

[9] Matsuo Sutejirō, "Onna nite mitatematsuramahoshi."
[10] Tamagami, *Genji monogatari hyōshaku*.

Women Wish a Male were Female

As though to compound the confusion, two other examples of the same pattern lack the erotic tone evident in [1] and [2], presumably because the watchers this time are women. In "Sakaki," Fujitsubo contemplates her young son, the future Emperor Reizei.

[3] The older he grew, the kinder his eyes became, as though Genji's face had slipped over his own. Mild decay affected his teeth, darkening the inside of his mouth and giving him a smile so winsome that she would gladly have seen such beauty in a girl *(onna nite mitatematsurahoshū kiyora nari).*[11]

The translation, "would gladly have seen such beauty in a girl," is ambiguous, since it could mean that girls as pretty as this boy are rare. In the original, Fujitsubo clearly would prefer to see him as a girl. Why? His being Genji's son, not the emperor's, has caused her anxiety now multiplied by his recent appointment, in a hostile political environment, as heir apparent. Things might indeed be easier if he were a girl, but that seems not to be the issue; nor, presumably, is desire. Passage [3] has given scholars seeking to grasp the *onna nite miru* pattern particular trouble. At any rate, something similar appears in this description of retired emperor Suzaku ("Eawase"):

[4] His Eminence's looks were such that one would have gladly seen him as a woman *(onna nite mitatematsura-mahoshiki o),* but Her Highness [Akikonomu] did not seem unworthy of him, and they would have made a handsome pair.[12]

The observer is probably a generalized one, resembling above all a gentlewoman like the narrator.[13] Her high but somewhat conventional-

---

[11] TTG, 205; GM 2:116.

[12] TTG, 322; GM 2:372.

[13] It could also be Genji who appraises Suzaku this way. Most modern editors refrain from committing themselves on the subject, but one explicitly includes this sentence in an interior monologue passage attributed to Genji (Abe Akio, *Kanpon Genji monogatari*, 387-388). In Yanai, *Genji monogatari* 2:170, n. 7 (SNKBT), *onna nite mitatematsuramahoshiki o* is interpreted as "be a woman in his intimate company";

sounding praise of Suzaku's looks seems intended mainly to extol Akikonomu's. Despite the repetition of *onna nite miru*, these two passages seem remote from the first pair cited.

The Hypothesis of Imperial Beauty

A thread that might link them after all involves a hypothetical conception of imperial beauty. The beginning of the thread can be found in the possibility, suggested by all four passages, that the author and her audience subscribed to an ultimately feminine standard of beauty. If so, then to wish a male were female is to find his beauty wasted on a male. A passage from "Miyuki" seems to point in this direction. From within her carriage Tamakazura has surveyed the gentlemen of the court and found "none to compare with His Majesty [Reizei] seen in profile, stock-still in his red robes." Then her eyes turn to the commander of the right (Higekuro, her future husband, although she does not know that yet):

> The Commander of the Right, ever weighty and imposing, served His Majesty in great style today with a quiver on his back, but his heavy, black beard was thoroughly unprepossessing. What could such a face ever have had in common with a prettily made up woman's?[14]

The context suggests that Reizei's incomparable looks (so similar to Genji's) are, in contrast, wholly compatible with a woman's. Tamakazura is keen on Reizei and would gladly enter his service, but the narrative is discreet about desire. Her gaze is admiring and perhaps, like Fujitsubo's, affectionate, but its mood little resembles that evoked in [1] and [2]. In the end, the significance of her appraisal of Higekuro slips away. After all, the narrator praises Genji's beauty repeatedly, chapter after chapter, without feeling the need to associate it with a woman's.

---

but Abe Akio, *Genji monogatari*, and Ishida and Shimizu, *Genji monogatari*, take it as translated here.
14 TTG, 500; GM 3:292.

Yoshikai Naoto proposed the hypothesis of an all-but-feminine male beauty associated with the emperor and ranking princes. Noting that the object of desire or admiration in passages [1] to [5] is an emperor or an emperor's son, he suggested that male beauty capable of being extended by the imagination into a woman's is a mark of the imperial and lies beyond any commoner's reach.[15] Another passage from the same "Miyuki" scene appears to support this idea.

> Tamakazura] secretly paid particular attention to His Excellency her father [Tō no Chūjō], but despite his dazzling looks and weighty presence there was only so much and no more to be said for him *[kagiri ari kashi].*[16]

Kagiri ari: Tō no Chūjō's looks "go only so far and no further." Elsewhere, precisely these words may distinguish a commoner from an emperor: the commoner's standing "has a limit" *(kagiri ari),* while the emperor's has none *(kagiri nashi).* This is exactly what Suzaku means in his mournful speech to Oborozukiyo ("Miotsukushi"):

> "I wonder why you would not even give me a child," he said…
> "I know you will have one for [Genji], with whom your tie is so much stronger, and the thought makes me very sad indeed. After all, he is what he is and no more *[kagiri areba],* and your child will have a commoner father."[17]

Imperial standing seems to transcend power and wealth (the busy realm proper to commoners), and its special aura makes those endowed with it peculiarly desirable. Beautiful features, almost transcending gender as well, then confirm the imperial ideal.

This reasoning sounds promising, but it neither acknowledges nor explains the erotic mood of [1] and [2]; nor does it explain other instances, such as [7] or [9], below, in which the man viewed is not imperial. It also contributes nothing toward understanding the next motif: that of a man admiring or desiring another man from the imagined perspective of a woman.

---

[15] Yoshikai, *Genji monogatari no shinkōsatsu*, 338.
[16] TTG, 500; GM 3:292.
[17] TTG, 281; GM 2:281.

The Watching Man Adopts a Woman's Gaze

In four passages of the tale, a man looking at a beautiful man, or picturing him mentally, realizes that if he were a woman he would want to stay with the man forever. In two cases the watcher explicitly finds the man desirable, while in the third desire seems not to be involved. In the fourth, desire is likely but unstated.

The first passage occurs in "Aoi." Genji is mourning Aoi, his late wife, when Tō no Chūjō ("the Captain," Aoi's brother and Genji's great friend) enters the room.

> [5] The Captain, gazing at [Genji] with his mind as always on pleasure *(iromekashiki kokochi ni uchi-mamoraretsutsu)*, knew that if he were a woman *[onna nite]* his soul would stay with Genji instead of setting off for the hereafter. Genji was in a very casual state of dress, and he simply re-threaded the cords of his dress cloak when the Captain sat down beside him...The Captain could hardly keep his eyes off him.[18]

Tō no Chūjō watches Genji with a fascination encouraged by Genji's casual dress. Instead of wishing Genji were a woman, however, he imagines himself as one pointedly unlike his sister Aoi. Aoi never desired Genji, and she indeed left him for the hereafter. Could this roundabout way of elaborating on the desire explicit in the passage be meant to blur it, or to deflect attention away from it?

The next passage, however, lacks any obvious element of desire. In "Wakana One" Suzaku says to himself, as he considers marrying his favorite daughter to Genji,

> [6] I would want to be close to [Genji] if I were a woman *[onna naraba]*, even a sister. That is the way I felt when we were young. No wonder women cannot resist him![19]

He is probably thinking both of his beloved Oborozukiyo, who loves Genji instead, and of his daughter's future happiness. Desire returns in a much later passage that repeats the pattern of [5]. In "Agemaki" Niou

---

18 TTG, 181; GM 2:55.
19 TTG, 580; GM 4:28.

considers his friend Kaoru, who is wasting away with grief after the death of Ōigimi.

> [7] After so many days of tears [Kaoru's] features had changed, though not for the worse, because they now had so fine a beauty and grace that [Niou], who deplored his own waywardness [ono ga keshikaranu on-kokoro narai ni], saw that *he* would certainly lose his heart to him, if he himself were a woman [onna naraba].[20]

Niou contrasts Ōigimi's rejection of Kaoru with the way *he* would feel about Kaoru if he himself were in Ōigimi's position, and he explicitly does so in a mood of erotic excitement. In all three passages ([5] to [7]) a man therefore views another man from the perspective of a particular woman, one well known to himself and the reader. The only instance that breaks this pattern is the last, from "Tenarai." The governor of Kii, a retainer of Kaoru, appraises Niou.

> [8] His Highness of War is the one of really striking beauty, though. I would gladly be a woman in his intimate service [onna nite naretsukōmatsuraba].[21]

Since the speaker is talking to a group of women he hardly knows, his remark presumably puts personal feeling in conventionally accepted terms. This topic will reappear below.

Women See the Man as a Woman More Beautiful Than Any Woman

In the set of gender-shift motifs just discussed, a man imagines another man as a woman; a woman imagines a man or boy as female; and a man viewing another man imagines himself as a woman. The tale also contains a passage in which women watching a man see in him a perfection of feminine beauty unattainable by women themselves. The moment occurs in "Yūgiri."

After a journey through an uncharacteristically (for the author in this part of the work) theatrical landscape, Yūgiri has reached Ono, at the foot of Mt. Hiei, and stands before the house of Princess Ochiba,

---

[20] TTG, 912; GM 5:338.
[21] TTG, 1107; GM 6:359-360.

whom he is determined this time, at last, to possess. Her gentlewomen view him from behind blinds.

[9] He walked up to the double doors as usual and stood looking about him. The deep scarlet gown beneath his soft dress cloak, beaten beautifully transparent, glowed in the waning sunlight that lay guilelessly upon him, and with an entrancingly casual gesture he lifted his fan to cover his face, looking, so it seemed to the watching women, exactly as a woman should look, although none ever quite succeeds *[onna koso kō wa aramahoshikere, sore dani e-aranu o]*.[22]

The women's appraisal of Yūgiri exactly matches the stock explanation of why men perform female roles in kabuki: the kabuki *onnagata* is more feminine than any woman could ever be. This passage is unique in the tale. Yūgiri has been described as handsome, but nothing prepares the reader for this vision of him as a sort of trans-woman, and nothing later on supports it. The account of Yūgiri's journey to Ono and the scene of his arrival there is almost parodic. Intentionally or not, passage [9] especially parodies passage [11], quoted below from "Suma." The "Suma" scene is by the sea, the "Yūgiri" scene in the mountains; the "Suma" colors, centered on Genji's clothes, are blue and green, while the "Yūgiri" colors, centered on the costume worn by Genji's son, are red and sunset gold; the dazzled watchers in "Suma" are men, those in "Yūgiri" women; and while the watchers in "Suma" find Genji's male company even more consoling than that of their girlfriends at home, for those in "Yūgiri," Genji's son makes a better woman than a woman. In one way or another, and more or less diffusely, passage [9] reverses all the others quoted.

Men Admiring a Man

In a particularly interesting set of scenes, one more congruent with [1] to [8] than the anomalous [9], the male gaze contemplates Genji in a mood of erotic and aesthetic excitement, but without imagined gender

---

22 TTG, 738; GM 4:449.

transformation on either side. For quotation purposes, all three will be collapsed as much as possible.

[10] Two days later the Captain gave the loser's banquet... and... all joined happily in music making. One of [his] sons, a boy of eight or nine... sang and played the *shō* prettily...When the music picked up a little he gave full voice to a very fine rendition of "Takasago." Genji took a layer from his costume and placed the garment over the boy's shoulders. His face, flushed with unaccustomed excitement, gave forth a beauty beyond any in the world, and his skin glowed wondrously through the silk gauze dress cloak and shift, until the ancient scholars watching him from their distance wept.

"How I long for you, my lily flower!" the boy's song ended, and the Captain gave Genji a cup of wine. [He said],

> *"All have longed to see*
> *those first blossoms this morning*
> *burst into full bloom,*
> *yet I contemplate in you*
> *beauty just as great as theirs!"*[23]

In this full-flavored tribute to Genji's beauty there appears initially to be no feminine presence at all, real or imagined. The young singer's role is suggestive, and the scholars' tears of ecstasy make a wonderful touch. The moment seems to be among men only. However, the image of a woman is there after all, in the song. The *saibara* "Takasago" is a lover's passionate appeal to the woman he desires. "Oh white camellia on the hilltop, oh lovely willow," the lover cries, "I want you *[mashi mo ga na]*, I want you!"[24] The song therefore superimposes an imagined girl on the physical Genji, yielding an image analogous to the ones evoked in [1] and [2].

A passage in "Suma" achieves the same effect by different means. Genji and his small entourage are in exile on the shore.

[11] One lovely twilight, with the near garden in riotous bloom, Genji stepped out onto a gallery that afforded a view

---

[23] TTG, 216-217; GM 2:141-142.
[24] Tsuchihashi and Konishi, *Kodai kayō*, 381.

of the sea, and such was the supernal grace of his motionless figure that, in that setting, he seemed not of this world. Over soft, white silk twill and aster he had on a dress cloak of deep blue, its sash only very casually tied; and his voice slowly chanting, "I, a disciple of the Buddha Shakyamuni..." was to their ears more beautiful than any they had ever heard before. From boats rowing by at sea came a chorus of singing voices. With a pang he watched them, dim in the distance, like little birds borne on the waters, and sank into a reverie as cries from lines of geese aloft mingled with the creaking of oars, until tears welled forth and he brushed them away with a hand so gracefully pale against his black rosary that the young gentlemen pining for their sweethearts at home were all consoled *[furusato no onna koishiki hitobito, kokoro mina nagusaminikeri].*[25]

The languid, come-hither melancholy of this tableau exploits Buddhist piety to erotic effect in a manner developed further in Part Three of the tale. As in [1], [5], and [10], Genji is casually dressed, and the pallor of his delicate hand against the black rosary contrasts artfully with the picture of him, flushed and excited, presented two chapters earlier.

As in [1], the young men's eyes are riveted upon Genji. Instead of having them imagine him as a woman, however, the author this time appeals to the memory of the woman that each holds dear: his sweetheart in the city. In the reader's mind this image superimposes itself upon, or colors, or reshapes, or blurs the physical spectacle of Genji. Male-male desire seems to be evoked here, only to be rhetorically deflected. Under these ambiguous circumstances, the "consolation" experienced by the young men could conceivably be sexual relief. Genji's remark to the Akashi Novice in passage [12], below, suggests as much: "[Your daughter's] solace will see me through these lonely nights." It is true, however, that [11] follows a different pattern. Nothing can be excluded from it, but nothing can be proven.

---

[25] TTG, 244-245; GM 2:200-201.

In any case, the point of the passage is elsewhere. Before the spectacle of Genji's beauty, the young men experience a wave of relief at being with him, rather than with the comparatively insignificant girlfriends who had seemed so important to them until a moment ago. This relief combines emotional (as erotic as one pleases) and aesthetic satisfaction with a renewed conviction that, despite the risk, each has been right to follow him into exile. In Genji's perfect beauty, the token of his true worth, each sees boundless future advantage for himself. The young men love him not only for what he is in himself, but also for what he promises them.

Other "Suma" passages similarly evoke the young men's whole-hearted devotion to Genji. "[Genji] was so kind and such a delight to the eye that [his] four or five [companions] forgot their cares and found his intimate service a pleasure,"[26] the narrator assures the reader; and again, "In the depths of the night [Genji] would rinse his hands and call the Buddha's Name, which to his companions was so wonderful and so inspiring that they never left him."[27] However, it is a messenger from Rokujō at Ise who highlights a significant aspect of their feelings when he is "dazzled" and weeps at his glimpses of Genji's beauty.[28] He may believe that, through Rokujō, Genji's favor will reach him, too, but his very distance from Genji suggests a larger meaning for his tears. Through Genji's beauty he (or, rather, the reader) recognizes Genji's destined role as the pole star of the realm. Genji's personal beauty, like his celebrated light, is not merely an aesthetic matter. It signals a transcendent calling in which the viewer wishes, however humbly, to share. Genji's companions of course feel the same way. Being at once so powerful and so intimate, the spell cast by Genji naturally has an erotic dimension as well.

The last passage to be quoted on the theme of the desiring gaze illustrates the complexity of Genji's appeal. It is from "Akashi." Genji and his host, the Akashi Novice, drink together one evening and reveal their thoughts to each other. The occasion is momentous for both. Ever

---

[26] TTG, 244; GM 2:200.
[27] TTG, 249; GM 2:208.
[28] TTG, 242; GM 2:195.

since his daughter's birth the Novice has been begging the Sumiyoshi deity, the protector of the imperial line, to provide for her a man like Genji and so to restore the dignity of his house. Meanwhile, Genji is desperately lonely, despite his devotion to the absent Murasaki. Commanding longings converge from both sides.

[12] It was late...and the sinking moon shone with a pure light. When all was quiet the Novice poured forth his tale to Genji...describing his plans when he first moved to this shore...and, all unasked, his daughter herself...

...Genji...listened with tears in his eyes. "I had been wondering for what crime I was falsely accused and condemned to wander an alien land, but all that you have said tonight leaves me certain...that [the tie between your daughter and me] is indeed a bond of some strength from past lives...Distant rumor had told me of such a lady, but I had sadly assumed that she would recoil from a ne'er-do-well. Now, however, I gather that you wish to take me to her. Her solace will see me through these lonely nights *[kokorobosoki hitorine no nagusame ni mo]*."

The Novice was transported with delight.

> *"Do you know as well*
> *what it is to sleep alone?*
> *Think then how she feels,*
> *wakeful through the long, long nights*
> *by herself upon this shore!"*

he said...

"But surely, someone accustomed to the shore...

> *How traveling wears*
> *through the long melancholy*
> *of the wakeful nights*
> *that keep a grassy pillow*
> *from gathering even dreams!"*

Genji's casual demeanor *[uchi-midaretaru on-sama]* gave him intense allure and a beauty beyond all words *[ito aigyō-zuki, iū yoshinaki on-kehai naru].*[29]

The Novice intentionally seduces the willing Genji for his daughter, and once their understanding is reached, the last sentence sums up the moment. Manners and dress loosened by wine, Genji glows with excitement at the thought of what awaits him, while the equally tipsy Novice sees in him the answer to all his prayers, indeed a manifest divinity. Eros colors the whole scene. Genji anticipates lovemaking with a lady of greater personal distinction than he had ever thought to find, while the Novice presumably looks forward to his daughter's pleasure in Genji's beauty, rather as Tō no Chūjō, in passage [5], imagines the pleasure that should have been his sister's. However, in [5] Tō no Chūjō seems to desire Genji. Does the Novice, too? He alone is present to experience Genji's "intense allure," and no doubt he does so. However, there is no point in trying to define more precisely, and especially more materially, the object of his desire, when it encompasses, in a single movement of the affections, both personal and lofty aspiration.

Further Reflections on the Feminine Veil in Erotic Scenes

The fluidity of view in passages [1] to [12] imperils whatever value one might assign to the motif of the feminine veil. Some of these passages suggest an ideal of imperial beauty that others undermine. Some are erotic in tone, but not all. Why does Fujitsubo imagine her son as a girl? Why is Suzaku described as wishing to be a woman, even a sister, close to Genji? There being as yet no answer to these questions, it is possible only to propose, for the more clearly erotic passages, the hypothesis summarized above.

The men in these passages may imagine another man as a woman, view another man through an imagined woman's eyes, or enjoy elaborately evoked male beauty in a manner also mediated by a variously imagined feminine presence. Desire roams freely through

---

[29] TTG, 264-265; GM 2:244-247.

them, communicating itself to characters and audience alike. The feminine image that drifts in them between the seer and the seen seems to be, or at least makes sense as, a rhetorical device designed to temper, presumably out of respect for the audience's notion of propriety, a mode of feeling widely known and even appreciated but not openly discussed.

Two kinds of relationship can be discerned between the men involved in these scenes. The first is that between lower-ranking men and a great lord like Genji. The second is between men who are more nearly equals and so presumably less preoccupied with favor and patronage, although these elements cannot be excluded. Two passages of *The Tale of Genji* shed light on the first. They deal with relationships between great lords (Genji, Niou) and boys who are the sons of lesser fathers.

The first occurs in "Hahakigi." Most *Genji* readers remember the moment at the end of the chapter when, hurt and frustrated by Utsusemi's rejection, Genji spends the night instead with Kogimi, her little brother.[30] As the narrator tells the story, Genji's interest in Kogimi is inspired entirely by his pursuit of Utsusemi herself. This "Hahakigi" passage therefore recalls in its way the ones already treated: the image of Utsusemi mediates Genji's desire for her brother. However, the wider context of Genji's night with Kogimi is particularly suggestive. Genji selected him from the start for the access he could provide to Utsusemi, and he cultivated him to the same end, showering him with benefits and advantages, and taking him into his intimate service. Seduced by Genji's charm and patter, no doubt dimly aware of the long-term value of the relationship, and in any case too awed to question Genji's will, Kogimi sought to please Genji in every way, including in bed. This does not mean that he was Genji's sexual plaything, still less that Genji was addicted to little boys. The night mentioned at the end of "Hahakigi" simply arose in the natural course of events brought about by Genji's pursuit of Kogimi's sister. It was incidental both to this pursuit and to Genji's wider patronage of Kogimi. At the same time, however, such a relationship (close

---

[30] TTG, 44; GM 1:113.

patronage on one side, intimate service on the other) clearly allowed at least the possibility of such nights. It established the pattern still visible among mature young men in passage [11] at Suma.

Such relationships were presumably familiar in the author's time, at the level of private confidence rather than public discourse. However, it was probably more common for a gentlewoman to play Kogimi's role. The man who desired access to a lady would then similarly cultivate one of her gentlewomen and, to secure her allegiance, become her lover himself as a step toward possessing her mistress. No such case is acknowledged in the tale, but many hints suggest the idea. Genji has intimate relationships with gentlewomen (such as Chūnagon), and so, too, does Kaoru (Kozaishō). The narrative does not present these as bridges to anyone else, but Kozaishō, in service to the First Princess who obsesses Kaoru in "Kagerō," could probably be bent to that purpose if Kaoru wished. Meanwhile, other gentlewomen certainly provide access to their mistresses in response to intense pressure from the men concerned, and the possibility that a man might gain access to a lady by suborning one of her women is evoked repeatedly as all too real. Kogimi's machinations on Genji's behalf recall Ōmyōbu's maneuvers to bring Genji to Fujitsubo, and one wonders in that light what hold Genji has on Ōmyōbu, to be able to make her do things so dangerous and so distressing to her mistress. Perhaps she can imagined caught in a trap, laid by Genji, that includes a sexual relationship with her.

The second example of the pattern under discussion occurs in "Kōbai." After repeated overtures, Niou succeeds in seducing a boy (one of Tō no Chūjō's grandsons) away from the heir apparent in order to pursue, through this boy, one of the boy's sisters. The heir apparent has been using the boy for the same purpose. However, these related episodes in "Hahakigi" and "Kōbai" differ entirely in tone. In "Kōbai" there is none of the disarmingly troubled sincerity that characterizes Genji's headlong adventure in "Hahakigi." Instead, Niou's motivation comes across as a mixture of frivolity and cunning. In the end, the target sister goes as a consort to the heir apparent, while Niou gets the boy, through whom he sets out to pursue another of the sisters. "I thought [the heir apparent] would never to let you go," he says to the boy, "but it appears that someone else [the new consort] may have taken your place."[31] Niou may only be teasing, but this insinuation that the boy had earlier been the principal object of the heir apparent's erotic interest is out of keeping with anything else in the book. Also unusual for someone of her considerable rank, because so light-heartedly crass, are the boy's mother's remarks to her husband (a grand counselor) after their son comes home reeking of Niou's perfume:

> "Our son was [at the palace] for a night on duty, and he smelled so good when he left that the Heir Apparent knew straight off he had been with His Highness of War [Niou], though most people thought nothing of it. 'No wonder he no longer cares about me!' he complained. It was quite amusing.[32]

Far from disapproving, or from fearing her husband's disapproval, she is pleased with her son for capturing the interest of Niou, the darling of the court and a patron of unrivaled promise. Meanwhile, "most people" at the palace apparently take such carryings-on for granted.

This situation sheds light on passage [8]: "His Highness of War is the one of really striking beauty, though. I would gladly be a woman in his intimate service." The speaker, a man of the provincial governor class, is speaking casually. Presumably the remark is unexceptionable, first because he talks of wishing to serve Niou not because Niou is influential, but because he is beautiful. His appreciation of Niou's beauty makes a high-minded cover for more persuasive calculations of self-interest. Second, his talk of wanting to be a woman, etc., appears to legitimize the sort of relationship with Niou that could yield patronage most beneficial to himself. It is not that a man's "intimate service" to his lord necessarily involved erotic intimacy. However, service of this kind must have made such intimacy possible and advantageous in some cases.

Men already of very high rank, for whom the advantages of patronage and service (vis-à-vis each other) are more diffuse, are in a

---

[31] TTG, 799; GM 5:50.
[32] TTG, 801; GM 5:53.

different position. The current that passes between Genji and Prince Hyōbu in [2], between Tō no Chūjō and Genji in [5], or and between Niou and Kaoru in [7], makes no sense unless the sort of relationship it suggests could indeed occur. While *The Tale of Genji* acknowledges none openly, the slightly later *Sagoromo monogatari* is more explicit.

Although original in its way, *Sagoromo monogatari* betrays pervasive and at times startlingly obvious *Genji* influence. For example, one *Sagoromo* scene merges passage [3], above, with the moment in "Wakamurasaki" when Genji makes little Murasaki write a poem.[33] The *Sagoromo* hero has his little son, whom the emperor believes to be his own (another *Genji* motif), write a poem; and the boy's fetching looks, when he bashfully demurs, make the hero "wish he could turn him into a princess" *(onna miya ni zo semahoshige ni mietamau).*[34] The *Sagoromo* author's expression of this motif is distinctly the more assertive of the two ("make him into a princess," as compared with "see him as a girl").

A similar directness makes another *Sagoromo* scene unique, unless the intention is to make explicit something unstated in *Genji* but obvious to eleventh-century readers. The hero, who is languishing for the love of an unresponsive lady, calls after a long absence on his friend the heir apparent. Begging the heir apparent to excuse him, the hero holds out his arm. "Look!" he says, "See how thin I am! I doubt that I am long for this world." The heir apparent has never seen so white an arm before, even on a woman. He exclaims, "Ooh, I'd like to go to bed with *that!*" *(imijū fushiyoge ni anmere)* and pulls the hero down beside him. "Oh no," the hero cries, struggling adorably, "it's *so* hot!"[35] The two are apparently established lovers.

Suggestiveness and indirection are gone, and the feminine image that in *Genji* mediates every desiring glance between males has vanished. This suggests a further thought. The feminine veil is absent from surviving earlier fiction, except for a single precursor passage in *Utsuho monogatari* (late 10th c.?); and, apart from the direct *Genji*

---

[33] TTG, 108; GM 1:259.
[34] Komachiya and Gotō, *Sagoromo monogatari* 2:369. Suzuki Kazuo, *Sagoromo monogatari* 1:336 is even more direct: *onnamiya ni zo semahoshiki.*
[35] *Sagoromo monogatari*, vol. 1, pp. 72-73.

imitation just cited from *Sagoromo*, it is to be found neither in *Sagoromo* nor in the slightly later *Hamamatsu Chūnagon monogatari*, which also shows *Genji* influence. It might be assumed to represent a Heian literary convention. In fact, however, this convention seems to have been especially favored, and perhaps even invented, by the *Genji* author herself, presumably in consonance with her own taste or purposes, or perhaps also in response to those of her immediate patrons.

Distribution of "Feminine Veil" Outside and Inside Genji

The following account of the motif beyond *Genji*, *Sagoromo*, and *Hamamatsu* will rely on the work of Yoshikai Naoto. Yoshikai confined his search to items linguistically identifiable (because following or close to the *onna nite miru* pattern) with passages [1] to [4] and [5] to [8], above. The *Utsuho monogatari* passage just mentioned reads as follows:

> On first seeing [Prince Hyōbukyō], one wanted to turn him into a woman and have him for one's own, or else to [become a woman and] be his own oneself" *(kano kimi o onna ni nashite motaramahoshiku, sarazu wa, ware motaremahoshiku nan miyuru).*[36]

This so explicitly covers both fundamental *Genji* transformations (male viewer or male object changed into a woman) and is otherwise so unusual in *Utsuho* that, given the confused state of the *Utsuho* textual transmission, Yoshikai saw in it a possible "reverse import" *(gyaku yunyū)* from *Genji*.[37] However, the inclusion of both possibilities in a single sentence is unlike *Genji*, as is the assertive phrasing ("turn him into a woman").

Among surviving works of fiction written within a hundred years of *Genji*, only *Sagoromo monogatari* and *Yoru no nezame* (late 11th c.) include the pattern defined by Yoshikai. The *Sagoromo* passage, on the

---

[36] Yoshikai, *Genji monogatari no shinkōsatsu*, 338. The *Utsuho* passage is quoted from the "Naishi no kami" chapter (Nakano, *Utsuho monogatari* 2:160-161).
[37] Yoshikai, *Genji monogatari no shinkōsatsu*, 338.

model of [3], has just been discussed. *Nezame* is most plausibly attributed to the "Daughter of Takasue," who described in her *Sarashina nikki* the enchantment she felt upon reading *Genji*. She too, therefore, presumably wrote under *Genji* influence. However, on the present issue that influence was slight. The pattern of [1] to [4] is absent, and only one passage recalls [5] to [8]. A young man known as Saishō no Chūjō longs to be a woman in order to give himself *(nabiki-yorinan kashi)* to Dainagon, the devastatingly melancholy hero.[38] Otherwise, the main female character twice finds her own son so pretty that, like Fujitsubo in [3], she wishes to see him as a girl.[39] Later Heian-style fiction has three brief passages on the pattern of [1] or [2] (one each in *Torikaebaya*, *Ama no karu mo*, and *Matsura no miya monogatari).* The *Genji* legacy is therefore visible but restricted. No doubt the twelfth-century *Torikaebaya* (rewritten in the following century, the original now being lost) features a languid brother and a tomboy sister, both equally beautiful, brought up with great success as members of the opposite sex, until the inevitable complications unmask the deception. *Torikaebaya* certainly confirms an enduring, collective interest in gender shifts and shadings. Compared to *Genji*, however, it belongs to the realm of fantasy, and in any case it is some two centuries later.

The theme of the feminine veil might therefore be almost invisible in Heian fiction but for *The Tale of Genji*, where it appears more often than elsewhere, in greater variety, and in fuller form. In this respect, as in so many others, *Genji* is unusual. However, the theme is by no means evenly distributed in *Genji* itself, as this table shows.

---

[38] Yoshikai, *Genji monogatari no shinkōsatsu*, 342-343; Suzuki Kazuo, *Yoru no Nezame*, 133. Saishō Chūjō reflects in a flight of hyperbole unknown in *Genji* that, if he were a woman, he would gladly give up being empress in order to do so. This sentiment recalls the *Sarashina* diarist's statement that, when reading *Genji* as a girl, she was so entranced that "I wouldn't have changed places with the Empress herself" (Morris, *As I Crossed a Bridge of Dreams*, 55).

[39] Yoshikai, *Genji monogatari no shinkōsatsu*, 342-344; Suzuki Kazuo, *Yoru no Nezame*, 431, 506.

Passage	Part 1 (Ch. 1-33)	Part 2 (Ch. 34-41)	Part 3 (Ch. 42-54)
[1] Genji/young men	Ch. 2, Hahakigi		
[2]Genji/Hyōbu	Ch. 7, Momijinoga		
[3] Fujitsubo/son	Ch. 10, Sakaki		
[4] Suzaku/narrator	Ch. 17, Eawase		
[5] Tō no Chūjō/Genji	Ch. 9, Aoi		
[6] Suzaku/Genji		Ch. 34, Wakana 1	
[7] Niou/Kaoru			Ch. 47, Agemaki
[8] Kii/Niou			Ch. 53, Tenarai
[9] Yūgiri at Ono		Ch. 39, Yūgiri	
[10] Genji/Tō no Chūjō	Ch. 10, Sakaki		
[11 Genji/young men	Ch. 12, Suma		
[12] Genji/Novice	Ch. 13, Akashi		

All the major passages occur in the first thirteen chapters of the tale, with the exception of the elaborately parodic [9] and the brief, possibly derivative [7]. Only five of the twelve passages listed occur past chapter 13.

It seems natural that striking scenes like [1], [2], or [11] should occur during Genji's youth, if they are to occur at all. However, they are not inevitable. There are no such moments further on, with the exception of the anomalous [9]. In fact, in three passages later than chapter 13 the viewer (the narrator, Suzaku, the governor of Kii) sees the object only in memory. It is not that Part Three, in particular, lacks erotic scenes. Rather, in Part Three the theme or motif of the feminine veil came to the author's mind no more often, and no more fully, than it did to the mind of those who wrote later works of Heian fiction. Passages [7] and [8] resemble brief acknowledgments of established motifs.

It is striking that nothing in surviving pre-*Genji* literature, apart from that single, doubtful *Utsuho* passage, should announce such passages as [1], [2], or [11]. *Ochikubo monogatari*, by an unknown male author and slightly earlier than *Genji*, contains nothing similar; nor does Sei Shōnagon's *Pillow Book*, in its way an authoritative expression of accepted feminine court taste in the years immediately preceding the writing of *Genji*. The cluster of motifs discussed here under the heading of the "feminine veil" appears therefore to have been devised by the author of Part One of the tale—an author whose erotic wit, inventiveness, and daring distinguish this part of her work in many other ways as well and go far toward making it unforgettable.

ABBREVIATIONS FOR WORKS FREQUENTLY CITED

GM   Abe Akio et al, eds. *Genji monogatari*. 6 vols. SNKBZ.
          1994-1998.

NKBT   *Nihon koten bungaku taikei.* 102 vols. Iwanami, 1957-1968.

SNKBT   *Shin Nihon koten bungaku taikei.* 100 vols. Iwanami, 1989-
          2003.

SNKBZ   *Shinpen Nihon koten bungaku zenshū.* 88 vols. Shōgakukan,
          1994-2002.

SNKS   *Shinchō Nihon koten shūsei.* 85 vols. Shinchōsha, 1976-1989.

TTG   Royall Tyler, trans. *The Tale of Genji*. New York: Viking,
          2001.

WORKS CITED

All Japanese books were published in Tokyo unless otherwise indicated.

Abe Akio, ed. *Kanpon Genji monogatari*. Shogakukan, 1992.

_____ et al., eds. *Genji monogatari*. 6 vols. SNKBZ 20-25. 1994-1998.

Abe Toshiko. "Genji monogatari no 'mononoke,'" Part 2. *Kokugo kokubun ronshū* (Gakushuin Joshi Tanki Daigaku) 7 (1978).

Abe Yasurō. "*Iruka* no seiritsu." *Geinō shi kenkyū* 69 (1980).

_____. "Jidō setsuwa no keisei," Parts 1 and 2. *Kokugo kokubun* 53:8 (1984) and 53:9 (1984).

_____. "Taishokan no seiritsu." In *Kōwakamai kenkyū*, vol. 4, edited by Agō Toranoshin and Fukuda Akira. Miyai Shoten, 1986.

Abe Yoshitomi. "Genji monogatari no Suzaku-in o kangaeru: joshō, ōken o koeru mono." *Nihon bungaku* 38:3 (1989).

Akimoto Yoshio, ed. *Fudoki.* NKBT 2, 1958.

Akiyama Ken, ed. *Genji monogatari jiten* (Bessatsu *Kokubungaku* 36) 1993.

_____. *Genji monogatari no sekai*. Tōkyō Daigaku Shuppankai, 1964.

_____. "Kanketsuteki na seishin hatten ron." In *Genji monogatari o dō yomu ka* (*Kokubungaku kaishaku to kanshō* bessatsu), April 1986.

_____, ed. *Sarashina nikki*. SNKS, 1980.

Amano Naokata. *Genji monogatari taii*. In *Hihyō shūsei Genji monogatari*, vol. 2 *(Kinsei kōki hen)*, edited by Shimauchi Keiji et al. Yumani Shobō, 1999.

Andō Tameakira, "Shika shichiron." In *Hihyō shūsei: Genji monogatari*, vol. 1 *(Kinsei zenki hen)*, edited by Shimauchi Keiji et al., Yumani Shobō, 1999.

Arntzen, Sonja, trans. *The Kagerō Diary: A Woman's Autobiographical Text from Tenth-Century Japan*. Ann Arbor: Center for Japanese Studies, University of Michigan, 1997.

Aston, W. G., trans. *Nihongi* (various editions).

Baba Taeko. "Jiga no ishiki o motsu Murasaki no Ue." *Tōyoko kokubungaku* 22 (March 1990).

Bargen, Doris, "The Search for Things Past in the *Genji monogatari*," *Harvard Journal of Asiatic Studies* 51:1 (June 1991).

_____. *A Woman's Weapon: Spirit Possession in* The Tale of Genji. Honolulu: University of Hawai'i Press, 1997.

Bowring, Richard. *Murasaki Shikibu: The Tale of Genji*. Cambridge, England: Cambridge University Press, 1988.

_____, trans. *The Diary of Lady Murasaki*, London: Penguin, 1996.

Brown, Delmer M. and Ichirō Ishida, trans. *The Future and the Past*. Berkeley, Calif.: University of California Press, 1979.

Caddeau, Patrick. "Tree Spirits (kodama) and Apparitions (henge): Hagiwara Hiromichi's Analysis of Supernatural Events in Yūgao and the Uji Chapters." *Gobun* (Ōsaka Daigaku Kokugo Kokubungakukai) 80/81 (February 2004).

Carter, William C. *Marcel Proust: A Life*. New Haven: Yale University Press, 2000.

Chateaubriand, François-René de. *Mémoires d'outre-tombe*. 2 vols. Bibliothèque de la Pléiade. Paris: Gallimard, 1951.

Childs, Margaret H. "The Value of Vulnerability: Sexual Coercion and the Nature of Love in Japanese Court Literature." *Journal of Asian Studies* 58:4 (Nov. 1999).

Cranston, Edwin A. *A Waka Anthology, Volume One: The Gem-Glistening Cup*. Stanford, Calif.: Stanford University Press, 1993.

Dictionnaire historique de la langue française. Paris: Dictionnaires Le Robert, 1992.

Elias, Norbert. *The Court Society*, translated by Edmund Jephcott. Oxford: Blackwell, 1983.

Enchi Fumiko. "Genji monogatari no kōzō." in *Hihyō shūsei Genji monogatari*, vol. 3 *(Kindai no hihyō)*, edited by Shimauchi Keiji et al. Yumani Shobō, 1999.

_____. *Genji monogatari shiken*. Shinchōsha, 1974.

Endō Yoshimoto and Matsuo Satoshi, eds. *Takamura monogatari, Heichū monogatari, Hamamatsu Chūnagon monogatari*. NKBT 77, 1964.

Enomoto Masazumi. "Ukifune ron e no kokoromi." *Kokugo to kokubungaku*, May 1975.

D'Etchverry, Charo B. "Out of the Mouths of Nurses: *The Tale of Sagoromo* and Midranks Romance." *Monumenta Nipponica* 59:2 (Summer 2004).

_____. "Rethinking Late Heian: Sagoromo, Nezame, Hamamatsu, and the Rear Court" (dissertation submitted to Princeton University), 2000.

_____. *Love After* The Tale of Genji: *Rewriting the World of the Shining Prince*. Cambridge, Mass.: Harvard University Asia Center, 2007.

Field, Norma. *The Splendor of Longing in the Tale of Genji*. Princeton, N.J.: Princeton University Press, 1987.

Fujii Sadakazu. *Genji monogatari: shigen to genzai*. Isagoya Shobō, 1990.

_____. "Uta no zasetsu." In *Genji monogatari oyobi igo no monogatari: kenkyū to shiryō*, edited by Murasaki Shikibu Gakkai. Musashino Shoin, 1979.

Fujimoto Katsuyoshi. *Genji monogatari no 'mononoke': bungaku to kiroku no hazama*. Kasama Shoin, 1994.

Fukasawa Michio. *Genji monogatari no shinsō sekai*. Ōfū, 1997.

_____. "Murasaki no Ue: higekiteki risōzō no keisei," *Kokugo kokubun* 368 (April 1965).

Genji monogatari no makimaki. *Kokubungaku kaishaku to kyōzai no kenkyū* 32:13 (Nov. 1987).

Genji monogatari o yomu tame no kenkyū. *Kokubungaku kaishaku to kyōzai no kenkyū* 40:3 (Feb. 1995).

Goff, Janet. *Noh Drama and* The Tale of Genji. Princeton, N.J.: Princeton University Press, 1991.

Goodwin, Janet R. *Selling Songs and Smiles: The Sex Trade in Heian and Kamakura Japan*. Honolulu: University of Hawai'i Press, 2007.

Gotō Yasufumi. "Mō hitori no Kaoru: Sagoromo monogatari no shiron." In *Kenkyū kōza Sagoromo monogatari no shikai*, edited by Ōchō Monogatari Kenkyūkai. Shintensha, 1994.

Hagiwara Hiromichi. "Sōron." In *Hihyō shūsei Genji monogatari*, vol. 2 *(Kinsei kōki hen)*, edited by Shimauchi Keiji et al. Yumani Shobō, 1999.

Haraoka Fumiko. *Genji monogatari no jinbutsu to hyōgen: sono ryōgiteki tenkai*. Kanrin Shobō, 2003.

Hasegawa Masaharu et al., eds. *Tosa nikki, Kagerō nikki, Murasaki Shikibu nikki, Sarashina nikki*. SNKBT 24, 1989.

Hayashida Takakazu et al., eds. *Genji monogatari jiten*. Daiwa Shobō, 2002.

Hérail, Francine, trans. *Notes journalières de Fujiwara no Michinaga, ministre à la cour de Hei.an*. 3 vols. Paris: Librairie Droz, 1987-1991.

Higuchi Yoshimaro and Kuboki Tetsuo, eds. *Matsura no Miya monogatari,*
Mumyōzōshi. SNKBZ 40, 1999.

Hinata Kazumasa. "'Genji monogatari' no shi to saisei: Ukifune o chūshin ni." *Kokubungaku kaishaku to kanshō* 53:9 (1988).

Hirota Osamu. "Jusui shinai Ukifune, seichō shinai Kaoru." In *Genji monogatari: Uji jūjō no kuwadate,* edited by Sekine Kenji. Ōfū, 2005.

_____. "Monogatari ron to shite no ōken ron to Kiritsubo no mikado: Genji
monogatari no kōtōfu to Hikaru Genji." In *Genji monogatari to mikado,* edited by Takahashi Tōru. Shinwasha, 2004.

Horiguchi Satoru. "*Sagoromo monogatari* no kōsō: kōhanbu ni tsuite." In *Kenkyū kōza Sagoromo monogatari no shikai,* edited by Ōchō Monogatari Kenkyūkai. Shintensha, 1994.

Horiuchi Hideaki and Akiyama Ken, eds. *Taketori monogatari, Ise monogatari.* SNKBT 17, 1997.

Hyōdō Hiromi. *Heike monogatari no rekishi to geinō,* Yoshikawa Kōbunkan, 2000.

_____. "Monogatari no katarite to sei: Ukifune no monogatari kara." *Kokubungaku kaishaku to kyōzai no kenkyū* 44:5 (Bessatsu *Genji monogatari no datsuryōiki),* April 2000.

Ichijō Kanera. *Renju gappeki shū.* In *Renga ron shū,* vol. 1, edited by Kidō Saizō and Shigematsu Hiromi, Miyai Shoten, 1972.

Ii Haruki, ed. *Kachō yosei.* Genji monogatari kochū shūsei, vol 1. Ōfūsha, 1978.

_____, ed. *Naikaku Bunko-bon Sairyūshō.* Genji monogatari kochū shūsei, vol. 7. Ōfūsha, 1980.

_____, ed. *Rōkashō.* Genji monogatari kochū shūsei, vol. 8. Ōfūsha, 1983.

Iijima Hisako. "Murasaki no Ue no shitto." *Monogatari bungaku ronkyō* 6 (Dec. 1981).

Iimura Hiroshi. *Genji monogatari no nazo: Yūgao, Aoi no Ue, Ukifune o chūshin ni.* Yūbun Shoin, 1994.

Ikeda Kazuomi. "Tenarai no maki mono no ke kō: Ukifune monogatari no shudai to kōzō." In *Genji monogatari no jinbutsu to kōzō (Ronshū chūko bungaku* 5), edited by Chūko Bungaku Kenkyūkai. Kasama Shoin, 1982.

Ikeda Kikan. "Genji monogatari no kōsei to gihō." *Bōkyō* 8 (June 1949).

Ikeda Toshio, ed. *Hamamatsu Chūnagon monogatari.* SNKBZ, 2001.

Imai Gen'e, ed. *Hikaru Genji ichibu uta.* Genji monogatari kochū shūsei, vol. 3. Ōfūsha, 1979.

_____. "Murasaki no Ue: Asagao no maki ni okeru." In *Genji monogatari kōza*, vol. 3 *(Kaku makimaki no jinbutsu*, vol. 1), edited by Yamagishi Tokuhei et al. Yūseidō, 1971.

_____. "Ukifune no zōkei: Yūgao, Kaguya-hime no omokage o megutte." *Bungaku* 50:7 (1982).

Ino Yōko. "Kakusu/kakureru: Ukifune monogatari." *Genji kenkyū* 6 (2001).

Inoue Mayumi. "Sagoromo monogatari no kōzo shiron: Sagoromo no hatashita yakuwari." In *Kenkyū kōza Sagoromo monogatari no shikai*, edited by Ōchō Monogatari Kenkyūkai. Shintensha, 1994.

Ishida Jōji and Kayaba Yasuo, eds. *Genji ōkagami.* Koten Bunko, vol. 508. Koten Bunko, 1989.

Ishida Jōji. "Seihen kara zokuhen e." In *Genji monogatari kōza* (10 vols.), vol. 4 *(Kyō to Uji no monogatari, monogatari sakka no sekai)*, editd by Imai Takuya et al. Benseisha, 1992.

Ishida Jōji and Shimizu Yoshiko, eds. *Genji monogatari.* 8 vols. SNKBS. Shinchōsha, 1977-1985.

Itō Masayoshi. "Jidō setsuwa kō." *Kokugo kokubun* 49:11 (1980).

_____, ed. *Yōkyoku shū*, vol. 3. SNKS, 1983.

Izume Yasuyuki, ed. *Ichiyōshō*. Genji monogatari kochū shūsei, vol. 9. Ōfūsha, 1984.

Izumiya Yasuo. "Richū zenki no shinwateki seikaku." In *Nihon shoki kenkyū*, vol. 13, edited by Yokota Ken'ichi. Hanawa Shobō, 1985.

Kanda Tatsumi. "'Kaoru' no bunretsu o genzen saseru tasō na kotoba." *Kokubungaku kaishaku to kyōzai no kenkyū* 44:5 (Bessatsu *Genji monogatari no datsuryōiki)*, April 2000).

_____. *Monogatari bungaku, sono kaitai: Genji monogatari, Uji jūjō ikō*. Yuseido 1992.

Katō Gitai. "Shōkū kyōdan ni yoru ichinichikyō kuyō." *Seizan Gakkai nenpō* 6 (Nov. 1996).

Kawai Hayao. *Murasaki mandara*. Shōgakukan, 2000.

Kawakami Junko. "Toyotama-hime shinwa no ichikōsatsu." In *Nihon shinwa II*, edited by Nihon Bungaku Kenkyū Shiryō Kankōkai. Nihon bungaku kenkyū shiryō sōsho. Yūseidō, 1977.

Kawazoe Fusae. *Genji monogatari hyōgen shi: yu to ōken no isō*. Kanrin Shobō, 1998.

Keene, Donald, ed. *Anthology of Japanese Literature from the Earliest Era to the Mid-Nineteenth Century*. New York: Grove Press, 1955.

Kikuta Shigeo. "Azumaya, Ukifune, Kagerō, Tenarai, Yume no ukihashi." In *Genji monogatari kōza*, vol. 4, edited by Yamagishi Tokuhei and Oka Kazuo. Yūseidō, 1971.

Kitamura Kigin. *Kogetsushō*. 3 vols. Meicho Fukyū Kai, 1927.

Ko Shūbin. "Murasaki no Ue no ron: naka no shina no josei to shite." *Shirin* 4 (October 1988).

Kobayashi Masaaki. "Saigo no Ukifune." *Monogatari kenkyū,* April 1986.

_____. "Uji jūjō no genzai ni kaete: aku no zanshō." In *Genji monogatari: Uji jūjō no kuwadate*, edited by Sekine Kenji. Ōfū, 2005.

_____. "Ukifune no shukke." In *Genji monogatari kōza*, vol. 4, edited by Imai Takuya et al. Benseisha, 1992.

_____. "Uji jūjō no genzai ni kaete: aku no zanshō." In *Genji monogatari: Uji jūjō no kuwadate*, edited by Sekine Kenji. Ōfū, 2005.

Kojima Yukiko. "Murasaki no Ue." In *Genji monogatari kōza*, vol. 2 *(Genji monogatari o orinasu hitobito)*, edited by Imai Takuya et al. Benseisha, 1991.

Kokumin Tosho Kabushiki Kaisha, ed. *Genji monogatari*. vol. 2. Nihon bungaku taikei, vol. 7. Kokumin Tosho Kabushiki Kaisha, 1927.

Komachiya Teruhiko and Gotō Shōko, eds. *Sagoromo monogatari*. 2 vols. SNKBZ 29-30, 1999-2001.

Komachiya Teruhiko. "Yume no watari no ukihashi." In *Genji monogatari kōza*, vol. 4 *(Kyō to Uji no monogatari, monogatari sakka no sekai)*, edited by Imai Takuya et al. Benseisha, 1992.

Komashaku Kimi. *Murasaki Shikibu no messēji*. Asahi sensho 422. Asahi Shuppan, 1991.

Kawashima, Terry. *Writing Margins: The Textual Construction of Gender in Heian and Kamakura Japan*. Cambridge, Mass.: Harvard University Asia Center, 2001.

Konishi Jin'ichi. "Genji monogatari no imejerī." *Kokubungaku kaishaku to kanshō* (June 1965). Reprinted in *Nihon bungaku kenkyū shiryō sōsho (Genji monogatari I)*, edited by Nihon Bungaku Kenkyū Shiryō Kankōkai. Yūseidō, 1969.

_____. *A History of Japanese Literature*. 5 vols. Princeton, N.J.: Princeton University Press, 1986.

Koyama Toshihiko. *Genji monogatari: kyūtei gyōji no tenkai*. Ōfūsha, 1991.

Kubo Tomotaka. "Zokuhen sakusha ibun: *Kachō yosei* kara keiryō bunkengaku e." In *Genji monogatari: Uji jūjō no kuwadate*, edited by Sekine Kenji. Ōfū, 2005.

Kubota Takao. "Uji e no shiza: monogatari no 'ba' zenshi." In *Genji monogatari: Uji jūjō no kuwadate*, edited by Sekine Kenji. Ōfū, 2005.

Kuge Haruyasu, ed. *Hamamatsu Chūnagon monogatari*. Ōfūsha, 1988.

Kumazawa Banzan. *Genji gaiden*. In Kokubungaku chūshaku sōsho 14. Meicho Kankōkai, 1930.

Kurano Kenji and Takeda Yūkichi, eds. *Kojiki*. NKBT 1, 1958.

Kurata Minoru. "Murasaki no Ue no shi to Hikaru Genji: Wakamurasaki to igo no makimaki." in *Genji monogatari kōza*, vol 3 *(Hikaru Kimi no monogatari)*, edited by Imai Takuya et al. Benseisha, 1993.

McCullough, Helen Craig and William H. McCullough, trans. *A Tale of Flowering Fortunes: Annals of Japanese Aristocratic Life in the Heian Period*. 2 vols. Stanford, Calif.: Stanford University Press, 1980.

McMullen, James. *Idealism, Protest, and the* Tale of Genji: *The Confucianism of Kumazawa Banzan (1619-1691)*. Oxford: The Clarendon Press, 1999.

Maruya Saiichi. *Kagayaku hi no miya*, Kōdansha, 2003.

Maruyama Kiyoko. "Murasaki no Ue shōron: Murasaki no Ue rikai ni kakawaru sankasho no kaishaku o chūshin ni." *Kashiigata* 27 (April 1982).

Masuda Katsumi. "Genji monogatari kara mananda koto." In *Genji monogatari kōza*, vol. 1. *(Genji monogatari to wa nani ka)*, edited by Imai Takuya et al. Benseisha, 1991.

Matsuda Toyoko. *Genji monogatari no chimei eizō*. Kazama Shobō, 1994.

Matsumae Takeshi. "Toyotama-hime shinwa no shinkōteki kiban to hebi nyōbō tan." In *Nihon shinwa II*, edited by Nihon Bungaku Kenkyū Shiryō Kankōkai. Nihon bungaku kenkyū shiryō sōsho. Yūseidō, 1977.

Matsuo Satoshi. "Murasaki no Ue: hitotsu no yaya kikyō naru shiron," In Matsuo Satoshi, *Heian jidai monogatari ronkō*. Kasama Shoin, 1968.

Matsuo Sutejirō. "Onna nite mitatematsuramahoshi." *Kokubunpō ronsan*, April 1928.

Miner, Earl. *Japanese Poetic Diaries*. Berkeley, Calif: University of California Press, 1969.

_____. "The Heroine: Identity, Recurrence, Destiny." In *Ukifune: Love in The Tale of Genji*, edited by Andrew Pekarik. New York: Columbia University Press, 1982.

Mishina Shōei. "Ōjin Tennō to Jingū Kōgō," In *Mishina Shōei ronbun shū*, v. 4 *(Zōho Nissen shinwa densetsu no kenkyū)*. Heibonsha, 1972.

Mitamura Masako. "Genji monogatari no 'kuruma' no kūkan." Paper given at Genji Monogatari Kokusai Forum II, Kyoto, November 3, 2008.

Mitani Eiichi and Sekine Keiko, eds. *Sagoromo monogatari*. NKBT 79, 1965.

Mitani Eiichi. *Sagoromo monogatari no kenkyū (denpon keitōron hen)*. Kasama Shoin, 2000.

Mitani Kuniaki. "Genji monogatari daisanbu no hōhō: chūshin no sōshitsu aruiwa fuzai no monogatari." *Bungaku* 50 (August 1982).

_____ "Miotsukushi no maki ni okeru eiga to tsumi no ishiki: Yasoshima matsuri arui wa Sumiyoshi monogatari no eikyō." In Mitani Kuniaki, *Monogatari bungaku no hōhō II*. Yūseidō, 1989.

_____. "Torawareta shisō: Kaoru gensō to Kaoru no shisō aruiwa sei nashi no danjo kankei to iu gen'ei." In Mitani Kuniaki, *Genji monogatari no gensetsu*. Kanrin Shobō, 2002.

Mitoma Kōsuke. *Genji monogatari no denshō to sōzō*. Ōfū, 1995.

_____. *Genji monogatari no minzokugakuteki kenkyū*. Ōfūsha, 1980.

Miyake Kazurō. "Umi no sachi yama no sachi shinwa no keisei ni tsuite." *Kodai bunka* 33:12 (December 1981).

Morishita Sumiaki. "Jusuitan no keifu: Sagoromo monogatari o chūshin ni." In *Kenkyū kōza Sagoromo monogatari no shikai*, edited by Ōchō Monogatari Kenkyūkai. Shintensha, 1994.

Morita Yuka. "Murasaki no Ue no miryoku: shitto, jiritsu." *Ōtani Joshidai kokubun* 19 (March 1989).

Morris, Ivan, trans. *As I Crossed a Bridge of Dreams*. New York: Harper Colophon Books, 1971.

_____, ed. *Madly Singing in the Mountains: An Appreciation and Anthology of Arthur Waley*. Berkeley, Calif.: Creative Arts Book Company, 1981.

Mostow, Joshua S. "On Becoming Ukifune: Autobiographical Heroines in Heian and Kamakura Literature." In *Crossing the Bridge: Comparative Essays on Medieval European and Heian Japanese Women Writers*, edited by Barbara Stevenson and Cynthia Ho. New York: Palgrave, 2000.

Nagai Kazuko. "Murasaki no Ue: 'onna shujinkō' no teigiron." In *Genji monogatari sakuchū jinbutsu ronshū*, editd by Mori Ichirō. Benseisha, 1993.

_____. "Ukifune." In *Genji monogatari kōza*, vol. 4, edited by Yamagishi Tokuhei and Oka Kazuo. Yūseidō, 1971.

Nakano Kōichi, ed. *Jōyō Genji monogatari yōran*. Musashino Shoin, 1995.

_____, ed. *Utsuho monogatari*. 3 vols. SNKBZ 15-17. Shōgakukan, 1999-2002.

Nihon Tosho Sentā, ed. *Sagoromo monogatari kochūshaku taisei*. Nihon Tosho Sentā, 1979.

Nomura Seiichi, ed. *Mōshinshō*. Genji monogatari kochū shūsei 6. Ōfūsha, 1982.

Ōasa Yūji. *Genji monogatari seihen no kenkyū*. Ōfūsha, 1975.

_____. *Genji monogatari zokuhen no kenkyū*. Ōfūsha, 1991.

_____. "Monogatari no kōzō." In *Genji monogatari kōza*, vol. 1 *(Genji monogatari to wa nani ka)*, edited by Imai Takuya et al. Benseisha, 1991.

Ōba Minako. "Special Address: Without Beginning, Without End." In *The Woman's Hand: Gender and Theory in Japanese Women's Writing*, edited by Paul Gordon Schalow and Janet A. Walker. Stanford, Calif: Stanford University Press, 1996.

Odagiri Hideo, "Uji jūjō: chūsei bungaku e." In *Hihyō shūsei Genji monogatari*, vol. 3 *(Kindai no hihyō)*, edited by Akiyama Ken et al. Yumani Shobō, 1999.

Okada, H. Richard. *Figures of Resistance: Language, Poetry, and Narrating in* The Tale of Genji *and Other Mid-Heian Texts*. Durham and London: Duke University Press, 1991.

Okada Shōji. "Nara jidai no Naniwa gyōkō to Yasoshima matsuri." *Kokugakuin zasshi*, November 1979.

Okami Masao and Akamatsu Toshihide, eds. *Gukanshō*. NKBT. Iwanami, 1967.

Okami Masao, ed. *Yoshimoto renga ron shū*, vol. 3. Koten Bunko, vol. 92. Koten Bunko, 1955.

Ōno Susumu, ed. *Motoori Norinaga zenshū*, vol. 4 *(Tama no ogushi)*. Chikuma Shobō, 1969.

Philippi, Donald L., trans. *Kojiki*. University of Tokyo Press, 1968.

Pigeot, Jacqueline. *Femmes galantes, femmes artistes dans le Japon ancien*. Paris: Gallimard, 2003.

Proust Marcel. *À la recherche du temps perdu*, vol. 1, edited by Jean-Yves Tadié. Bibliothèque de la Pléiade. Paris: Gallimard, 1987.

_____. *Remembrance of Things Past*, vol 1. Translated by C. K. Scott Moncrieff and Terence Kilmartin. New York: Random House, 1981.

Robertson, Jennifer. *Takarazuka: Sexual Politics and Popular Culture in Modern Japan*. Berkeley, Calif: University of California Press, 1998.

Rowley, Gaye. *Yosano Akiko and The Tale of Genji*. Ann Arbor: Center for Japanese Studies, The University of Michigan, 2000.

Saigō Nobutsuna. "Genji monogatari no hōhō." *Bungaku,* Dec. 1950.

Saitō Akiko. "Murasaki no Ue no shitto: tai Akashi no baai (1)." *Kaishaku*, February 1973.

_____. "Murasaki no Ue no shitto: tai Akashi no baai (2)." *Kaishaku*, June 1973.

_____. "Murasaki no Ue no shitto: Akashi oyobi Asagao no Saiin." *Murasaki* 13 (June 1975).

Sakamoto Kazuko. "'Urazutai' kō." *Chūko bungaku* 16 (Sept. 1975).

Sakamoto Tarō et al., eds. *Nihon shoki*. 2 vols. NKBT 67-68, 1965-1967.

Sakamoto Tomonobu. "Ukifune monogatari no shudai." In *Genji monogatari kenkyū shūsei*, vol. 2, edited by Masuda Shigeo et al. Kazama Shobō, 1999.

Schalow, Paul Gordon. *A Poetics of Courtly Male Friendship in Heian Japan*. Honolulu: University of Hawai'i Press, 2007.

Sekine Kenji, ed. *Genji monogatari: Uji jūjō no kuwadate*. Ōfū, 2005.

Setouchi Jakuchō. "Genji no shiori." In Setouchi Jakuchō, trans., *Genji monogatari*, vol. 1. Kodansha, 1996.

_____. *Genji monogatari no joseitachi*. NHK Ningen Daigaku. NHK, April-June 1997.

_____. "Shinsaku nō *Yume no ukihashi* ni tsuite." In *Yume no ukihashi*, edited by Kokuritsu Nōgakudō Jigyōka. Nihon Geijutsu Bunka Shinkōkai, 2000.

Shigematsu Nobuhiro. "Murasaki no Ue no ningenzō." *Geibun* 10 (Nov. 1978).

Shimizu Yoshiko. *Genji no onnagimi*. Hanawa Shobō, 1967.

_____. "Yo o ujiyama no onnagimi." In *Genji monogatari: Nihon koten kanshō kōza*, vol. 4. Kadokawa, 1957.

Shinkawa Tokio. "Umi no tami." In *Sumiyoshi to Munakata no kami*, edited by Ueda Masaaki. Chikuma Shobō, 1988.

Shirane, Haruo. *The Bridge of Dreams: A Poetics of* The Tale of Genji. Stanford, Calif.: Stanford University Press, 1987.

Shun'ya jinki. In *Shintō taikei (Jinja hen 13, Kasuga)*, edited by Shintō Taikei Hensankai. Zaidan Hōjin Shintō Taikei Hansan Kai, 1985.

Stinchecum, Amanda Mayer. "Who Tells the Tale? 'Ukifune': A Study in Narrative Voice." *Monumenta Nipponica* 35:4 (Winter 1980).

Sumiyoshi engi. In *Muromachi jidai monogatari taisei*, vol. 8, edited by Yokoyama Shigeru and Matsumoto Takanobu. Kadokawa, 1979.

Sumiyoshi jindaiki. In *Nihon shomin seikatsu shiryō shūsei*, vol. 26 (*Jinja engi*), edited by Miyata Noboru et al. San'ichi Shobō, 1983.

Suzuki Chitarō et al., eds. *Tosa nikki, Kagerō nikki, Izumi Shikibu nikki, Sarashina nikki*. NKBT 20, 1957.

Suzuki Hideo. "Fujitsubo kara Murasaki no Ue e: Asagao no maki ron." In *Ronshū Heian bungaku*, vol. 4 *(Genji monogatari shiron shū)*, edited by Gotō Shōko et al. Benseisha, 1997.

_____. "Kaoru ni okeru dōshin to shūshin." In *Genji monogatari*, vol. 4, edited by Yanai Shigeshi, et al. SNKBT 22, 1996.

_____. "Uji no monogatari no shudai." In *Genji monogatari kenkyū shūsei*, vol. 2, Masuda Shigeo et al. Kazama Shobō, 1999.

_____. "Ukifune monogatari shiron." *Bungaku* 44:3 (1976).

Suzuki Kazuo, ed. *Sagoromo monogatari*. 2 vols. SNKS, 1985-1986.

_____, ed. *Yoru no nezame*. SNKBZ 28. Shōgakukan, 1996.

Takada Hirohiko. *Genji monogatari no bungakushi*. Tōkyō Daigaku Shuppankai, 2003.

_____. "Suma, à la croisée du lyrisme et du destin." *Cipango* (Numéro Hors-série, *Autour du* Genji monogatari), 2008.

Takahashi Kazuo, *Genji monogatari no sōsaku katei*. Yūbun Shoin, 1992.

Takahashi Tōru. "Aishū no tsumi: Ukifune no genzoku to bukkyō." In *Genji monogatari: Uji jūjō no kuwadate*, edited by Sekine Kenji. Ōfū, 2005.

_____. *Genji monogatari no shigaku: kana monogatari no seisei to shinteki enkin hō*. Nagoya: Nagoya Daigaku Shuppankai, 2007.

Takeda Kō, ed. *Genji kokagami, Takai-ke bon*. Kyōiku Shuppan Sentā, 1978.

Takeda Munetoshi. *Genji monogatari no kenkyū*. Iwanami, 1954.

Tamagami Takuya. *Genji monogatari hyōshaku*. 12 vols., Kadokawa, 1964-1968.

_____, ed. *Shimeishō, Kakaishō*. Kadokawa, 1968.

Tanabe Seiko. *Genji monogatari kami fūsen*. Shinchōsha, 1981.

Tanaka Mitsuru, ed. *Mikan yōkyoku shū*, vol. 1. Koten Bunko, vol. 194. Koten Bunko, 1963.

Tanaka Suguru. *Sumiyoshi Taisha shi*. 3 vols. Osaka: Sumiyoshi Taisha Hōsankai, 1963-83.

Tanaka Takeshi, ed. *Mingō nisso*, vol. 4. Genji monogatari kochū shūsei, vol. 14. Ōfūsha, 1983.

Tenshō Daijin kuketsu. In *Shintō taikei, ronsetsu hen 2 (Shingon shintō 2)*, edited by Shintō Taikei Hensankai. Zaidan Hōjin Shintō Taikei Hensankai, 1992.

Terada, Sumie. "Présentation." In *Cipango* (Numéro Hors-série, *Autour du* Genji monogatari), 2008.

Toyoshima Hidenori. "Suma, Akashi no maki ni okeru shinkō to bungaku no kisō: *Sumiyoshi taisha jindai ki* o megutte." In *Genji monogatari no tankyū*, vol. 12, edited by Genji Monogatari Tankyūkai. Kazama Shobō, 1987.

Tsuchihashi Yutaka and Konishi Jin'ichi, eds. *Kodai kayō shū*. NKBT. Iwanami, 1957.

Tsunoda Bun'ei and Katō Shigefumi, eds. *Genji monogatari no chiri*. Shibunkaku, 1999.

Tyler, Royall. "Marriage, Rank and Rape in The Tale of Genji," *Intersections* 7 (2002).

_____. *Japanese Tales*. New York: Pantheon, 1987.

_____, trans. *The Tale of Genji*. New York: Viking, 2001.

_____. "The True History of Shido Temple." *Asian Folklore Studies* 66:1-2 (2007).

Ueda Masaaki. "Kaijin no genzō." In *Sumiyoshi to Munakata no kami*, edited by Ueda Masaaki. Chikuma Shobō, 1988.

Wada Shigeki et al., eds. *Setonai jisha engi shū*. Hiroshima: Hiroshima Chūsei Bungaku Kenkyūkai, 1967.

Wakashiro Kiiko. *Genji monogatari no onna*. Nippon Hōsō Shuppan Kyōkai, 1979.

Waley, Arthur. "Review of *Ivan Morris's The World of the Shining Prince: Court Life in Ancient Japan*. In *Madly Singing in the Mountains: An Appreciation of Arthur Waley*, Ivan Morris, edited by Ivan Morris. Berkeley, Calif.: Creative Arts Book Company, 1981.

Washiyama Shigeo. *Genji monogatari shudai ron*. Hanawa Shobō, 1985.

Watsuji Tetsurō. "Genji monogatari ni tsuite." In *Watsuji Tetsurō zenshū*, vol. 4. Iwanami, 1962.

Yamagishi Tokuhei and Imai Gen'e, eds. *Yamaji no tsuyu, Kumogakure rokujō*. Shintensha, 1970.

Yamaguchi Masao. *Tennōsei no bunka jinruigaku*. Iwanami gendai bunko. Iwanami, 2000.

Yamakami Yoshimi. "Suzaku-in." In *Genji monogatari kōza*, vol. 2 *(Monogatari o orinasu hitobito)*, edited by Imai Takuya et al. Benseisha, 1991.

Yamanaka Yutaka et al., eds. *Eiga monogatari*. 2 vols. SNKBT 31-33. Shōgakukan, 1995-1997.

Yanai Shigeshi et al., eds. *Genji monogatari*. 5 vols. SNKBT 19-23. Iwanami, 1993-1997.

Yoshida Kōichi, ed. *Sagoromo monogatari, Renkū-bon*. 3 vols. Koten Bunko, vols. 96-97, 100. Koten Bunko, 1955.

Yoshikai Naoto, *Genji monogatari no shinkōsatsu: jinbutsu to hyōgen no kyojitsu*. Ōfū, 2003.

Yoshimori Kanako. "*Kakaishō* no Hikaru Genji." *Kokugo kokubun* 65:2 (Feb. 1996).

"Zadankai 'Genji monogatari no seiritsu katei'." In *Nihon bungaku kenkyūshiryō sōsho (Genji monogatari 3)*, edited by Nihon Bungaku Kenkyū Shiryō Kankōkai. Yūseidō, 1971.

Made in the USA
Middletown, DE
14 August 2016